Myth, Ritual, and Shakespeare

Myth, Ritual, and Shakespeare

A STUDY OF CRITICAL THEORY AND PRACTICE

Rajiva Verma

SPANTECH PUBLISHERS PVT LTD

© Rajiva Verma

All rights reserved. No part of this publication may be reproduced or transmitted, in any form or by any means, without prior permission

First published 1990

Published in India by
Spantech Publishers Pvt Ltd
5/58 Old Rajendra Nagar, Shankar Road
New Delhi 110060

Published in England by
Spantech Publishers
Spantech House, Lagham Road
South Godstone, Surrey RH9 8HB

ISBN 81-85215-07-3

Phototypeset in Bembo by
Spantech Publishers Pvt Ltd, New Delhi
and printed in India

To the memory of my father
VISHWANATH VERMA

Contents

Preface	ix
Introduction	1
1. Allegorical Mythography	6
2. Ritual in Drama: Drama as Ritual	76
3. Mythical Thought and Vision	128
4. The Structural Approach to Myth	149
5. Myth, Ritual and Society	169
Conclusion	187
Notes	192
Bibliography	203
Index	222

Preface

It is generally conceded that literary criticism is, even at its worst, a necessary evil, but most people would still draw the line at criticism of criticism, though it is as 'natural' and inescapable an activity as the former and often indistinguishable from it. The idea that we can get to the creative work directly, without the mediation of any criticism, is of course an illusion. In the case of Shakespeare in particular our response is determined, with or without our knowledge, directly or indirectly, and to a lesser or greater extent, by a long and continuous tradition of critical commentary, a tradition of which commentaries on the commentaries are an inseparable part. It is, therefore, hardly possible to approach his works in a condition of critical innocence, nor indeed would it be desirable to do so even if it were possible, for the most likely consequence of such an attempt would be the repetition of outdated or, what is perhaps worse, the latest critical cliches rather than fresh insight. Our confrontation with a literary classic necessarily involves quarrels or collaborations with other critics with regard to both theory and practice, and progress in our knowledge of the text is also a progress in critical self-knowledge. We must of course try to ensure that in our inevitable involvement in the criticism the creative work itself is not forgotten altogether.

The present work examines various theories of myth and ritual and their application to Shakespeare. Critical theory is best studied in relation to actual critical practice, and the criticism of Shakespeare is the obvious choice to illustrate the working of any theory since his works provide the test case for all theories. However, this book is not interested in Shakespeare criticism merely as an example to illustrate an approach, or rather approaches. It includes a comprehensive survey of readings of the individual plays and poems as well as more general studies in terms of myth and ritual which, it is hoped, will not merely clarify these concepts and bring out the possibilities and limitations of 'myth criticism' but also, in the process, throw light, however obliquely, on some aspects of the works themselves. Indeed the importance of 'myth' and 'ritual' in the criticism of Shakespeare can scarcely be exaggerated, for they feature significantly in the works of three of the most important critics after Bradley: 'myth' is a crucial concept in the criticism of G. Wilson Knight and Northrop Frye, and the idea of festive rites is central to C. L. Barber's study of the comedies. The appearance during the last ten years of some valuable and interesting work on Shakespeare in the light of anthropological theories about individual passage rites and social rites like carnival points to the continuing interest in the idea of ritual and its relation to Shakespearean and other drama. And though the great diversity of the 'myth and ritual criticism' of Shakespeare—a consequence of the wide lexical and theoretical range of the two terms themselves— makes generalization difficult, one can say that broadly speaking such criticism involves an attempt to see the individual work in a cross-cultural or universal perspective, or in relation to other forms of symbolic action within a specific culture. In thus moving away from an exclusive focus on character or on the play as an isolated poetic object, it is in harmony with what is perhaps the major trend in contemporary criticism.

The book has grown out of a doctoral dissertation submitted to the University of Warwick, and my first and greatest debt is to Professor G. K. Hunter, my supervisor, for his faith in the work and his invaluable guidance. The comments of Professors Philip Edwards and E. A. J. Honigmann were also of great help and saved me from many errors of fact and interpretation. I alone of course am responsible for those that still remain.

I owe a special debt of gratitude to Professor Vinod Sena, without whose constant prodding and encouragement this book would never have been completed. Professor G. K. Das and Mr K. G. Verma have also shown keen interest in the work and have been unfailing in their support and encouragement. I am also grateful to Professor Amritjit Singh for some useful advice on style and phrasing, to Mr Anand Prakash for his careful scrutiny of the text, and to my brother Rakesh Verma for preparing the index.

I would like to thank the Commonwealth Scholarships Commission for the award of a scholarship for research at the University of Warwick, and Kirori Mal College and the Department of English at the University of Delhi for periods of study-leave which enabled me to pursue the present study to its completion. I am also grateful to the American Studies Research Centre at Hyderabad for a grant which enabled me to visit the Centre for a month. It was a pleasant surprise to find how much the Centre's library had to offer even to those who were not specializing in American studies. Apart from this library, research for the book was carried out at the following places, and I am grateful to the concerned staff for their courtesy and helpfulness: the libraries at the Universities of Warwick and Birmingham; the Shakespeare Institute; the Central Reference Library, Birmingham; and the Central Reference Library and the South Campus Library, University of Delhi.

My wife, Meera, has been a constant source of help and encouragement. She has closely followed the evolution of this book through its different stages and has been full of helpful suggestions on matters of style and organization. Grateful as I am for these, I am even more grateful to her and to my sons, Niraj and Rajat, for their patience and forbearance.

University of Delhi RAJIVA VERMA
Delhi

Introduction

The term 'myth' has a truly protean existence in contemporary thought and criticism, with the capacity to assume a bewildering variety of meanings. 'Myth' or 'mythical' can, for example, signify any of the following: stories about gods and heroes; philosophical fables such as those of Plato; a special and 'higher' kind of insight that is denied to the merely rational man; the kind of thinking behind such diverse cultural practices as alchemy, astrology and magical rites; powerful social and political ideas which impel men to collective action, generally of a violent sort; ideologically distorted history; or plain lies and errors. Often, the term is used so loosely that it is difficult to assign any meaning to it at all. It is not surprising therefore that several writers should have thought it necessary to write on the 'meanings' of this extremely slippery term, or that some others, driven almost to despair, should have written on 'the myth of myth'.[1]

What is generally known as 'myth criticism', or the 'myth and ritual approach', has occupied an important place in twentieth-century criticism and has consequently elicited hostile as well as enthusiastic responses. For example, Herbert Weisinger claims in an article written in 1957 that the myth and ritual approach is now 'one of the high gods in the pantheon of contemporary criticism', numbering among its devotees 'not a few eminently respectable names'. He himself is willing to be counted in, though his devotion is not of the fanatical kind. On the other hand, William K. Wimsatt and Cleanth Brooks, writing in the same year, express alarm at the advent of this new god. 'Surely the hugest cloudy symbol,' they write, 'the most threatening, of our last ten or fifteen years in criticism is the principle of criticism by myth and ritual origins.' Writing a little earlier in the same decade, R. S. Crane gives a largely adverse verdict on the myth and ritual approach in the course of a rigorous analysis of the assumptions about poetic structure underlying some of the dominant modes of contemporary criticism.[2] The promise or the threat of this approach dissipated somewhat in the following decades, but there has been a revival of interest in it in recent years: the figure of Bakhtin's Carnival is already looming large over the critical horizon, particularly in the area of Renaissance studies, as Frazer's Dying God did in the earlier part of the century.

In spite of the strong views for and against myth and ritual criticism, there is some uncertainty about the identity of the myth and ritual critics. Weisinger, for example, writes in one essay:

> To prove how widespread is the application of the myth and ritual approach to Shakespeare I simply call attention to the reversal in attitude toward G. Wilson Knight in the thirty years since *Myth and Miracles* [sic] was first published. The map of Shakespeare's spiritual progress 'from spiritual pain and despairing thought through stoic acceptance to a serene and mystic joy' which Knight first sketched and which was greeted with derision and hostility has now been accepted as the most illuminating guide of all; and indeed, one can almost plot the widening acceptance of Knight by graphing the increasing amount of space given Knight and his followers in each succeeding issue of *Shakespeare Survey*.

But in another note on the same subject Weisinger doubts whether Knight can be considered a myth and ritual critic at all; besides, it is difficult to test the statement given above as we are not told who Knight's followers are. There is a similar vagueness about the critics concerned in Robert Hapgood's survey 'Shakespeare and the Ritualists' (1962). Hapgood seems to assume, like Weisinger, that such criticism stems from the theories of Frazer and the so-called Cambridge School of anthropologists. But he includes in his survey criticism which has little to do with these theories, such as Philip Wheelwright's discussion of the 'myth of love and the myth of divine and earthly governance' in the plays of Shakespeare.[3] Similarly, when C. L. Barber, author of *Shakespeare's Festive Comedy*, is described as a 'mythicist' or an exponent of the 'anthropo-archetypal approach', these terms throw light neither on his work nor on the myth and ritual approach, especially as the terms 'myth' and 'archetype' do not appear in his book at all.[4]

Both Hapgood and Weisinger are aware of the diversity of 'myth and ritual' criticism, the latter, in fact, using the plural in the title of a brief note on the subject—'Myth and Ritual Approaches'. Nevertheless, in practice they take the field to be far more unified than it actually is. Weisinger, for example, concentrates on only one of the approaches, namely that which seeks to examine literary works in the light of a universal 'myth and ritual pattern'. This is indeed the most common form of myth criticism and the one generally referred to by the terms 'myth criticism' and 'the myth and ritual approach', but as there are other kinds of criticism using the concepts of myth and ritual there is little justification for such exclusive focus on a single approach.[5] Hapgood covers a large amount of very diverse material in his brief survey and provides a valuable bibliography, but one is still left wondering what, if anything, all the critics that he mentions have in common. The blanket term 'ritualists' prevents him from making many essential discriminations and imposes a merely factitious unity on the subject-matter.

The present work provides a classification of the various uses of the terms 'myth' and 'ritual' as well as the theories associated with these uses, and examines the application of these theories in the criticism of Shakespeare. Each chapter discusses a theory or a group of theories about myth or ritual, then the application of these theories to literature and drama in general, and finally their application to the works of Shakespeare. It has not, however, been possible to follow this plan strictly and uniformly, especially while dealing with the first two steps down the ladder of abstraction. The criticism of Shakespeare was an obvious choice in this attempt to examine the actual working of these concepts and theories because Shakespeare, in the words of Murray Krieger, is a 'shaping force in modern literary criticism',[6] and in the criticism of his works can be seen the largest variety of critical approaches and nuances of critical usage, both representative and eccentric. Moreover, the subject is interesting in its own right, and it is hoped that this book will not only bring some order into a rather confusing area of literary theory but also manage to throw some light on the works themselves.

Chapter 1 discusses some theories of myth that I have described as allegorical and then gives a play-by-play survey of the criticism of Shakespeare which exemplifies this approach. For this purpose the plays have been divided into four groups: comedies, tragedies, history plays and romances, and within each group they have been discussed in chronological order. The purpose of this extensive survey is to show that the majority of what goes under the name of myth criticism represents an extension to literary works of the ancient tradition of allegorical mythography and owes little to the theories of Frazer and other anthropologists, actually antedating them in many cases. In fact the 'discovery' of Sanskrit, the growth of comparative mythology, and the new direction that these gave to the study of Shakespeare's sources were more important factors in the rise of the myth criticism of Shakespeare.

Chapter 2, which follows the same plan as the previous chapter, focusses on theories of ritual and on how ritual is related to myth, literature and drama. It is in this area that the theories of Frazer and others have made their greatest impact, though in recent years van Gennep's paradigm for rites of passage and the idea of popular festive rites have been applied more frequently.

Chapter 3 discusses theories which postulate a special 'mythical' mode of thought, of which not only myths but a wide variety of other cultural phenomena are supposed to be expressions. Cassirer considers myth to be one of the symbolic forms in which man constructs reality, and much of his work on myth is devoted to analysing the structure of mythical thought—just as a large part of Freud's work is concerned with analysing the structure of unconscious thought. As Cassirer is concerned with the possibilities as well as the limitations of the mythical mode of thought, his attitude to it is a neutral one. There are, however, other writers who seem to assign, though sometimes only implicitly, a special status to myth as the reflection of a consciousness which is somehow privileged to grasp aspects of reality denied to the merely rational man. In the actual criticism of Shakespeare it is more common to find the term myth used in this honorific sense. The play-by-play survey of the relevant criticism is abandoned here, and in the two chapters that follow, because most of this criticism is of a general nature rather than concerned with the analysis of individual plays. Besides, though the theories discussed in these chapters, particularly in Chapter 3, have been very influential as theories, they have not had a corresponding influence on practical criticism.

Expediency has been a factor in the lumping together of Northrop Frye and Lévi-Strauss in Chapter 4, but there is logic as well, for both are concerned not only with myth but also, in their different ways, with structural analysis. Frye combines anthropological theories of myth and ritual with Aristotelian concepts and considers myth a structural principle in literature. Lévi-Strauss is concerned with the structure of myth rather than with myth as a structural principle, but he too seems to believe that in myth one can observe the structure of the human mind in its least distorted form, so that by analysing the structure of myth one can arrive at the structure of the human mind itself. Both Frye and Lévi-Strauss, in other words, attach great importance to myths as 'elementary structures'. Finally, Chapter 5 discusses the relationship between myth and society. Although anthropologists from Malinowski onwards have emphasized the social role of myth in primitive cultures, there are very few applications of this idea in Shakespeare criticism, where a concern with the universal meaning of myth has been more common.

The classification of the various approaches to myth and ritual outlined above can claim to be neither exhaustive nor the only one possible.[7] There may be many meanings of the terms that I have failed to catch, while such common significations of the word myth as 'distortions' or 'lies' have been deliberately excluded because they are not of much significance in critical theory or practice. There is a great deal of simplification and slurring over important differences within the approaches that I have outlined, and there is a good deal of overlap as well. Some of it is inevitable in a work of this scope, and I hope that with all its shortcomings the classification suggested here will help to organize a large and confused mass of material in a way that is useful for critical theory and for the criticism of Shakespeare.

This book is not concerned with another kind of interest in myth associated with the criticism of Shakespeare, namely the study of similes, metaphors and allusions drawn from the realm of mythology. This kind of 'imagery' study has been done with admirable thoroughness by Douglas Bush and Robert Kilburn Root. Among the critics who discuss Shakespeare's conscious use of myths, only those have been considered as 'myth critics' who try to show that these allusions to myths have a structural function and determine the significance of the plays in a substantial way. Such critics form a minority among myth critics, most of whom are content to use myths to unify *their* perception of the plays, without implying that Shakespeare consciously tried to unify the plays by what T. S. Eliot has called the 'mythical method'.[8]

CHAPTER 1
Allegorical Mythography

The theory of myth as an allegory embodying a timeless truth is the oldest of all theories of myth. As early as the sixth century BC, when Xenophanes complained of the immorality of the Homeric gods, Theagenes attempted to justify Homer by arguing that they were really personifications of human faculties and the natural elements. In spite of Plato's criticism of the allegorical interpretation of myths, it continued throughout antiquity.[1] One common form of allegorization was to equate the gods with the planets or constellations. In the Middle Ages this kind of equation was active not only in astrology but also through the concept of man as a microcosm, in medicine and alchemy.[2] Max Müller's 'solar mythology' is a later variant of the same approach.

The moralizing of myths is as old as the naturalizing of them. It was most extensively used by the Stoics and the Neoplatonists. The still current idea of myth as a mystery whose true meaning is apparent only to the initiate can be traced back to them.[3] The same idea can be traced in Renaissance Neoplatonists such as Pico della Mirandola and Ficino. There was initial hostility to the allegorical interpretation of myths from the early Christian fathers, but it was a method which Jewish theologians had begun to apply to the Old Testament even before Philo (b 20 BC), and Origen (b AD 185) finally laid the theoretical foundation of allegorical Christian interpretations of the Bible.[4] Origen argued that while some of the passages in the scriptures are to be taken purely literally, others are to be construed only in an allegorical sense. In the case of still other passages, 'it is useful and necessary for us to accept them in an allegorical sense, in addition to accepting their literal truth'.[5]

Another mode of Biblical exegesis was the typological. Two kinds of typology have been discerned. The first involves a recognition of correspondences between events or persons in the Old Testament and similar events or persons in the New, the latter being considered as clarification and 'fulfilment' of the former.

This kind of typology has been distinguished from allegorical commentary since the latter is not controlled by any teleological perspective.[6] Often, however, typological exegesis amounted to no more than the finding of parallels between the Old Testament and the New. Gregory of Nyssa, for example, found a parallel between Moses stretching his hands to stay the plague of frogs and Christ stretching his to banish 'frog-like thoughts'.[7] From such analogizing to the finding of parallels between pagan myth and Christian scripture was only a short step, one which, in fact, was taken by the Gnostics, who combined allegorical interpretations of the mystery cults and of the myths associated with them with Biblical material.[8]

Such syncretism, as well as allegorization, is inherent in the second kind of typology, which assumes a 'quasi-Platonist' doctrine of the relation of the literal sense to 'eternal spiritual realities' hidden behind the literal sense. Philo, for example, uses the term 'archetype' to refer to ideas conceived by God himself; this is reproduced as 'type' or 'paradigm' in the minds of the prophets, and the 'copy' or 'shadow' of the 'type' is in turn transmitted to the many.[9] If an archetype is thus shadowed forth in a type and thence in a copy, and is otherwise unknowable, a multiplicity of types and copies could be thought of as shadowing forth the one and only archetype. This kind of typology can hardly be distinguished from allegory since it involves not only the reduction of many individual stories to one paradigm, but also the assumption that behind the diversified manifest content of these stories is a single latent spiritual truth.

There has been a long tradition of such allegorical-cum-typological commentary on the Bible despite theological objections to its syncretism. In the Middle Ages, as Jean Seznec has pointed out, the medieval genius for allegory finds 'anticipations of the New Covenant in Old Testament characters and episodes of Fables as prefigurations of Christian truth'. Thus, Moses and Hercules are often equated, and in a text from the fourteenth century, *Ovid Moralisé*, Actaeon is equated with Christ himself.[10]

Specifically in relation to classical myths, this tradition of commentary is most notably represented in the Middle Ages by Fulgentius's *Mythologiae* (sixth century) and Boccaccio's *Genealogy of the Gods* (c. 1350–60). Their allegorical mythography is continued in the works of the mythographers of the Renaissance such as

Lilio Giraldi, Natali Conti and Vincenzo Cartari. All of them were widely read and translated, and at least one of them, Cartari, may have been read by Shakespeare. A new element in the works of these writers is the use of illustrations from non-European myths. Seznec cites the example of an early-seventeenth-century reprint of Cartari's *The Images of the Gods* which has an appendix on the gods of Mexico and Japan. Conti, significantly, was hailed as a precursor by French historians of religion in the nineteenth century. Syncretism is even more marked in the Renaissance Humanists, in whose hands allegory becomes an instrument to reconcile pagan myth with Christian scripture. As Seznec points out, with the help of Neoplatonic doctrine the Humanists discovered in mythology not merely a concealed morality but the Christian doctrine itself. Thus, Plato is equated with Moses and Socrates is held to 'confirm' Christ. Erasmus maintains that there is more benefit to be had from the classical fables read allegorically than from the Bible read literally. Seznec also mentions Mutianus Rufus, who reaches the brink of heresy when he writes that there is but 'one god and one goddess, but many are their power and names: Jupiter, Sol, Apollo etc.'. However, Rufus points out, one should have care in speaking these things: 'They should be hidden in silence as are the Eleusinian mysteries; sacred things must needs be wrapped in fable and enigma.' He adds the further comment (dictated perhaps by prudence): 'When I say Jupiter, understand me to mean Christ and the true God.' Douglas Bush cites another instance of syncretism in William Lily's Latin Grammar where 'Our Father...' becomes 'O Pater omnipotens, clarique habitator Olympi'.[11]

The attempt to syncretize mythologies continued through the seventeenth and eighteenth centuries into the early years of the nineteenth. In a book called *Shores of Darkness*, Edward B. Hungerford has given an entertaining account of the mythographers of the period who attempted, like George Eliot's Casaubon, to provide a key to all mythology: people like Samuel Bochart, Jacob Bryant, Jean Sylvan Bailly, Pierre Hancarville (or d'Ancarville) and Francis Wilford. They all relied on dubious etymologies, among other evidence, to prove their particular hunches. Euhemerism was a marked tendency in this mythography. Francis Wilford, for example, was convinced, though only for a time, that he had discovered the secret of the lost Atlantis; it was none other than Albion itself, the selfsame Albion or England which the Hindus referred to in their myths as the *Sweta Dwipa* or 'White Island'. Blake, who had read widely in this literature, remarks: 'The antiquities of every Nation under Heaven, is no less sacred than that of the Jews. They are the same thing, as Jacob Bryant and all antiquaries have proved.'[12]

Max Muller's 'solar mythology' is in the tradition of the speculative mythology mentioned above, though with the development of Indo-Germanic philology the wilder speculations are replaced by a more 'scientific' comparison of words and roots. Max Müller insists on the allegorical nature of myths, criticizing Grote for taking Greek myths purely literally. He observes that two of the common ingredients of ancient languages are what he terms 'polyonymy' and 'synonymy'—i.e. a plurality of names for a single object and a single name for a plurality of objects—and also that primitive speech is essentially metaphorical. On the basis of these two postulates he goes on to interpret nearly all myths, Greek, Indian and others, as dealing with the one theme of the rise and fall of the sun. As an illustration, we can consider his interpretation of the myth of Kephalos and Prokris. He first reduces the myth into its 'constituent elements' thus:

1. Kephalos loves Prokris;
2. Eos loves Kephalos;
3. Prokris is faithless, yet her lover is still Kephalos in disguise;
4. Prokris is accidentally killed by Kephalos.

Kephalos is taken to represent the 'head' of the sun, i.e. the rising sun, since in Greek it is the word for head. Prokris is interpreted as the dew, the etymology of the name being traced to the Sanskrit for rain-drops. Eos is the dawn. The whole myth is thus a natural allegory of the sun, who is loved by both the dawn and the morning dew; the third constituent element listed above refers to the 'rays of the sun being reflected in various colours from the dewdrops'. The accidental killing of Prokris signifies the final absorption of the dew. At the end of the myth Kephalos throws himself into the sea, and this obviously refers to the setting of the sun. Max Müller is similarly able to show that Hercules also is a sun-god, and the poisoned coat given to him by Deianeira is really a metaphor for the clouds which engulf the sun at sunset. The whole of mythology, in fact, stems from a gigantic pathetic fallacy:

There is much suffering in nature to those who have eyes for silent grief, and it is this tragedy—the tragedy of nature—which is the lifespring of all the tragedies of the ancient world. The idea of a young hero, whether he is called Baldr, or Sigurd, or Sifrit, or Achilles, or Meleager, or Kephalos, dying in the fulness of youth, a story so frequently told, localised, and individualised, was first suggested by the Sun, dying in all his youthful vigour either at the end of a day, conquered by the powers of darkness, or at the end of the sunny season, stung by the thorn of winter.[13]

This looks back to the interpretation of myths as allegories of natural phenomena that began in early antiquity and looks forward to Sir James Frazer and the Cambridge anthropologists, because Frazer's prototypical Vegetation Spirit and Dying God and Jane Harrison's *Eniautos-daimon* are basically similar figures. There is in them, as in Max Müller, a reduction of the multiplicity of gods to a single god whose life-history is seen as an allegory of the progress of the year, of the sowing and harvesting of corn, of winter and spring, death and rebirth.

Carl Jung, in a sense, continues from the point where Max Müller leaves. Accepting the latter's 'monomyth' of the solar hero, Jung goes a step further and allegorizes this hero as a projection of the libido. In opposition to Freud, Jung maintains that the libido is not to be equated with sexuality or desire since it is in itself just a potentiality, a 'psychic energy'. The concept of libido as desire is, according to Jung, an *interpretation* of it; what it is *per se* we cannot know; we can at best symbolize it in various forms. In fact, a large variety of symbols (e.g. the sun, fire, the phallus, the snake) can be reduced to a 'common denominator—the libido and its properties'. Jung goes on to suggest a parallel between this simplification and 'the historical attempts of civilizations to unify and simplify, in a higher synthesis, the infinite number of gods'. The attempt of Amenophis IV to replace all the gods of Egypt by 'the great living disc of the sun', and similar attempts in the case of Greek and Roman polytheism (Jung also refers with approval to the syncretism of Mutianus Rufus mentioned earlier) were psychologically valuable since the reduction of the many gods to one merely reflected the fact that they were but different symbols for the same psychic force.[14]

Jung's concept of archetypes also leads to allegory. The idea of the 'collective unconscious' and of inherited archetypes has been the subject of much controversy which lies beyond the scope of this book. It may be pointed out, however, that Jung repeatedly emphasizes that he does not intend to imply that the *contents* of images can be inherited. What is inherited in 'the anatomical structure of the brain' is rather a 'potentiality', a form. As examples of archetypal forms he gives the following: chaotic multiplicity and order; duality; the opposition of light and dark, upper and lower, right and left; the union of opposites in a third; the quaternity (square, cross); rotation (circle, sphere); and finally the centring process and a radial arrangement. In thus reducing the immense variety of images and motifs taken from myths and 'visionary' literature as well as from dreams to a few basic structures, Jung would seem to be anticipating Lévi-Strauss's structural analysis of myths in which they are reduced to a number of binary opposites—which in turn are supposed to reflect the binary structure of the human mind. However, the similarity between Lévi-Strauss's constraining structures of the mind that determine even the making of myths (which are apparently the freest of all human activities), and Jung's 'inborn possibilities of ideas that set bounds to even the boldest fantasy and keep our fantasy activity within certain categories', is only superficial. For Jung's 'ideas' and 'forms' are transcendental realities, existing in the collective unconscious as in a Platonic world of ideas, whereas Lévi-Strauss's structures are only the structures of the human mind.[15]

Jung uses the term 'archetype' in precisely the sense in which Philo uses it. For him, as for Philo, the archetype in itself is unknowable. He therefore makes a distinction between the archetype as such and archetypal or primordial images, the latter bearing the same relation to the archetype as 'type' does to 'archetype' in Philo's terminology. Archetypal images

are very varied structures which all point back to one essentially 'irrepresentable' basic form. The latter is characterized by certain formal elements and by certain fundamental meanings, although these can be grasped only approximately. The archetype as such is a psychoid factor that belongs, as it were, to the invisible ultraviolet end of the psychic spectrum. It does not appear, in itself, to be capable of reaching consciousness. I venture this hypothesis because everything archetypal which is perceived by consciousness seems to represent a set of variations on a ground theme.

The relation between the archetype *per se* and the archetypal images is thus a relation of the One to the Many, the many images being variations on the one 'irrepresentable' theme. Jung compares this to the situation in physics where the smallest particles are themselves irrepresentable but have effects on the basis of which a model of the particle can be built up. 'The archetypal image, the motif or mythologem, is a construction of this kind.' Further, Jung argues that where two or more irrepresentables are assumed to exist, there is no logical argument against the hypothesis that they are really identical—the one timeless reality, in short.[16]

The inclusion of psychoanalytical interpretations of myth in this survey may appear far-fetched or arbitrary. Freud himself distinguished psychoanalysis (which attempted causal explanations of symbols) from allegorical commentary (which merely translated symbols in a 'two-dimensional' fashion).[17] However, without going into the merits of the scientific claims of psychoanalysis, it can safely be said that psychoanalytical studies in comparative mythology often turn psychoanalysis into a 'dictionary of symbols' which helps the analyst bypass the tedious process of clinical investigation. In other words, they proceed by comparison and analogy, which are the basic tools of allegorical criticism. Freud, of course, was aware that psychoanalysis can never provide such a dictionary, but any assumption of the universality of certain symbols inevitably leads to such an idea, in practice if not in theory.

Psychoanalytical interpretations of myths, rituals and dreams are allegorical in another, more general sense. Kenneth Burke has argued that 'any sense in which one order is interpreted as the sign of another' would be the modern equivalent of the allegorical level of the fourfold medieval system of interpretation, and as examples he has suggested a psychoanalytic interpretation of Venus in *Venus and Adonis* as mother, or a 'flat' Marxist equation of Venus, Adonis and the boar with three different social classes. It is in this sense that Northrop Frye considers all commentaries that seek to relate a work of art to moral, social or philosophical concerns as allegorizations.[18]

Yet another sense in which psychoanalytical interpretation is allegorical is in its basic assumption that myths and dreams are modes of 'other speaking', i.e. allegory in its original sense. At the same time, it must be admitted that the effect of Freudian interpretation is to demythologize myth. In the traditional view of myth and allegory, 'other speaking' was considered necessary because it was the only way in which truths otherwise inexpressible could be expressed, or because it provided a veil which protected sacred truth from desecration by creating 'difficulties for the understanding' which only a chosen few could overcome. For Freud, on the other hand, the veil of allegory hides something not sacred but sordid; it is a subterfuge to elude the super-ego rather than the comprehension of the profane or the uninitiated. For the mythologists, including Jung, myth is something positive, shadowing forth some profound truth about the external world or the internal world of the spirit; for Freud, myth has become entirely neutral. Nevertheless, in actual practice Freud does attach a great deal of importance to myths, fairy tales and folk tales because they seem to him to represent the 'natural language' of the unconscious.

II

Theories about the nature of myths or scriptures can easily be extended to literature, and have been. It is easy to see how the view of myths as allegories embodying profound truths can have literary application. Once the term 'myth' ceased to signify a story about gods which is believed to be true, and began to imply a 'fiction' expressing a universal truth, it became synonymous with 'great art' or 'great literature'. Perhaps it would be more appropriate to call myth 'literature', rather than vice versa. At any rate, the idea of art-as-myth-as-allegory is implicit in a good deal of contemporary criticism.

Colin Still, who wrote a study of *The Tempest* in 1921, belongs more completely to the allegorizing tradition of mythologists than perhaps any other modern literary critic. Art, for Still, is a mirror to reality: external and internal. Lesser art is concerned with the reflection of mere external reality, but it is the quality of great art to reflect internal reality. This internal reality can be of two kinds: (a) realities peculiar to the individual consciousness, and (b) realities existing in the 'universal consciousness'. This reality is not on the surface of the work of art and has to be discovered through interpretation. The critic must be a 'reader of riddles', a priest or hierophant ceremoniously initiating the reader into the mysteries of the work.[19]

Still then goes on to formulate a system of 'universal imagery', the basis of which is in the 'permanent facts of mankind's material existence', and the relevance of which is to the 'permanent facts of his inner experience'. The origin of this system of 'universal imagery' goes back to the ancient concept of man as a microcosm. This imagery consists of the four elements of earth, water, air and fire (ether), and the three transitional substances, mire, mist and the rainbow. Their significance is twofold: they are symbolic of what Still (following Bergson) calls 'planes of consciousness' as well as of 'mythical regions'. Fire, for example, corresponds to paradise in the mythical realm and to 'redemption' on the plane of consciousness.[20]

In myth, according to Colin Still, this system of natural imagery is most conspicuous. Still does not see any fundamental distinction between myth and great art. Genuine myth, in his view, 'is a living tree growing slowly out of the seed which was sown by the genius of some poet or mystic of old, and which has been quickened and developed by the collective imagination of countless generations of men and women'. If a work of art by an individual genius contains the seed of inspiration it will go on living and will achieve 'a larger life than its original creator could give it'. It will, in short, eventually become myth. And the sum of all such myths and mysteries 'forms the main substance of a universal tradition which is a living organism'. Still writes (and the sentiment here, if not the actual words, brings to mind the writings of Northrop Frye, though, of course, these come later):

THIS UNIVERSAL TRADITION IS THE LIVING ART OF ALL HUMANITY. It is a perfected reflection of the entire sum of man's spiritual wisdom and experience. It is THE WORD MADE FLESH, begotten by the universal spirit, as by the archangel Gabriel, through the soul of all mankind, as through the Virgin Mary Herself.

The common theme of this universal or organic tradition is the cycle of the Fall and Ascent, and it is this theme (the 'Timeless Theme' of the title of the book) which is the 'Absolute Standard' by which individual works are to be judged. Still applies this theory to *The Tempest* and comes to the conclusion (after comparing the play with the initiation rites of the Eleusinian mysteries) that like the ancient myths and mystery cults, and like all great works of art, it deals with the theme of initiation and redemption.[21]

For Still, then, great art is mythical, and myth is the embodiment of a timeless reality; rather, all myths embody the same reality. For G. Wilson Knight, too, great art is mythical. In myth, as in poetry and religion, 'fact and value are reintegrated, and an immediate unfalsified reality created'. It is in this sense that Shakespeare's last plays are 'myths of immortality'. Knight discerns three orders of facts:

1. Imaginatively true but factually insignificant or false;
2. Factually true but imaginatively insignificant;
3. Factually as well as imaginatively true.

The facts of the life of Jesus are, according to Knight, of this last order, so that his life itself becomes symbolic, but the synthesis of the imaginative and the factual can also be seen, in varying degrees, in great works of art, including Shakespeare's.[22] There is a parallel between the factual-imaginative distinction and Origen's distinction between the literal and the allegorical sense of the Bible; Knight's literary criticism may thus be seen as an extension of this method of Biblical exegesis to works of literature.

For Knight, then, a work of art, like the Bible itself, could be taken literally as well as allegorically, that is, as a myth. What the myth expresses is a mystery that can never be grasped intellectually, the mystery of immortality or eternity, for example. Other writers have used the term 'myth' in the sense of a story expressing truths which are beyond the grasp of the intellect. Thus, D. G. James defines the purpose of myth as 'the showing forth of that which cannot be set out by the representation of a merely human situation; its function is the conveyance, to whatever degree possible, of the divine as well as the human'. Similarly, Richmond Y. Hathorn has defined myth as 'a tissue of symbolism clothing a mystery'. In his view, all myth is literature, though all literature is not myth. This view of myth relates it to what is normally called a symbol rather than to allegory. Indeed, it is more common in modern criticism to find both myth and symbol distinguished from allegory. If by allegory is meant a work in which, as Northrop Frye puts it, 'a poet explicitly indicates the relationship of his images to examples and precepts, and so tries to indicate how a commentary on him should proceed', then, of course, myths are not allegories, nor is 'mythical' literature allegorical. But we are concerned here with allegorization rather than with allegory itself. And we get allegorical commentary, as Kenneth Burke and Frye have argued, whenever the critic tries to relate the images or events in the work to 'examples and precepts', even when the writer himself has not explicitly indicated any such relationship. In the passage just cited, Frye suggests that one of the reasons for the widely prevalent dislike of formal allegory is that it 'prescribes the direction' of the critic's commentary and so 'restricts its freedom'. Explicit allegory, in other words, invites (or tolerates) the least amount of allegorization; and it is precisely the fact that myth, whether Classical or Biblical or literary, has invited the greatest amount of allegorization that can explain the usual distinction between myth or symbol and allegory [23]

Myth invites allegorization. But, at the same time, allegorization helps to preserve the mythical status of myth. Allegorical interpretation, in other words, reinstates myth in the sense of a story about the gods which is believed to be true as myth in the sense of a story containing a hidden timeless truth, allegorically expressed to protect it from the desecration of being understood by the uninitiated masses. The *O.E.D.* gives as an obsolete sense of the word 'mythologize', 'to expound the symbolism of', and illustrates with a quotation from Swift: 'This parable was immediately mythologized. The whale was interpreted to be Hobbes's *Leviathan*.' In other words, to mythologize is to allegorize. But often the converse is even truer: to allegorize is to mythologize, i.e. raise to the status of 'myth' in the second sense just noted.

Edwin Honig has argued that there is a resemblance between the 'endowed quality of mystery in myth and the allegorical quality derived from a text'. Both represent what anthropologists would term the 'mana' in the object. Honig continues:

The priest endows the object with mana and the communicant apprehends its existence there. The object with mana, like the religious allegory, becomes an instrument of faith, something to worship, an artefact. If, as in Christianity, for example, a single god has created the text as well as the world, the text is the means of apprehending the presence of divinity in nature; there is 'the good book' and there is 'the book of nature' which it interprets. So, too, one might say of creations in art that they take on the quality of mana by lending themselves to many varieties of interpretation. There is also an obvious parallelism between object and mana, text and allegory, myth and mystery: in each case the original creation invites, is followed by, and frequently is wholly consumed by a variety of interpretative re-creations.[24]

That last clause could serve very well as a description of the fate of a writer like Shakespeare. His works certainly have taken on this quality of mana and thus become myths. However, Honig's position needs some qualification. Not all allegorization of a text corresponds to the mana in an object; Freudian allegorization would seem to belong to what Frye calls the ironic mode, which is at the other pole from the mythical. The intention of his exegesis is not to endow the object with mana or mystery but rather to divest it of it, though fortunately he does not always succeed. The kind of historical allegorization by which a character in a play or novel is related to a contemporary figure is also, obviously, not a mythologizing kind of allegorical commentary.

Allegorical commentary that can properly be described as myth criticism is characterized by two elements: a conviction that the truth that the work is allegorically presenting is of a higher, spiritual order, and a marked tendency towards syncretism. Both have been conspicuous in the allegorical theory of myths from very early times, though in modern criticism the former element has been complicated by the insistence that this truth is not only of a higher order, but also inexpressible in any other way. Yet this need not be a position in conflict with the allegorical theory since allegory too was considered to be the only way in which sacred truth could be revealed.

Syncretism in literary studies is an obvious development from a similar trend in theories about myth and scripture. It has been shown how typological exegesis led from finding anticipations or 'types' of Christ in the Old Testament to finding similar 'types' in classical myths. When G. Wilson Knight argues that each of Shakespeare's tragic heroes is 'a miniature Christ', or when Northrop Frye reads the romances as plays which have Orpheus as their hero, they are extending the scope of this typology. Such analysis usually involves allegorization. The urge towards perfection leads such typological analysis to a synthesis of several mythical or literary narratives or characters into a single pattern or figure which is considered to be a symbolization of some one timeless theme. The commonest of these patterns is that of the life-cycle of a god or hero who is born under exceptional circumstances, has many adventures and undergoes many trials, dies, and is finally reborn. This, broadly speaking, is Weisinger's 'myth and ritual' pattern mentioned earlier. In his book *Tragedy and the Paradox of the Fortunate Fall* (1953), Weisinger suggests that this pattern, more simply the pattern of death and rebirth, has exercised a peculiar fascination on the imagination of man from very early times. He further suggests that its development can be traced from its genesis in ancient seasonal rituals, through the myths of the Near-East, including the myths of Christianity, to its culmination in the tragedies of Shakespeare and others. The myth and ritual approach is described by Weisinger as the application of this pattern to an individual work to see how far it corresponds to the original in its form and emotional content.[25]

Closely associated with the death–rebirth pattern are the patterns of separation and reunion or reconciliation, the loss and regaining of paradise, and the seasonal cycle. Yet another related pattern is that of initiation rituals, in which the initiate suffers a temporary loss of identity before acquiring a new one. The loss of identity (like the loss of paradise) is often symbolized by death and the regaining of it by rebirth. The central myth of Christianity—the death and resurrection of Christ—is also obviously related. It is this cluster of themes and patterns that is implied by the term 'the myth and ritual pattern'. 'Myth and ritual criticism' would thus include all interpretations of literary works in terms of any of the patterns just mentioned, even when there is no explicit reference to myth and ritual or to any anthropological theory. In fact Weisinger uses the term to refer to practically any criticism which sees the theme of 'reconciliation' in a work. Myth criticism of this kind can therefore be better understood when seen in the context of the allegorical-typological tradition of mythography and Biblical exegesis, rather than in relation to any specifically anthropological theory. This is borne out by the fact that there are many examples of such myth criticism, especially in relation to Shakespeare, which actually precede Frazer and other anthropologists. The actual content of this kind of myth criticism, the pattern or theme that is discerned beneath the variety of literary and mythic materials, also derives from pre-Frazerian sources. For example, the pattern of the seasonal rituals of renewal and of the myths associated with them does not vary significantly from the pattern of 'solar mythology', the seasonal cycle being, after all, a function of the solar rounds. Even more importantly, the theme of rebirth has been central to esoteric cults from very early times down to our own.

The connections between myth, allegory, typology, esotericism and syncretism is brought out very clearly in the work of W. F. C. Wigston, whose *A New Study of Shakespeare* first appeared in 1884. E. A. J. Honigmann has rightly emphasized the pioneering role of Wigston with respect to myth criticism of *The Winter's Tale*, but his role appears to be even more significant than Honigmann suggests if one considers his contribution to the criticism of the final plays as a group and to myth criticism generally. A rather lengthy quotation is necessary to give the reader an idea of Wigston's general argument and the tone of his writing:

The secret knowledge, or *Gnosis*, had never been extinguished during the dark ages, and in this profound fact we have an explanation of much that would otherwise perplex and embarrass us. One of the vehicles of this Gnosis was the form of popular tales, with an allegorical meaning well understood by the initiated....

The habit of finding personal allegories in every metaphysical poem of the 16th and 17th centuries, is pernicious and absurd. The study of the classics, of Plato, and the ancient philosophers, had given rise to great subtlety of deductive thought, which is to be found not only in all the sonneteers of the period, but in secret societies, who seem undoubtedly to have renewed touch with the opinions, sentiments, *and mysteries* of the *ancient world* prior to the corruption of Christianity. We find the society of the Rosicrucians arising suddenly into notice, about the beginning of the 17th century. A study of the Hermetic philosophy, as far as we can gather, certainly suggests that this strange brotherhood and its kindred allies, had anticipated much of the results of modern critical inquiry. For example, a study of Sir George Cox's Mythology of the Aryan Nations, leaves us as result, the essence of the old Iranian dualism, in the conflict of Light and Darkness, of Day and Night, as the protagonists of most of the ancient mythology. This conflict of Light and Darkness seems, however, to have formed one of the leading doctrines of the Rosicrucians and Hermetic Brethren. The learned authoress of Isis Unveiled tells us that with the exposure of the mythical nature of Christianity, a return to the Hermetic philosophy is certain.[26]

In another passage, where he is discussing *The Tempest* in particular, Wigston writes:

We confess that (to ourselves) it seems highly possible that Miranda (the Marvel) *is no less than the daughter of Ceres and Jupiter* (Prospero), viz.,

Proserpine,—we mean the *spiritual* life of the poet's art,—asleep under power of his spells,—a type of the resurrection and rebirth of this art promised through the wooing of Ferdinand—ourselves (?). If so, the introduction of this classical vision or masque, is a revelation in itself. *Ceres is summoned, to preside over the marriage of her daughter.* And this *Midsummer* or *August* vision, is the crowning self-reflecting portrait of the poet's art, *come full circle,—its Winter* (crowned with new life), *become Summer*! Then in Miranda, we have Perdita and Marina again, under a fresh aspect. And the profound student will mark *the sleep* that Prospero puts Miranda under. A sleep that is not difficult to understand, if this be the sleep of Persephone in Hades, viz., the sleep of the *Winter's Tale*, the poet's *entire art*, slumbering during the Winter of its uninterpretation. (p. 326)

Most of the characteristics of myth criticism can be observed here. There is, first of all, the conviction that the individual work under consideration is of profound significance; secondly, that this significance is hidden or esoteric rather than explicit or exoteric; and thirdly, that this significance is shared by the myths and rituals of the past. The association of syncretism and esotericism is also clearly brought out. Especially noteworthy is the application of the term 'mythical' to Christianity. Wigston also gives an interesting twist to the rebirth theme, suggesting that it hints at the discovery of the true meaning of Shakespeare (by faithful Rosicrucians like himself) after nearly two centuries of 'uninterpretation'. He seems to cast himself in the role of the priest in a mystery cult, 'revealing' the hidden meaning of the cult symbols to the initiate. In fact the word 'revelation' and its derivatives appear very frequently in the book. Also recurrent are the themes of rebirth, the seasonal cycle and reconciliation—which are the stock-in-trade of the myth and ritual approach. It is interesting to note that according to Wigston the aim of Shakespeare's art 'seems to have been both to obscure and reveal at once' (pp. 7–8). This, as already pointed out, is precisely what the ancient and medieval allegorists thought was the function of allegory in a sacred text. It threw a veil over it so that none but the initiate could see its true significance.

III

The survey that follows includes, in addition to the kind of myth criticism described above, some criticism which seems to be concerned merely with pointing out sources or analogues of elements in Shakespeare's plays in myths, folk tales and fairy tales. The motivation in such studies is primarily antiquarian, but they prepare the ground for more significant critical works. Besides, cumulatively such source-and-parallel-hunting works to modify our response to the plays. Broadly speaking, it prepares the way for two approaches, both of them anti-naturalistic. One of these approaches seeks to emphasize the 'depth-psychology' aspect of the plays rather than the 'surface' psychology of character analysis in the Bradleyan mode; the other seeks to deny psychology altogether and to examine the plays in the light of conventions. An example of the former approach is J. I. M. Stewart, as Northrop Frye is of the latter.

Myth and ritual criticism has been applied not merely to individual plays but also to the spiritual development of Shakespeare as inferred from the works. Weisinger, for example, as pointed out earlier, cites G. Wilson Knight's map of Shakespeare's spiritual development as an instance of the myth and ritual approach, while suggesting that it is not really very different from Dowden's map of Shakespeare's progress. If we accept Weisinger's argument, we will have to consider Knight's role in myth and ritual criticism as crucial. But his influence has been of a general kind rather than related to the criticism of individual plays in terms of specific myths. His chief contribution to the myth and ritual approach lies in his concept of the last plays as myths—myths being understood as embodiments of transcendental intuitions of reality—and in the popularizing of the rebirth pattern in a language relatively free from the esoteric jargon found in Wigston.

THE COMEDIES

The genre of comedy was related to the pattern of seasonal rituals of *renouveau* by Cornford in *The Origin of Attic Comedy* (1914). Even when not approached from the angle of anthropology, the relation of comedy to the myth and ritual pattern is obvious. Since two of the key ideas in this pattern are rebirth and reconciliation, and since comedy ends on a note of some kind of deepened awareness and reconciliation after a period of discord and confusion, it is believed by some critics to be nearest to the ideal pattern. Northrop Frye, in particular, has written about the 'comic myth' in this sense. Many other critics, as I try to show in the rest of this chapter, also discern the mythic pattern in Shakespeare's comedies, all comedies being concerned, in some sense, with loss or confusion and reconciliation. An important conclusion that can be drawn from the myth criticism of the comedies is that they are continuous with the last plays, the same individual mythic and folk motifs as well as the same broad pattern emerging in both groups of plays. The relation of comedy to the Christian myth is also obvious since the history of the world viewed in the perspective of Christian eschatology is a divine comedy.

The Comedy of Errors

I have discovered only one example of mythical-cum-allegorical interpretation of this play, though no doubt there could be many, since the pattern of loss and reconciliation is present in this play as much as in any of the later romances. Jean Paris (1960), employing some ideas of Paul Arnold, interprets the play in the light of Rosicrucian and other esoteric doctrine. Briefly, his thesis (anticipated by Wigston) is that in the Renaissance there was a flowering of occult doctrine, and that occultism and the theatre were closely connected then, as indeed they have been throughout history. In this connection he mentions the popularity of alchemy and the introduction of Rosicrucian doctrine into England around this time. Esotericism he defines generally as a 'quest for the absolute'. Cabbalistic doctrine, in particular, holds that in the beginning there was absolute unity—*Ain Soph*. A series of divisions in this unity, beginning with the division between the masculine and the feminine principles—the *voluntas* and the *noluntas*—was the source of all creation. The goal of life should be the reattainment of the original unity. Paris sees a reflection of this doctrine in *The Comedy of Errors*. The cities at war at the beginning of the play symbolize the first rupture of unity. The story, he writes, 'relates a series of disasters, each of which seems marked by the rupture of a couple'. The action thus parallels, in the realm of human affairs, the progress of the universe as described in Hesiod's *Theogony*. Thus, this comedy, which is one of Shakespeare's earliest plays, 'contains the basic pattern of his entire theatre'. The divorce between the masculine and the feminine is found again in *Pericles*, *As You Like It*, *A Midsummer-Night's Dream* (which may be described as 'the New Comedy of Errors'), *Cymbeline*, *The Winter's Tale*, and *The Tempest* (?). In *The Two Gentlemen of Verona*, also, Paris sees 'a real initiative method' reflected in the pattern of separation and then union and regeneration.[27]

Although they do not invoke esoteric doctrine, other critics have come to similar conclusions about the play. Thus, G. Wilson Knight sees the play as representing the pattern of birth, 'the dispersal of a family in tempest, and then a final reunion'. And although he believes that there is less 'religious and mythical suggestion' in this play than in *Pericles*, he still maintains that Ephesus is presented as a land of supernatural mystery. Northrop Frye describes the play as possessing a 'metamorphosis structure' of 'descent into illusion and emergence into recognition'. This, we might remark, is the pattern of many initiation rituals, in which the initiate has to undergo a period of wandering in the wilderness before the mystery can be imparted to him. The 'errors' or illusions through which the characters in the play pass thus correspond to 'the labyrinth of the wilderness of error' of the Eleusinian mysteries, of which Christ's wandering in the wilderness is the Christian counterpart. It is interesting in this connection that Northrop Frye comments upon the 'curiously eerie' atmosphere of the play, with Adriana's melancholy, the insistence on madness and the repeated references to jugglers and wizards. He also contrasts Shakespeare's treatment of Antipholus with Plautus's treatment of his counterpart, arguing that Shakespeare's Antipholus enters the house of his brother's wife 'with almost the feeling of being initiated into a mystery'. Frye further argues that the effect of the doubling of the identical twins is not to turn the Plautine comedy into complete farce, but rather to suggest 'the primitive horror of the doppelgänger'.[28]

The Taming of the Shrew

The taming of a shrewish wife is, of course, a well-known and widely-distributed folk-tale motif. It seems to be a comic version, as Peter Alexander has pointed out, of 'one of the great themes of literature', namely the theme of 'the perilous maiden', where the lady is death to any suitor who woos her except the hero—who alone knows how to turn her vices into virtues.[29]

The Two Gentlemen of Verona

An obvious interpretation of this play would be in terms of the Proteus myth, and this is what William O. Scott has done in an article written in 1965. The assumption in this article, unlike what obtains in many other examples of analogizing with myth, is that Shakespeare is using the myth of Proteus consciously to give a deeper significance to the character of Proteus and hence to the play as a whole. Thus, the allusion to the myth of Proteus is more than mere rhetorical ornament. Scott argues that in the mythography of the Renaissance, Proteus is seen in three aspects: as shape-shifter, as a type of lust and as 'a type of nature or the truth of things obscured by material appearance'. Shakespeare's Proteus is like this mythical figure, and the use of the myth helps to suggest 'an underlying reality of character which will remain after the fickleness, and its resultant treacheries, have been purged away'. In fact, he argues, the theme of identity implied in the Proteus myth is the subject of the play. The redeeming heroine brings her man to a true conception of himself. 'If Proteus can be bound firmly, he holds his true shape.'

Love's Labour's Lost

Wigston argues that the author of *Love's Labour's Lost* is more than an erudite writer, for he writes with 'direct and plenary inspiration, with knowledge of rites pertaining to certain classic Mysteries, which the learned can discover for themselves'. His theory is, as he puts it, 'to connect the poet's art with the cycle of the seasons, in connection with the mysteries'. Associated with the cycle of the seasons is the theme of rebirth, and Wigston argues that this is suggested in the following lines:

> LONG. Berowne is like an envious sneaping frost
> That bites the first-born infants of the spring.
>
> BER. Well, say I am; why should proud summer boast
> Before the birds have any cause to sing?
> Why should I joy in any abortive birth?
>
> (I. i. 100)

Berowne, he goes on to argue, suggests Apollo, and the show of the Nine Worthies is said to be 'the greatest mystery of all the poet's plays'. Rosaline, according to Wigston (who constantly refers to her as Rosalind), represents the Ephesian Diana because she is described as 'black', and the Ephesian Diana is none other than the Great Mother Earth herself in her underground darkness. Wigston mentions in this connection the Aryan mythology of George Cox, which revolves round the conflict of light and darkness.[30]

A Midsummer-Night's Dream

Some of the earliest uses of the word 'myth' (or 'mythology') in the criticism of Shakespeare occur in connection with *A Midsummer-Night's Dream*. This play has been a favourite among folklorists, and one of them, W. J. Thoms (who was in fact the man who coined the term 'folk-lore') wrote on the subject of Shakespeare's use of folklore in this play. The word 'myth' appears more frequently in the form of its derivative, 'mythology', usually qualified by the adjective 'fairy'. Thus, James O. Halliwell (later Halliwell-Phillips) wrote in 1841 that Shakespeare 'formed his beautiful creations out of the popular fairy mythology of the age'.[31] Much of the folklore criticism of Shakespeare is not, however, very relevant to our purpose since it is concerned merely with pointing out the folklore elements (also referred to as 'popular mythology' or 'fairy mythology'). For example, Arthur S. Way (1906) traces some elements in the plays to Aryan folklore and mythology dealing with natural phenomena. The evidence adduced is largely etymological, although a few instances of actual folk customs are also mentioned. To cite an example, the elves in the play are held to be descendants of certain creatures in Aryan mythology called Ribhus, which meant sunbeams. Hence the nature of the elves in Shakespeare, which partake, like the sunbeams, 'of the shifting and unstable character of aerial phenomena'. The word 'nightmare' is traced back to the Sanskrit 'Marut', which refers to the mythical personification of clouds as demons continually changing shapes. Such examples of 'solar' mythologizing are more than mere tracing of etymologies in one respect; their aim is to suggest not merely that many words used by Shakespeare have origins going back to Aryan mythology (so, after all, have many other words in contemporary usage) but rather that Shakespeare uses these words with some awareness of their mythic resonance. And insofar as such studies can help us to recapture this resonance in words which have become dead metaphors, they can be said to be useful contributions.

Wigston relates this play also to the mysteries, but this time with special reference to the doctrine of idealism, which he sees the play as setting forth. After stating that the mysteries 'were in effect an allegorical death and rebirth', he asks rhetorically: 'Is the *Midsummer-Night's Dream* derived from Virgil's VIth Book, which has profound connection with Plato's idealism, as taught in the Mysteries? Is this art, in short, the Mysteries themselves?' Wigston relates the mystic doctrine of idealism with the 'Buddhist' concept of "Maya' (illusion), and sees a further confirmation of his theory about the relation of the play to the mysteries in the fact that the boy who is the cause of the quarrel between Oberon and Titania is of Indian origin. He suggests that this boy might be Bacchus-Dionysus himself, who also was believed to have come originally from India (pp. 313–17).

Sinclair Korner interprets the play in terms of Max Muller's 'solar mythology' in an article written in 1891. Korner's is a rather impressionistic essay, concerned with little more than pointing out the solar references in the play, very much in the manner of some modern studies of imagery: it is simply a study of the sun-image in the play. Korner suggests that both Hippolyta and Theseus are solar figures. Hippolyta's name means 'horse-woman', and the horse is a familiar symbol for the sun. Korner also mentions a myth in which Hippolyta is given away by Hercules (another solar figure) to his kinsman Theseus, 'who is an Athenian parallel of the Teutonic Sifrit, a renowned sun-champion'. Theseus, in mythology, is 'the offspring of brightness and radiance'. The Indian boy also features in this solar interpretation of the play because, as Korner points out, 'from the brightest and sunniest region where men dwell, she [Titania] carries away a choice victim to the shadowy underworld, or to roam about in her train beneath the subdued beams of the moon'. In conclusion, this critic describes the play as 'a beautiful mosaic of old-world myth and modern folk-lore' in which 'the solar element is as pronounced as in the poems of Homer'.

In *The Fairy Mythology of Shakespeare* (1900), Alfred Nutt argues that in *A Midsummer-Night's Dream* Shakespeare has managed to synthesize two strands of fiction: Arthurian romance (to which belongs the figure of Oberon) and peasant belief (in Puck or Robin Goodfellow). He traces the origin of Puck to certain Irish deities called the Tuatha de Danann, who were fertility spirits with the attributes of both gods and mischievous spirits. They are thus the link between the Oberon of Arthurian romance and the folk figure of Puck. Shakespeare's association of the two is not, therefore, according to Nutt, arbitrary. It brings out the fact of the common mythology of the 'Aryan speaking people of Europe'. Nutt also maintains that the deities whose different transformations are presented by Shakespeare as Oberon and Puck were associated with cults related to agriculture. In thus relating the fairies of Shakespeare with gods of fertility and agriculture, Nutt finds himself in agreement with the 'chief recent students of myths and rite in Britain and the continent'. Once again, then, we find the idea of rebirth associated with myth, for, as Nutt argues, the Celtic doctrine of rebirth (which was the subject of his earlier book, *The Voyage of Bran*) and the cults associated with it had an agricultural basis, as indeed had ancient mythology. Puck and Oberon are therefore to be seen as fertility spirits, as personifications of the dying and reborn vegetation god. A reference to Nashe clinches the point. According to Nashe, as quoted by Nutt, elves and Robin Goodfellow are the same as the fauns and satyrs associated with Dionysus, the god of growth and vegetation.[32] Nutt's study of the sources of the play thus leads to the mythical gods whose life-histories constitute the myth and ritual pattern. He is, nevertheless, closer to the folklorists of the nineteenth century than to the myth critics of the twentieth as he does not concern himself with the mythical pattern of the play as a whole.

According to C. Cambillard, who interprets the play as an astrological myth, Titania represents the moon, which at the beginning of the play is said to be in her last quarter, i.e in her most pernicious phase. She also represents the female principle, microcosmically as well as macrocosmically. Oberon represents the sun as well as the male principle. The Indian boy is spiritual energy, which is symbolized in alchemy by Mercury. The problem of the play is to restore the child to Oberon, spiritual energy to the male principle. Only thus can the energy of the child be directed towards growth and fertility. In association with the moon in its destructive last quarter, the child can only have a baleful influence, as at the beginning of the play. Cambillard goes into more complicated astrological and alchemical details, but the outline of his interpretation follows a familiar pattern: he too sees the play as moving from disorder and infertility to harmony and fertility, these latter being symbolized by marriage.

Jean Paris brings out clearly the initiation pattern which is only implicit in Cambillard. He refers to the Orphic mysteries celebrated under the new moon and suggests that the play itself may be dealing with such a mystery:

> This moon (i.e. the new moon), under whose sign the final scene of *The Merchant of Venice* unfolds, reveals the cosmic mechanism of initiation in *A Midsummer-Night's Dream*. It reappears at various intervals to illuminate, as the tale progresses, the path of those in search of the absolute. Described as 'waning' in the opening scene, it will complete a full cycle, from death to resurrection, toward that new moon which will sanctify the marriage of the King and Queen.

Paris also compares the 'sterility' in Theseus's kingdom at the beginning of the play with the sterlity in the castle of Amfortas in the fisher-king legend. The earth, he suggests, is represented at the beginning of the play as 'suffering from some sort of curse' under the baleful influence of the old moon. But finally the sun dispels the gloom cast by this old moon, and the characters return to celebrate 'the redeeming marriage and bury the old moon as an effigy is burnt at Mardi Gras'.[33] We see in this interpretation a neat synthesis of esoteric lore with seasonal myth and ritual.

The Merchant of Venice

The fairy-tale, ultimately mythic, sources of the two plots of the play have been commented upon by several writers, including Freud. In his famous essay 'The Theme of the Three Caskets' Freud also refers to a book, *Astralmythen der Hebraeer, Babylonier und Aegypter* (1907), in which the author E. Stucken interprets the play as an 'astral myth' as follows:

> The identity of Portia's three suitors is clear from their choice: the Prince of Morocco chooses the gold casket—he is the sun; the Prince of Arragon chooses the silver casket—he is the moon; Bassanio chooses the leaden casket—he is the star youth.

Freud further cites Stucken's reference to an Estonian folk epic, *Kalewipoeg*, in which the three suitors appear undisguisedly as the sun, the moon and the star youth (the last being 'the Pole-star's eldest boy') and here too the bride is won by the third suitor. According to Freud, however, this is an incomplete explanation of the play:

> The question is not exhausted, for we do not share the belief of some investigators that myths were read in the heavens and brought down to

earth; we are more inclined to judge with Otto Rank that they were projected on to the heavens after having arisen elsewhere under purely human conditions. It is in this purely human condition that our interest lies.

In spite of the slight hint of a mythoclastic rather than a mythologizing attitude in this passage, Freud goes on to evoke marvellously the mythic dimensions of the story, investing it with mystery rather than divesting it of it. Suggesting that the situation in which a woman chooses between three suitors is really an inversion of the theme of a man's choice between three women, who are symbolized in the three-caskets story by the caskets, he goes on to draw parallels between this story and the choice of Lear among his three daughters, and between both these on the one hand and a number of myths and fairy tales on the other. He gives the examples of Paris and the three goddesses, of Cinderella and her two sisters, and of Psyche, the youngest again of three sisters in Apuleius's story. His interpretation of this recurrent motif is that the three sisters represent 'the Fates, the Moerae, the Parcae or the Norns, the third of whom is called Atropos, the inexorable'. The story is thus a 'triumph of wish-fulfilment' in which death is transformed into a beautiful woman, and what is inevitable is made a matter of conscious choice.[34]

Whatever one might say of Freud's interpretation of this myth, of which he considers the three-caskets story in *The Merchant of Venice* to be a variation, it cannot, I think, be denied that once pointed out the analogies between the story and the myth do make the former resonate or reverberate with a sense of deeper significance. One note in this reverberation is, I think, the uncanny feeling of having seen it before. Some works of art, like 'The Ancient Mariner', for example, resonate even without the aid of the myth critic, though the resonance becomes deeper once the mythic parallels are pointed out (e.g. the myth of the Wandering Jew, the curse of Cain); there are other works which seem to be quite without mystery till the critic indicates these mysterious parallels and thus transfers, as it were, the 'mana' of the myth on to them. Freud's comments on the three-caskets theme in *The Merchant of Venice* achieve this mystifying of the apparently unmysterious very effectively.

Theodor Reik (1952) also comments on the theme of the three caskets in the play, but comes to a very different conclusion. He considers this story a new version of 'the mythological theme shaped in the legend of the Sphinx and in the Turandot tale'. He argues that Portia is like the Sphinx, even to the point of having a cruel streak in her. In opposition to Freud, who assumes implicitly that collective representations like myths are manifestations of the unconscious wishes of the male population, Reik argues, on the basis of the fact that it is a *woman* posing a riddle, that the myth expresses the unconscious feelings of women, especially their penis envy and hostility to men generally. Reik concludes: 'The myth, the fairy tale and the play seem to prove the unconscious meaning of certain feminine behaviour that has not changed much through the ages and appears even in the extraordinary situation of psychoanalysis.' Two almost opposite myths have thus been held to be behind the three-caskets plot in the play—the myth of the fatal sisters (to put it in its most general form) and the myth of the Sphinx. There is the common element in them, however, of a rather sinister woman, however superficially attractive, who poses riddles or pulls down the hero, like lead, to death. 'All that glisters is not gold' seems to be as applicable to Portia as to the golden casket. Norman Holland, on the other hand, interprets Portia as a 'bountiful mother', with Belmont as the primal matrix.[35]

The folk and mythic origins of the other plot in the play, namely the story of the pound of flesh, have also been pointed out by several writers. Several analogues of the tale in folk tales and mythology have been found. Even more important, perhaps, have been commentaries on Shylock's origin in myth and legend. Among the prototypes of the 'Shylock myth' that have been suggested are Loki, Oedipus, and the Wandering Jew.[36] The origin of the Wandering Jew legend in turn has been traced down to a very different figure, that of the prophet Elijah (Sinsheimer, pp. 114–17). Others have seen behind the figure of Shylock the mythic dimension of the Christian story. Antonio has been compared to Christ, and Shylock, either to the Devil or Jehovah—by Reik for example, who also mentions non-Christian counterparts of Christ like Attis and Adonis. Even Antonio's nastiness towards Shylock is explained as a parallel to Christ's abusing and whipping of the moneychangers in Jerusalem during Passover. Reik writes: 'Shakespeare wanted to present a Jewish figure as he and his contemporaries saw it, but the character grew beyond human measure into the realm of the mythical, as if the God of the Jews stood behind the stage.' Reik also mentions the feeling, which may be described as a resonance, that the awareness of the myth behind

ALLEGORICAL MYTHOGRAPHY

the figure of Shylock arouses, but he writes of it as 'a moment of glow' when he discovered for the first time the 'traces of the old myth in the plot'.[37]

The play has also been interpreted in terms of esoteric rituals of death and rebirth. Paul Arnold (1951) interprets the story of the three caskets as a representation of the initiation ritual of the Eleusinian mysteries. Antonio's ordeal is also represented by him as initiatory. Following him, Jean Paris (1960) relates Antonio's ordeals to the initiatory rites of the masonic brotherhood. Concerning the esoteric theme of the play he writes:

> As a final proof—one which, as a matter of fact, occurs in the masonic rites of initiation—Antonio, like Hamlet, had felt the 'bare bodkin' pressed against his breast. Victorious, he in turn can enter the ideal temple at Belmont and, under the aegis of Portia, found a sort of lodge together with Bassanio, Lorenzo, Gratiano, Jessica, and Nerissa, a superior society governed only by the laws of poetry and music.[38]

A similar pattern of a new life emerging after a period of trials is seen by Paula Brody (1967) as the essence of the plot relating to Antonio. His experience is described by her as that of 'tribal initiation, whereby he is reborn as an adult'. She believes that this postulate regarding the role of Antonio is the logical and valid conclusion 'growing out of a myth and ritual approach to *The Merchant of Venice*'. The ritual of initiation is described as a 'ceremonial death and rebirth' which Antonio (described as 'a youth') goes through in order to attain full manhood. After his initiation, Antonio can rejoin the society at Belmont:

> A privilege which has already been enjoyed by everyone else within the group. (This includes even Jessica, who has been made eligible by marriage to one of the Venetian 'tribe'.) Three times Portia welcomes Antonio. (v, lines 139, 239 and 273) Antonio, reborn, says, and rightly, 'Sweet lady, you have given me life and living' (v. i. 286). Initiation is complete.

Thus we see that this play too can be seen in terms of the pattern of death and rebirth. The question remains, however, whether Antonio really does undergo any kind of rebirth. Graham Midgley (1960) takes the opposite view of Antonio's role in the play, arguing that he, like Shylock, remains an outcast, a view which, it would seem, receives support from the image of the 'tainted wether of the flock'. But although Brody quotes from Midgley's article, she completely ignores this point of vital difference between their different interpretations. One could possibly argue that this image occurs not at the end but during the course of Antonio's trial and that, at the end of the play, Antonio is a different sort of character. However, the evidence for such a view seems to be slight. There is no reason why Antonio could not have been married to someone at the end if Shakespeare intended to suggest his integration into the society at Belmont.

To sum up: both the plots of the play have been traced by the myth critics to primitive mythic origins, even though one of the plots is developed in a realistic mode while the other retains the fairy-tale atmosphere of the original. Shylock, indeed, is held to be mythic not merely by virtue of his mythic prototypes but because he seems to have acquired a place in popular imagination quite independent of the play in which he appears. In this respect he is like the other great mythic characters of the European tradition such as Faust, Don Juan, Don Quixote, Hamlet and Falstaff. It is in this sense that critics have written about the 'Shylock myth' or the 'myth of the Jew'. But it is usually maintained that the mythic status of Shylock is due not only to Shakespeare's literary skill but also to the fact that he is able to reach down to the mythical prototypes behind his sources. Shylock, in other words, is held to have had a past beyond Shakespeare's play.

Much Ado About Nothing

The mythical pattern of death and rebirth is as obvious in this play as in *The Winter's Tale*. The figure of the slandered woman is also frequently found in folk tales and myths. Northrop Frye points to the connection between the two themes when he argues that in *Much Ado* Shakespeare has put the theme of calumniation in 'something much closer to a primitive context by suggesting so strongly that Hero actually dies and revives during the play'.[39] Shakespeare's handling of the theme is thus closer, in his view, to Kalidasa's *Abhijñāna Śakuntalam* than to the comedies of Terence and Plautus.

As You Like It

The folk-tale aspect of this play has been pointed out by H. Coote Lake (1928), who classifies it, along with *Hamlet* and *Macbeth*, under the folk tale of the Orestes type: of 'rightful heir deprived by relative whom he finally slays and regains throne'.[40]

Wigston compares Rosalind as an agent of reconciliation with Imogen and Viola. All of them, as well as Perdita in *The Winter's Tale*, are considered to be representatives of Diana-as-Proserpine:

> If the poet has planned a profound reconciliation through rebirth, of his spiritual unity with its outer symbolic vehicle, then we can imagine no better *classical* type of this reconciling power than Diana—particularly in her character of Proserpine.... In *As You Like It*, it is Rosalind who brings about the reconciliation and restitution of the Banished Duke.... In *Pericles* Diana is introduced *directly as reconciling divinity*.... Diana as Proserpine typified *the sleeping power of the earth* during *winter*. She is, therefore, closely connected *with death*. Her reconciling power is the reconciliation that belongs to the immortality of Nature, that gives back what it takes away, through the grave. (pp. 336-7)

M. Sennet (1949) interprets the play within a theosophical framework as depicting the myth of paradise lost and regained. Referring to the phrase 'mangled forms' (II. vii. 42) he writes:

> The symbolism of 'mangled forms' may be traced in myth and folklore and religions. It is an ancient teaching that humanity, coming forth from the Edenic state of wholeness or undifferentiation, becomes split asunder, or loses a sense, or is in some way broken up into diversity and multiplicity as a result of its earthly existence. And it is the function of true Philosophy to teach man how to return again, with all its garnered harvest of experience, to unity, or at-one-ment, which is a state very different from simplicity.

Sennet brings the play within this broad pattern through the following equations: the three 'brothers'—Oliver, Jaques and Orlando—represent what in the mysteries are referred to as 'Will', 'Wisdom' or 'Intellect' and 'Love' respectively; it is the youngest of these, Orlando, who is successful in the quest for 'Ideal Love', which is represented by Rosalind; Celia is held to represent 'Holiness'; with a little 'hammering it out' Fredrick is equated with 'Friedrich', and hence with 'state of Peace'; the Duke Senior is equated with the 'Natural Man', and Frederick-Friedrich with the 'Spiritual Man' who finally attains peace; the forest of Arden is related to the 'Dark night of the Soul' (in support of this interpretation Sennet mentions the examples of Dante, Bunyan, Ibsen's *Peer Gynt*, *The Faerie Queene* and *Macbeth* as well as Babes in the Wood, Red Riding Hood, Sleeping Beauty, and *Through the Looking Glass*. From the name of Sir Roland de Bois (= Master of the Forest), Sennet infers that he represents 'Man before his Fall'.

A parallel is also drawn between the play and the story of Noah, which can be taken to represent the passage from 'tribulation to the regenerate life'. The forest in *As You Like It* is made to correspond to the flood in the Biblical story. While the details of Sennet's interpretation may not be very clear, the broad outline is familiar enough. Remarking that the play, both in its beginning and ending, can be 'matched with the old tales' (this matching being, we might remark, one of the main features of myth criticism), Sennet sums up the theme of these tales and the play as the 'Restoration of fallen man and Paradise Regained'. In conclusion he sets out in tabular form the parallels between the play and the stages of the mystical experience as described by Evelyn Underhill. The five acts of the play are thus seen to correspond to the five stages through which the mystic is led to the culminating experience of 'Union'.[41]

Richard Knowles (1966) argues that there is a need to combine myth interpretations, which generally neglect specific mythological allusions, with historical studies of mythology (like Douglas Bush's) which generally tend to ignore the broad mythic patterns. He mentions Don Cameron Allen as one of the very few critics who approach 'Shakespeare's mythmaking through his use of an established mythological tradition'. Knowles makes a similar attempt with reference to *As You Like It*. He argues that Hercules is the dominant mythological figure, even though he is mentioned only once in the play. This and other allusions 'consistently make the literal action reverberate beyond itself'. Orlando, according to Knowles, is a Hercules figure, and Hercules in Renaissance mythography is a type of Christ. He also finds other, though less important, mythological parallels (e.g. between Duke Senior and Moses in the wilderness; Oliver and Cain; Frederick and the Pharaoh or Herod; Rosalind and Heavenly Rose, etc.). Some of the parallels seem to be rather strained, as when Knowles interprets Rosalind's comment on Oliver and Celia that 'Clubs cannot part them' (v. i. 38) as alluding to Hercules's weakness before love. One would have thought that the reference was to pairing dogs. Nevertheless, Knowles's suggestion that the mythical allusions in the play refer not merely to the myths but also to the Renaissance interpretations of them is valuable. He also suggests that there is no necessary contradiction between this historical approach to the mythical allusions and the archetypal approach of the myth critics, since the figures of Christ and Hercules are 'intermediary between Orlando and an archetype of heroic struggle' which may be consistent with 'those outlined by Rank, Raglan, Campbell, and others'.[42]

Twelfth Night

Wigston's association of Viola in this play, along with Rosalind, Imogen and others, with Diana considered as a deity of reconciliation has already been mentioned. The general pattern of discord and harmony, which is found as early as *The Comedy of Errors*, can easily be discerned in this play. Also discernible is the pattern of a period of confusion and loss of identity followed by the regaining of social identity that Northrop Frye traces in the comedies generally.

Barbara Lewalski (1965) interprets the play in the light of Christian typological exegesis. Her argument is that the themes and motifs of the play 'contain something of religious significance associated with Epiphany and with the Spirit of Christmastide'. Shakespeare's method is one of 'Christian typology , 'whereby certain real historical events and personages from the Old Testament and (more significantly for the present purposes) from certain classical fictions such as the *Metamorphoses* or the *Aeneid* were seen to point to aspects of Christ and of the Gospel story without losing their historical or fictional reality'. This idea is applied to *Twelfth Night* as follows: Illyria, as Professor Lewalski points out, is different from what Frye has called the 'green world' and John Vyvyan, 'retreats in the wilderness' because the characters stay on in this world at the end of the play instead of returning to the former society. It may therefore be equated with 'Elysium'. Illyria, she argues, is a place of 'Good Will' where the 'Bad Will' of Malvolio has no place. But she also suggests, inconsistently, that Illyria, by virtue of its first syllable, may be associated with Illusion (witness the self-love and disorder of Malvolio, Olivia, Orsino). The roles of Viola and Sebastian are interpreted as representing the 'dual nature and role of the incarnate Divine Love, Christ', Viola standing for the suffering aspect of Christ and Sebastian for his divine exaltation. The final scene is described as containing an 'epiphany' when Sebastian is finally 'manifested'. In brief, Sebastian and Viola, together, 'do indeed bring the "peace" of the season to Illyria through a reordering of its life and its loves'.[43]

The Merry Wives of Windsor

John M. Steadman has interpreted Falstaff in the light of the figure of Actaeon in Renaissance mythography. According to him, Shakespeare's portrayal of Falstaff is 'an obvious burlesque of the Actaeon myth', that myth being interpreted in the Renaissance as an instance of the 'ravages of desire'. Thus, even though Shakespeare's predominant mode in this drama is one of 'bourgeois realism', he adopts the technique of 'mythological symbolism and parody' in its three episodes dealing with the gulling of Falstaff.

All's Well That Ends Well

Northrop Frye argues, characteristically:

The 'problem' of *All's Well* is not any Shavian social problem of how a woman gets her man, but the mythical problem of how Helena, like her ancestress Psyche, is going to solve her three impossible tasks: first of healing the sick king, then of presenting Bertram with a son of his own getting, and with his own ring, the talisman of recognition that, in *All's Well* as in *Sakuntala*, awakens his mind to reality.

This argument is built upon earlier studies of the folk-tale and mythic elements in the play. Karl Simrock, for example, had noticed the parallel with the story of 'Sacontala' as early as 1850. H. Coote Lake (1928) had suggested that the whole play is based on folk tales and pointed out the following folk motifs: the curing of the king, forced marriage, impossible tasks, substitutions, ring or token, and twin sons. He had also suggested the story of Judah and Tamar (Genesis 38) as an analogue. W. W. Lawrence (1931) had also discussed the folk tale motifs in the play and suggested that their origin is to be traced not in the Orient but rather in 'primitive manners and customs, in the domains of anthropology and folklore'.[44]

James L. Calderwood (1964) relates some of these folk motifs to the theme of micro- and macro-cosmic sterility and revitalization that has been popularized through the writings of Frazer and Eliot's *The Waste Land*, thus bringing the play within the framework of the 'myth and ritual pattern' of death and rebirth. Calderwood argues that the king's illness is a kind of sexual impotence corresponding to the sterility in the community at large. The community is ultimately revitalized through Helena's magical powers. While conceding that the play has elements of realism, parody and satire, Calderwood argues that 'the myth is nevertheless in the play—though subdued like the dyer's hand to the stuff it works in—and following its traces can be instructive'. He points to the traditional association of social sterility with sexual impotence and suggests that the healing of the king becomes 'a kind of intellectual-spiritual coitus as a result of which the king is, paradoxically, "rais'd... from [his] sickly bed" (II. iii. 109) and restored to cultural potency'. This sexual symbolism, he suggests, relates the healing to the bed trick later in the play. Calderwood also draws, briefly, a parallel between this play and *Venus and Adonis*, Helena corresponding to Venus (which helps to bring out the erotic aspect of Helena's cure), Bertram to Adonis, and Parolles to the boar (which symbolizes death).[45]

Regeneration or rebirth in a more spiritual sense has been seen in the play by some other critics. In his essay on the play in *The Sovereign Flower* (1958), G. Wilson Knight relates Helena's healing power to the mystic concept of the Third Eye. Beryl Pogson interprets the play as dramatizing a stage in the initiation of the Hero. She traces a common theme in all the plays of Shakespeare, namely 'the theme of Man's inner life and his possible redemption and re-birth through the spiritual influence within him which is represented externally in the drama as Woman'. *Romeo and Juliet*, *All's Well* and *The Winter's Tale* belong, she argues, to three successive periods of Shakespeare's work, in each of which the heroine plays an important role. Juliet, according to her, plays her part in the redemptive process as a sacrifice, Helena as a healer, and Perdita as 'the Lost Child of the King whose return signifies his re-birth'. About *All's Well*, specifically, Pogson writes that it represents allegorically 'not Man's search for God but God's search for Man and the ultimate triumph of divine love over all human difficulties'. Helena is the Soul seeking after Bertram the Man, and is shown as taking the initiative because 'on some inner planes the feminine principle is said to be more active'. The union of Bertram and Helena symbolizes the planting of 'the seed of Second Birth', which is why the twins born from the encounter in the dark in the source are changed by Shakespeare into one child.[46]

A similar interpretation of the play, but with greater claims to historical validity, is put forward by Eric La Guardia (1963), who maintains that the major poetic objective of the play is 'to dramatize the re-generation of man and imitate the condition of *concordia mundi*'. The study concentrates on what is described as the 'two regenerative narrative actions in the play', namely initiation and purification. Apart from the relevance of this to the familiar myth and ritual pattern of rebirth, La Guardia's analysis suggests that the play is mythic in another sense, in that, belonging to what Frye has called the romantic mode, the play presents an interaction of the divine and the natural through Helena and her chastity.

Measure for Measure

Hanns Sachs has related Angelo to Oedipus, whom he considers to be the prototype of the man who judges himself. The ethical principle, he argues, is especially associated with the 'Oedipus-crime'. Admittedly, there is no hint of this in *Measure for Measure*, but it is brought out clearly in *Hamlet*.[47] The comparison between Oedipus and Angelo does, I believe, throw a useful light on the play, whether we choose to emphasize the ethical aspect of their dilemma or the psychological.

THE ENGLISH HISTORY PLAYS

The history plays, with the important exception of the two parts of *Henry IV*, have, not surprisingly, elicited few commentaries in terms of the myth and ritual pattern. Nevertheless, some critics have discerned the shape of the Christian myth of the fall and redemption when the plays are taken as a group. Honor Matthews (1962) describes this as the myth of Lucifer. She writes:

Shakespeare accepted the myth of Lucifer's rebellion as the archetype of sin and, like his contemporaries, found an acceptable reflection of it in the recent history of his own country.... Among them [the Elizabethan dramatists] Shakespeare alone traced in English history a picture of sin, justice and redemption such as his fathers had found in the Bible stories, and the Greeks in the legends of Agamemnon and Oedipus.

But Matthews points out that in the *Henry VI* plays man's sins are explained not in terms of the archetypal rebellion of Lucifer but rather in terms 'of its derivative, the more general breach of degree'. Tillyard (1944) sees a basically similar pattern in the whole cycle of Shakespeare's history plays: 'the beginning in prosperity, the distortion of prosperity by a crime, civil war, and ultimate renewal of prosperity'.[48]

1. *Henry VI*

Otto Rank pointed out in *The Myth of the Birth of the Hero* (1909) that Joan's denial of her parentage followed the well-known mythical pattern of the birth of the hero. 'There seems a certain necessity,' writes Rank, 'for the prophet to deny his parents.'[49] Shakespeare's attitude towards this 'mythical' heroine is, of course, far from uncritical, but in including this episode in the play he shows, it seems, an awareness of this common feature of mythical heroes.

2. *Henry VI*

Samuel M. Pratt (1965) argues that Humphrey is not merely historical but also 'mythic', his story symbolizing 'the perilous path that the good public servant has to travel in this world'. But even more importantly, in popular thought he had become the victim of the Roman Catholic Church, and hence his myth became 'the archetype of what the English Renaissance in its political, religious, and humanistic concerns was all about'. 'Myth' in such usage is associated with social pressures at a particular moment in history rather than with universal, non-historical patterns.

3. *Henry VI*

H. Coote Lake (p. 314) suggests that the episode in II.v showing a father who has killed his son and a son who has killed his father should be classed as myth, along with such other myths and legends as those of Sohrab and Rustam, Odysseus and Antigonus, and Balan and Balin. However, such an episode would perhaps have had greater mythical reverberation in the *Henry IV* plays since the theme of fathers and sons is of central significance there.

Richard III

H. C. Goddard (1951) briefly suggests a Jungian interpretation of the play. Richard III, he writes, 'has failed to come to terms with the nocturnal world—the other side of life—the unconscious. Of that unconscious world, from the myth of Pegasus to the White

Horses of Rosmersholm, the horse has been the symbol, standing for the living stream of unconscious energy on which consciousness rides.' Goddard also suggests that the red and the white rose stand for blood and spirit respectively, the political conflict thus also representing an internal psychic conflict in keeping with the mythological principle of the continuity between the macrocosm and the microcosm. Elements of the hero myth are discerned in the play by Honor Matthews in the figure of Richmond who, like many other mythic heroes, escapes as a child overseas, finally to return to kill the usurper. This helps to link the idea of the 'Tudor myth' with the general pattern of myth and ritual.

Clifford Leech (1964) argues that the play presents not only the Tudor myth but also the 'tragic myth' of rebellion and Nemesis (represented by Richard and Margaret) in which the spectator identifies with the 'challenger of order'. Finally, Norman Holland (1964) sees the following simple mythic pattern in the play:

Good King Henry VI is murdered by a bad king in the image of a boar (as in the myths of Osiris or Adonis) and mourned by three queens. The boar-king, now his successor, lays the land waste, but he is finally killed by good king Henry VII who comes from across the sea to kill the boar-king and set the wasteland free.[50]

An important point to note, however, is that unlike the hero myths *Richard III* focuses attention on Richard, who corresponds to the evil giant or the boar, rather than on Henry VI. In *Macbeth*, similarly, Macduff has all the attributes of the mythical hero but the centre of interest is the evil Macbeth.

King John

I have not seen any discussion of this play in terms of myth.

Richard II

There is no interpretation of this play in terms of 'solar myth', so far as I know, though the sun-king imagery in the play could easily be associated with such a myth.[51] The play has, however, attracted 'Christian myth criticism' or mythologizing in the tradition of typological-allegorical exegesis. J. A. Bryant, for example, has argued that one of the characteristics of Shakespeare's dramaturgy from this play onwards is his 'persistent use of the Biblical story as an analogue for his secular fable'. Richard is thus presented as *microchristus* as well as *microcosmos*. Glynne Wickham similarly argues that the relationship of the content of this play to the form springs 'naturally from the native English dramatic tradition, grounded on Biblical narrative treated typologically'.[52]

Henry IV and *Henry V*

These plays have been the subject of several commentaries in terms of myth and ritual, the mythic or ritual origins or analogues of Falstaff being the chief preoccupation. Falstaff's connection with the magico-mythical realm is hinted at by Frazer himself in the only allusion to Shakespeare in *The Golden Bough* when he cites the description of Falstaff's death, 'even just between twelve and one, e'en at the turning o'th'tide' (*Henry V*, II. iii. 13) as an example of belief in the homoeopathic magic of the tides.[53]

John Heath-Stubbs (1949) relates Falstaff to a recurring type in mythology, folklore and heroic saga, namely the figure of the 'fabulous glutton' of divine origin. Other such figures cited are Gargantua, Heracles, the Norse god Thor, the Irish Dagda, and the Celtic deity Beli or Belinus. Heath-Stubbs also draws a parallel between Hal-Falstaff and Dido-Aeneas, both Dido and Falstaff being symbols of passion or 'corporeal humanity'. W. H. Auden (1959) makes a similar comparison between Falstaff in love with the prince and stories in which an immortal mermaid falls in love with a mortal, only to lose both her immortality and her beloved.

Martin Lings (1966) interprets the play (*Henry IV*) in terms of esoteric lore. He distinguishes between esoteric and exoteric art in the following way: exoteric art is concerned only with salvation; esoteric art, on the other hand, 'looks beyond salvation to sanctification'. Sanctification is the regaining of man's lost paradise, and Lings argues that it has been the object of all esoteric cults, including those of the Freemasons and the Rosicrucians. *Henry IV* is a dramatization, according to Lings, of the Prodigal Son story, which he interprets esoterically and 'anagogically' as depicting 'the exodus of the soul from the state of original sin to the state of sanctification'. This could be the meaning of the play, Lings argues, even without Shakespeare's intending it, though it does seem to be intentional. The rejection of Falstaff, in his view, represents the soul's final purification, the victory of the Red Cross Knight over the Dragon.[54]

Sitansu Maitra (1967) attempts to explain the figure of Falstaff and the effect of his rejection in the light of Jungian psychology. He argues that Falstaff is the Renaissance variant of the trickster symbol. This figure is seen as a manifestation of the shadow side of the personality; he has the 'syncretic nature of assimilating to himself his older archetypes'; and he rises from the unconscious when conscious life becomes too one-sided. The rejection of Falstaff is right because 'Prince Hal could integrate the trickster [Falstaff] in himself and as he attained a higher degree of psychic stability the trickster lost his hold over the Prince, which is what is meant by the rejection of Falstaff'.[55]

Finally, a minor mythic motif in the play may be noted. The presence of an adversary to the hero-prince in the figure of Hotspur, whom Shakespeare deliberately and unhistorically makes of the same age as Hal, has parallels in myths and legends. In the Indian epic *Mahabharata* there is such a pair in Arjuna and Karna, who are actually brothers without being aware of it and are closest to each other in terms of talent, though belonging to rival camps. Hector and Achilles are perhaps a similar pair, and in Shakespeare's drama we have other examples of such pairs in Hamlet and Fortinbras, Hamlet and Laertes, and Macbeth and Banquo. Psychologically, this motif seems to express sibling rivalry.

Henry VIII

G. Wilson Knight considers this play the culmination of the entire work of Shakespeare. From our point of view the interesting aspect of Knight's criticism of the play is the emphasis on the play's 'national statement'. This seems to suggest that for Knight the play is a synthesis of myth and history. This would be especially the case with the prophetic vision centred in the infant Elizabeth. Knight relates this 'prophetic emphasis on a child' to the Virgilian and Christian traditions, and also remarks that the works of Aeschylus and Sophocles 'show similar completions in national statement'. R. A. Foakes and Howard Felperin, however, split up between them Knight's synthesis of the anti-theses of myth and history. Foakes (1957) argues that the play marks Shakespeare's return from the magic of the romances to the world of historical fact. On the other hand, Felperin (1966) argues that the play merely represents 'an orthodox translation of the heterodox myths of process rendered in the romances', the symbolic pagan deities of the earlier plays being superseded by the familiar God of Christianity. The play shows, according to Felperin, that like other ageing English poets Shakespeare finally 'embraces traditional answers to questions which he had spent his career formulating on both sides'. Shakespeare, in other words, goes from one set of myths (in the romances) to another myth, but with great loss of intensity.[56]

THE TRAGEDIES

The genre of tragedy has attracted more studies in terms of anthropological theories about primitive rituals of the scapegoat than the other genres. The 'Cambridge Anthropologists' were primarily concerned with tragedy, although Cornford extended their theories to comedy as well. Frazer himself saw the lineaments of tragedy in the primitive sacrificial rituals of king-killing that he documented at such length. In specifically mythic (rather than ritual) terms, too, critics have seen individual tragedies as variations on what has been termed by Philip Wheelwright 'the myth of tragedy'. Clifford Leech also, as we saw in the discussion of *Richard III*, uses the term 'tragic myth', implying by it not merely that the myth of rebellion and Nemesis is tragic, but also that it is the myth of tragedy as a whole. As already pointed out, Herbert Weisinger sees tragedy in terms of the myth and ritual pattern of death and rebirth, the 'monomyth', we might call it, of which the individual tragedies are variations. The genre has also been related to the Christian myth, especially by G. Wilson Knight who argues that 'each of Shakespeare's tragic heroes is a miniature Christ', and that the Christian Mass can be seen as central to Shakespearean tragedy. Northrop Frye includes Christ among the tragic heroes. Roy Battenhouse (1969) also sees, at least in Shakespearean tragedy, the presence of the Christian myth, although, in opposition to Frye and Knight, he suggests that it is not Christ but rather Adam who is the 'ultimate archetype for the tragic hero'. This view links up with Clifford Leech's description of the tragic myth as one of rebellion and Nemesis, and with the Aristotelian concept of the tragic flaw.[57]

Titus Andronicus

Honor Matthews points out that Lucius, who comes back from over the mountains to establish order in Rome, is like the hero figures or saviours that we find in myths. Matthews also makes the interesting observation that in this play, as well as in some others, Shakespeare splits the mythic figure of the saviour-hero into two, so that while one figure wins the victory and establishes order, the actual slaying of the tyrant is done by the other (e.g. Macduff kills Macbeth but Malcolm takes over the reign of Scotland; Edmund does the slaying of the old year, Lear, but Edgar becomes king). In this way Shakespeare is able to resolve the problem that the action of revenge creates by setting the law of talion in motion, the law of an eye for an eye, a tooth for a tooth.[58]

Romeo and Juliet

As early as 1850 Karl Simrock related the play to the stories of Hero and Leander, Pyramus and Thisbe, and Tristan and Isolde. 'The last mentioned,' writes Simrock, 'is only the most modern form, the last *renascence* of the ancient myth, which represents the idea of love, and of its tragic fate, in the simplest and most consistent manner.' Simrock also mentions parallels to the story in oriental myths, though he does not name any.[59] William Archer (1884) mentions Simrock's derivation of the plot of the play from the myths of Pyramus and Thisbe and Hero and Leander, and says that 'no one who realizes the true nature of the mythopoeic tendency will find this theory either far-fetched or startling'. All these stories, he suggests, 'are collateral outgrowths of some primitive legendary embodiment of the sweet vehemence of young desire'. Shakespeare, according to Archer, 'instinctively recognized' the 'primitiveness and well-nigh symbolic universality of the subject he had chosen'. We see in Archer's essay the close relation that 'myth criticism' has with source studies, myths being the earliest of the possible sources for the plays. Archer also suggests that a fairy tale is 'myth adapted to the nursery-fireside view of life', and that myth itself is 'unconditioned by time or place'. Myth, in other words, is at once the most universal and the most primitive, timeless as well as the first in time. Finally, it might be mentioned that Archer considers the story of the play to be one of the 'age-old myths of the Aryan race' to which Shakespeare was attracted by choice rather than chance.

Wigston (pp. 201–38) argues that the play celebrates Love's martyrs, 'but in some profounder sense than metaphor'. Romeo, according to him, is none other than Eros or Phanes, because he has a torch in I. iv. Phanes, the God of Love in Orphic mythology, is also associated with a torch, that being the meaning of his name. Wigston writes that 'Dadouchos or Torchbearer at Eleusis was this mystic Love, Phanes himself'. Romeo-Eros-Phanes is also equated with Bacchus-Priapus, the thumb-biting in the first scene being taken as a priapic gesture. Juliet, in Wigston's equations, represents Night, the Moon, and Diana; Mercutio = Mercury = Hermes = the sacred herald. Wigston also compares Juliet to some other heroines in Shakespeare: like her, Hero, Imogen, Hermione and Thaisa also fall 'into a death sleep or simulated death, that has no reality *except in appearance.... They return to life with restoration to their husbands.*' As for Romeo, he seems 'the very incarnation of Love, as the creative energy of life itself personified and deified, suffering as the Logos, as Adonis, Bacchus descending into the tomb, the Divine Word crucified in the sepulchre of this transcendent art, yet immortal as the divine principle he represents—Love deified, to be reborn'. This may appear to be mythological syncretism run riot, but it is curious how many of the ideas that became common currency in later myth criticism are anticipated by Wigston—the idea of death and rebirth, the equation of Christ with the other dying gods, the emphasis on the figures of Persephone and Dionysus, and, though not here, the myth of the seasons.

Theodore Heline (1936) also interprets the play in terms of occult thought. It is best summarized in the author's own words in the following passage which, incidentally, plays many variations on the One Timeless Theme, the Monomyth:

Romeo and Juliet is deeply occult. It depicts the tragedy of separateness; it is a poetic version of the Biblical episode of Cain and Abel. It is an esoteric treatment of the one becoming two. It is a story of the children of the 'sorrowful star', the earth, with emphasis placed on humanity's passage through the place of duality.

The characters, Romeo and Juliet, voice the longing of the human soul for completeness; they portray humanity's struggle to surmount separateness and to regain unity; they represent all mankind in its effort to regain the spiritual vision which it possessed before taking on the veils of dividing forms.[60]

Finally, very briefly, three other discussions of the play: Beryl Pogson considers the play as dealing with the theme of dualism, pointing out that Verona was the centre of Dualism, 'the secret faith of the Cathari'. Dualism in another form is also emphasized by Harry Levin (1960), and by Caroline Spurgeon and others who have commented on the contrast between light and darkness in the play. Levin subsumes various imagistic oppositions in the play under the 'all-embracing one of Eros and Thanatos, the *leitmotif* of the Liebestod, the myth of the tryst in the womb'. Sitansu Maitra (1967) considers Mercutio as a trickster figure representing the shadow side of the personality who is no longer needed once Romeo matures. 'Mercutio,' he writes, 'is the simple Hans in Grimm's *Tales* who becomes King Romeo after the sea-journey, i.e., death.'[61]

Julius Caesar

Edward T. Herbert (1970) undertakes a 'mythic interpretation' of the play in the light of Freud's theory of the primal horde. In its bare outline, he suggests, 'the plot is a dramatization of an archetypal situation such as that discussed by Freud in *Totem and Taboo*'. Julius Caesar, according to this interpretation, corresponds to the ruler of the primal horde, and his murder to the primal crime. The conspirators, like the patricidal brothers, enter into a blood bond, signifying that the entire clan assumes responsibility for the crime. Caesar is thus the totem figure, a father to the conspirators, who are all young men. Caesar's continuing power even after death results from the remorse that follows the primal crime. Herbert concludes: 'Actions, therefore, which seem at first to be contradictory or inconsistent, are seen to be natural and deeply rooted in the human psyche when viewed in light of Freudian insights. A mythic approach in interpreting the play, consequently, shows the aptness of naming the tragedy after one who was sacrificed on the Ides of March.'

Hamlet

The close connection between source studies and myth criticism is brought out very clearly from the history of Hamlet criticism. Karl Simrock, in the course of a discussion of the sources of this play, relates it to the Norse myth of Odin and Vali, and that myth, in turn, to the solar theme, suggesting that Odin is a sun-god who descends to the lower regions and stays there for seven years

(= seven months) so that Rinda, the frozen Earth, might, after the death of Baldur, the God of Light, give birth to another son, Vali, who should avenge the death of Baldur and bring back the light of returning spring. Reviewing Simrock's book *Die Quellen des Shakespeare* (1870), Felix Liebrecht points out that Simrock had already, in an earlier book, traced the shadow of old popular legends behind the episode of the journey to Britain. Liebrecht continues: 'In the present work he carries this idea still further, and inclines to believe that this legend, like most others, was originally mythological, and referred to the life of the world in the annual revolution of the seasons, and from its greatest antiquity might have been known to the Romans.'[62]

Simrock's theory about the mythological origin of the Hamlet saga has been adopted and elaborated upon by several writers. John Fiske (1873), a 'solar' mythologist, takes up Simrock's point that the story of Hamlet, 'when traced back to its Norse original, is unmistakably the story of the quarrel between Summer and Winter, and the moody prince is as much a solar hero as Odin himself', but suggests that, of course, Shakespeare was not conscious of this solar myth. It is nevertheless present in the play as a 'faded nature myth', just as, one supposes, there are faded metaphors behind many words. Another writer, in the course of a review of a book on *Hamlet* which advanced the theory that the play depicts not an individual but a type illustrating the conflict between will and passion, traces the transformations of the Hamlet story thus:

> Hamlet, or *Amleth*, first emerges from the night of the past as a mythical Norse hero who typified the quarrel between Summer and Winter; next he appears in the guise of an historical prince upon whom the poet seizes to make of him 'what we see...' Finally the critic, sooner or later, unconscious of the original mythical character of the hero, yet utterly unable to resist the relentless wheels of fate, reduces him again to a myth, though of another sort. Having started a type of the warfare of nature, he ends up a type of the warfare of mind.

Almost as if in illustration of what this reviewer writes, thirty years later John T. MacCurdy (1918) relates the seasonal myth to the Oedipus complex in the course of a comparative study of Hamlet and Orestes, arguing that the conflict between Winter and Summer is merely a metaphorical version of the Oedipal conflict.[63]

Sinclair Korner, whose interpretation of *A Midsummer-Night's Dream* has already been mentioned, interprets *Hamlet* too as a solar myth. Hamlet—either father or son—represents summer and sunshine; Claudius, winter and darkness; and Gertrude, the earth-goddess Flora, equally at home in the arms of either brother. Korner's essay brings out one aspect of myth criticism very clearly, namely its similarity to the imagery approach. For the solar myth in the play is discovered largely through a study of the imagery of the play. Korner refers to the prevalence of 'solar similes' in the speeches of Hamlet, though his concept of 'solar' includes not only Jove, but also Mars, Mercury, and the sea and the wind. Both the myth and the imagery approach to a work attempt to reveal the pattern which is below the level of plot and character and which is revealed through the indirections of similes and metaphors. The chief difference between the two approaches lies in the formulation of this subliminal pattern, the myth critic trying to go beyond mere imagery in relating the pattern to archetypal or universal themes, especially as found in the myths of antiquity. The myth critic therefore generally concentrates on those images which can most fruitfully be related to these universal patterns. Such images tend to be associated with natural phenomena like the changes of the seasons, the annual and diurnal progress of the sun and the growth of vegetation. It is such images that Colin Still includes in his list of universal symbols, although he simplifies the list even further by reducing these natural phenomena also to their elemental level.

Gilbert Murray's famous essay on 'Hamlet and Orestes' (1914) is important because it relates the seasonal or solar myth (from Korner's essay it is clear that the two amount to the same thing) to Frazer's anthropological studies in rituals of king-killing. But it is interesting to note that although Murray interprets *Hamlet* in terms of its origin in 'that prehistoric and world-wide ritual battle of Summer and Winter, of Life and Death', he complicates (or confuses) the pattern by equating the hero not with Summer but with Winter.[64] In thus presenting a view the very opposite of Simrock's and others', Murray puts a very big question mark to the very idea of there ever being such a pattern as that of the battle of Summer and Winter. Murray's description of Hamlet, it seems to me, is closer to our experience of the play, but it does not make much sense to associate Hamlet (as Murray does) both with the right cause and with winter (and death). The moral and the seasonal themes seem to coexist rather uneasily, but where they are harmonized, as in Simrock, Korner and others, it is done with considerable violence to our experience of Hamlet as a predominantly melancholy figure and hence as associated with winter rather than summer. One could, of course, argue that Hamlet is the sun during the winter of Claudius's reign, but the association of Claudius with winter is not at all evident.

In addition to being seen as the spirit of summer or winter, Hamlet has been compared with both Orestes and Oedipus, the comparison with Orestes going back to at least 1709.[65] The comparisons are made within varying theoretical frameworks, ranging from the purely literary to the psychological and anthropological. William Ward Crane (1891) compares the three figures of Hamlet, Laertes and Fortinbras to similar triads in Greek and other mythologies, referring to Prometheus (interpreted to mean 'fore-thinker', i.e. Hamlet), Epimetheus ('after-thinker', i.e. Laertes) and Atlas (the 'strong in arms', i.e. Fortinbras), and to the Indian triad of Brahma, Shiva, and Vishnu. Crane suggests that this recurrence of triads might have something to do with the superstitious regard for the number three which, in turn, might have grown out of 'the same ancient idea of two opposing forces in nature, with a third principle beneficiently supplying what they lacked or left wanting'. This is probably true as a general principle, but one wonders where Horatio fits into this triadic scheme.

Joseph Campbell (1949) briefly refers to the play in the course of a discussion of that stage in his 'monomyth' in which the hero encounters Woman-as-temptress.[66]

D. S. Savage (1952) examines the alchemical images in the play and suggests that what the images refer to is 'transmutation in reverse'. In other words, 'they are used to point a tendency, not towards regeneration, but degeneration'. Nevertheless, Savage suggests, 'the process of degeneration shows the unity which underlies the triple theme of generation, regeneration and degeneration which the play explores'. Jean Paris (1959) relates the play to the primal theme of Creation, Fall and Redemption. Like Crane (although he does not mention him) he interprets the three sons in the play as representing three attitudes to revenge and to thought and action generally, and like Crane, again, he interprets Fortinbras as the synthesis of the attitudes represented by Hamlet and Laertes.

Both Hamlet and Laertes are men divided within themselves, just as the society to which they belong is torn with strife and division. Paris writes:

Beginning with a profound corruption in the existing nature of men and things—'there is something rotten in the state of Denmark'—Shakespeare leads us through spiritual strife, division, and war toward an ultimate purification and recapture of the pristine state of innocence. Hamlet's world is the rotten world destined to return to dust, while Fortinbras's is the 'shape of things to come', perfect once more in its order, unity and purity.

Paris also refers to D. S. Savage's article on the alchemical imagery in the play and suggests that alchemy gives us an archetype of tragic catharsis, in that according to it 'all must rot and rust in order to be changed into gold'. Finally, Paris argues that this dialectic of fall and redemption can also be found in all of Shakespeare's historical dramas. Alexander A. Vannovsky (1962) also discusses the play in terms of the myth of paradise, but in a rather obscure manner, as the title of his book itself might lead one to expect: *The Path of Jesus from Judaism to Christianity, as Conceived by Shakespeare (Disclosure of a Hidden Jewish Plot in Shakespeare's Tragedy "Hamlet")*. Claudius, according to Vannovsky, represents the Serpent, Gertrude's seduction resembles that of Eve, and the play of Gonzago also represents the same Biblical myth of the fall. In Vannovsky's own words: 'Gonzago represents a screen behind which is hidden the staging of the eternal myth about the fall of a heavenly entity into the midst of the sensuous world, and how this fall is being utilized for its own aims by the evil power. Therefore, Gonzago serves as a screen to the staging of the eternal myth, just as the Danish plot of *Hamlet* serves as a screen for the Jewish plot of the tragedy.'[67]

Richmond Y. Hathorn (1962), using the speech about the rugged Pyrrhus (II. ii. 444) as a starting point, compares the story of Hamlet to that older story. It seems that Hathorn's conclusion that Hamlet represents an individual in the state of *Acedia* precedes, instead of following, this comparison. Taking for granted that the speech is meant to reflect upon the roles of the central characters of the play, he goes on to suggest that Hecuba is 'obviously' Queen Gertrude, who 'would sincerely mourn' if Claudius were dead; Priam 'then' becomes not the elder Hamlet but Claudius; the 'hellish Pyrrhus must accordingly be Prince Hamlet'. (In a footnote

Hathorn points out that he is the first to make this identification.) Now Pyrrhus, according to Hathorn, represents the 'Renaissance Man of Honour'. Hence, 'Hamlet is Shakespeare's pointing up of the ideal's shortcomings'. Hathorn's book is entitled *Tragedy, Myth, and Mystery*, but it seems that the only mystery is whether Hamlet's death 'is a herald of eternal day or a summoner to fast in fires'.[68]

For Sven Armens (1966), however, Hamlet's ultimate fate is not all that much of a mystery. He is certain that for him, as for the Moor, there were to be no flights of angels. The basis for this certainty is Armens's Jungian psychology. According to him, there are two archetypes of the family, the patriarchal and the matriarchal, and corresponding to each are certain basic attitudes. For example, the matriarchal child is 'passive', whereas the patriarchal child is 'active'. The archetypal masculine or patriarchal is symbolized as the Hero and the Father, while the archetypal feminine is symbolized as Kore and the Mother. The Jungian 'True Self' is achieved through a union of the two, but Hamlet 'fails to unite with the Kore in a bond of love, and thus, losing his soul, he falls back into the embrace of the "world dragon"'.[69]

Harry Slochower (1970) considers *Hamlet* not as a myth but as an example of 'mythopoesis', i.e. a conscious individual creation which arises when 'the literal account of the legend [can] no longer be accepted'. Slochower proceeds from this idea to draw some interesting parallels between episodes in *Hamlet* and mythical motifs. Thus Hamlet's mission, as in all mythopoesis, is 'to rid the body politic of its deceased state'. Among specific mythical motifs pointed out are fratricide, son versus mother (e.g. Marduk and Tiamat), usurping uncle (e.g. Kansa *versus* Krishna in Indian mythology), sea-voyage, and rescue from water. Slochower also points out that the play is full of mythic allusions 'evocative of Hamlet's own situation', and suggests that like other mythic heroes (e.g. Hercules) Hamlet can be considered to be the offspring of a union between a god (the elder Hamlet) and an ordinary mortal, Gertrude, since Hamlet's father is almost deified. Slochower also argues that the play can be divided into three acts corresponding to the three stages in the life of the mythic hero which he terms the Quest, the Journey, and the Recreation, but suggests that Hamlet is 'the first hero in mythopoesis who questions himself from the beginning, the first who fails to carry out his mission, until it no longer really matters to him'.[70]

Troilus and Cressida

There is only one article on this play that I have come across that uses the concept of myth. R. A. Foakes (1963) argues that the audience's awareness of the myth of Troy conditions its response to the play as a whole, creating, as it were, a double awareness of the characters as ordinary mortals as well as types of great warriors or beautiful women.

Othello

Lilian Winstanley (1922/4) interprets *Othello, Lear, Macbeth* and *Hamlet* in term of 'the vast body of contemporary mythology relating to the history of the time' which was common, according to her, to all the countries of Europe. 'Mythology' in her usage means 'the method of writing in vivid metaphor', and she maintains that most of the great works of the period deal with recent history in terms of this body of commonly used metaphors. Thus, *Othello* in her view is a symbolic expression of 'the Tragedy of Italy', with Desdemona as the symbol of Italy, which was under threat from Spain at the time, and Othello representing the 'idea' of Spain. Similarly she argues that both *Lear* and *Macbeth* should be seen as 'symbolic mythology' dealing with important recent events such as the Darnley Murder and the St Bartholomew Massacre. Such interpretations, which can be traced back to Horace Walpole's *Historic Doubts on the Life and the Reign of Richard III* (1768), where *The Winter's Tale* is seen as an indirect apology for Ann Boleyn, and to James Plumptre's attempt to see *Hamlet* as a political allegory in his *Observations on 'Hamlet'* (1796), may be said to derive from the Euhemerist tradition of mythography, though Winstanley herself compares her method with the Higher Criticism of the Bible. But there is this important difference: Euhemerism (after Euhemerus, a Greek philosopher of the fourth century BC) sought to 'demythologize' mythology by reducing the mythical gods and heroes to real historical persons, Winstanley's purpose, on the other hand, is to raise rather than lower the status of the particular work. As she writes, with reference to *Othello*, Shakespeare's subject 'is a *human* story of *human* interest, a real story taken from real life; but it is also a story which is made the symbol of a *national* destiny'.[71]

Othello has also been seen by several critics in relation to the Christian myth. A full equational model of the play has been built by Hugh Brown (1930), who considers *Othello* an analogue of the Divine Drama of the Christian scheme of the world. The simplest way to present Brown's interpretation is to tabulate his equations:

God the Father	= Shakespeare's imagination
Devil	= 'the Adversary'
Christ	= the Heroine
Man	= Othello
Holy Spirit	= Shakespeare's inner personal spirit, 'awakened to full knowledge of himself by the death of the Beloved', but not incarnated
The Wicked	= Iago
The Gentile	= Emilia

The figures that would normally be the signified have been deliberately put on the left hand side of the equations, which is usually reserved for the signifiers, because, according to Brown, it is not the study of theology that throws light on *Othello*, but rather 'the best approach to systematic theology is through the study of dramatic creation, and particularly the creation of *Othello*'.[72]

Maud Bodkin (1934) examines Iago in terms of the 'devil archetype' as the 'shadow-side of Othello'. She links this up with the idea that tragedy represents a conflict between assertive and submissive impulses, which in turn is related to our ambivalent attitude towards our parents. According to her the theme of the conflict between generations is also central to *Hamlet* and *Lear*.[73]

Beryl Pogson (1950) interprets the play in terms of occult doctrine. The handkerchief, she suggests, is the symbol of Othello's divine origin, and his fate is woven into it. Iago is the divine Tempter testing Othello. Miss Pogson also refers to the *Zohar* to show that the kiss with which Othello dies has an 'occult' meaning and concludes:

In depicting the death of the hero at his own hand, by his own will, for the purpose of union with his spiritual Self on a higher plane, Shakespeare is here following in the tradition of the Drama of the Mysteries, where the candidate suffers the Mystical Death as a Prelude to Re-Birth. The word on which Othello is pierced by his own will is the symbol of the Cross. He slays himself on the altar, as it were, of Desdemona's body, upon a kiss' which is the sign of spiritual union.[74]

Honor Matthews links the play to the romances by suggesting that as in those plays, a person of the younger generation becomes the reconciler and restorer of order. This young person is Cassio, who is like a 'son' to Othello. Finally, David Kaula (1966) points out that Othello, 'like the standard mythic hero', achieves eminence by tracing his progress 'from slavery, dangerous exploits, and exposure to monsters and wild landscape' up to Brabantio's drawing-room.[75]

King Lear

In the criticism of *Lear* we once again find myth criticism emerging from source studies. In his introduction to the Temple edition of the play (1895), Sir Israel Gollancz traces the story to Celtic legend, and beyond that to 'the more remote realm of simple nature myths'. In a footnote Gollancz mentions, without naming, 'some Celtic folk-lorists' according to whom 'Lir', the prototype of Lear in the Celtic legends, represents the sea-god Neptune. The two evil daughters, in this view, represent 'the rough winds' and Cordelia, 'the gentle Zephyr'. Gollancz comments on this: 'I know of no better commentary on the tempestuous character of the play; Shakespeare has unconsciously divined the germ of the myth' (p. ix). As already pointed out, the idea that Shakespeare somehow managed to grasp the essential mythic import of the stories that served him as sources recurs among commentators.

The play has been related to the 'Oedipus motive' (in a non-Freudian sense) in an article in *Poet Lore*. This Oedipus motive is in turn related to the solar myth because 'to-day's sun is the child of yesterday's sun and kills it in order to live'.[76]

Charles Creighton (1912), like Lilian Winstanley later, interprets the play in a manner which corresponds to Euhemerism in the interpretation of myths. The search for symbolism in the story is justified by Bacon's canon: 'It may pass for a further indication of a concealed and secret meaning, that some of these fables are so *absurd* and *idle* in their narration as to show and proclaim an allegory even afar off'. According to Bacon, the purpose of allegory and parables is to instruct as well as to conceal. 'Let this,' writes Creighton, 'be our encouragement to go on searching for something below the surface of Shakespeare's recension of the Lear legend.' Creighton then goes on to suggest that the play 'is an allegory of the Reformation in its peculiarly English form', with the characters representing actual historical figures.[77]

Freud's comments on the play have already been briefly referred to in the discussion of *The Merchant of Venice*. Cordelia, according to Freud, represents Death, one of the three forms in which woman confronts man, and he compares the scene in which Lear carries her dead in his arms to the Valkyrie carrying the hero dead from the battlefield, the latter situation being reversed in the play in accordance with the demands of wish-fulfilment. Freud also suggests, like Israel Gollancz and others, that Shakespeare manages 'a reduction of the theme to the original myth' which recaptures the 'moving significance' that had been lost by distortion in the other versions. It is this 'return to the original' that creates that profound effect that the play has upon us.[78]

F. Hiebel (1940) interprets the play in the light of 'anthroposophy' as 'a mythical mystery play'. 'In every old fairy story,' he argues, 'the king with his three princesses represents the state of the human soul, and the king's youngest child always shows the salient point of future development.' From a different point of view, Geoffrey L. Bickersteth (1946) tries to explain the 'golden' effect of the play in terms of the theme of the transmutation of and victory over evil or suffering as symbolized in the myths of Prometheus and Christ, Lear resembling Prometheus and Cordelia, Christ.[79]

J. I. M. Stewart, writing in 1949, observes that the first anthropologist to approach *Lear* (and Stewart suggests that he had not yet arrived) would, on observing how paternal figures in the play are deprived by their children, 'aver that these incidents are symbolical as such things in dreams are symbolical: they veil an unconscious fantasy of the kind classically expressed in the myth of Uranus and Cronus'. Shortly before this Stewart remarks that there is 'something unmistakably atavistic about the play'.[80] Once again we have the idea that Shakespeare's treatment of his sources represents a 'return to the original'.

The folk-tale nature of the story of *Lear* has been often remarked upon. In fact one type of folk tale is named after this play. The subplot of the play is also of a familiar folk type, namely, the 'expulsion and return type'.[81] Remarking on the widespread prevalence of the type of folk tale to which Lear belongs, Arpad Pauncz (1954) suggests that the name 'Lear complex' could be given to a congeries of complexes which appears in literature and life in the relationship between fathers and daughters, mothers and sons, young women and ageing men, and in the rivalry between fathers and sons for young women. *Lear* thus acquires a mythical status as the ideal, archetypal (though not the prototypical) representation of certain universal unconscious emotions.

Richmond Hathorn has written a far more interesting essay on this play than the one on *Hamlet* already referred to. He argues that Shakespeare is concerned in this play with refuting certain naturalistic 'equations', but that he does this by having recourse to three myths 'at least'. The false naturalistic equations are: that words are equal to things (logic); that things are equal to things (causality); and that human beings are equal to things (analysis). Against these equations Shakespeare puts forth, respectively, the mythic motifs of the 'Riddle', the 'Debasement of the King', and the 'Duel with the Unknown Champion'. The Ordeal of the Riddle refutes the logical equation because it emphasizes the mystery of the word; the ritual Debasement of the King refutes the causal equation because, if I understand Hathorn rightly, the mock-king both is and is not the king; the third naturalistic equation, according to Hathorn, is refuted by the Duel with the Unknown Champion who strikes a blow for heavenly justice and shows that mere patient suffering, in accordance with the Stoic-Cynic doctrine of *autarkeia*, is not enough. Hathorn also relates the Gloucester-Edgar plot to initiation myths. In this connection he refers to a book by Guiseppe Cocchiara (*La Legenda de Re Lèar*) in which the following motifs that occur in the play are traced to initiation rites and seasonal festivals: sacrifice of a younger son, estrangement between father and son, a father's supersession by his son, the wandering of the son in the wilderness, the meeting with a 'wild man' or spirit in the wilderness, the abasement of the father, and the final reconciliation.[82]

Honor Matthews argues that although the play is primarily about Lear's personal fall and redemption, yet viewed from another angle it is also concerned with the redemption of a community. Again, the hero-figure is split, with Edmund doing the job of destroying the 'old year', thus allowing Edgar to succeed the old king without staining his hands with blood. Warren Stevenson, on the other hand, considers that it is Albany who is the archetypal saviour, 'pointing to the spiritual reintegration not merely of the British people, but of mankind'. Three reasons are suggested for this view of Albany 'as a figure with mythic and symbolic overtones': Albany is related to Albion, who was the giant son of

Neptune and hence a symbol for Britain; he lacks individuality (hence he is symbolic); and finally, there is a parallel between a speech of Albany (IV. ii. 46) and a speech by God in *Everyman*. None of these reasons, I suspect, will strike those who are not already determined to see archetypes everywhere as very compelling. Sven Armens sees the play within the framework of his Jungian psychology as dealing with the patriarchal Lear's redemption through the sacrifice of Cordelia, the 'mother figure of the physical hearth'. Albany and Edgar are both, according to Armens (in opposition to Matthews and Stevenson), figures of unregenerate 'solar patriarchy'.[83]

Judging from the various discussions of the play outlined above, then, *King Lear* would seem to be rather full of saviour figures, with Edgar, Albany and Cordelia all staking their claim to the title of the Saviour-Hero, whether as the sun-god, or Zephyr, or the spirit of England, or Christ, or the Great Mother Goddess.

Macbeth

We have seen *King Lear* interpreted as a nature myth, and we also observed how Freud (and other psychoanalytical critics) interpreted the nature myth itself as an expression of unconscious emotions and desires. A similar process can be observed in interpretations of *Macbeth*. Karl Simrock traces the 'mythical basis' of the Birnam Wood episode to nature myths and rituals of renewal through the intermediary stage of German folk tales, especially the legend of King Grünewald, in which there is an episode of a moving forest. According to Simrock, this legend originated in the 'German religious custom of May festivals, or Summer-welcomings', King Grünewald being originally 'a Winter-giant, whose dominion ceases when the May-feast begins and the greenwood draws nigh'. Simrock also relates Macduff, with respect to the manner of his birth, to legends from several cultures and observes that in many other instances 'heroes and demi-gods were similarly ushered into the world, and it always implied power and heroic strength'.[84]

Simrock's suggestion has been followed up by several critics, including psychoanalysts, of whom two may be mentioned. Ludwig Jekels tries to combine the mythic view of the play with the psychological. Taking up Simrock's nature myth, he relates it to Freud's observation that the play is concerned with the theme of fertility and barrenness, and also to the theme of the son's rivalry with his father. The play, he suggests, presents the tragic realization that a bad son (Macbeth being a bad 'son' to Duncan) is also a bad father. Jekels also suggests that it is Macduff, not Macbeth, who is the true hero of the play, and attempts to relate the play to Shakespeare's life and to certain historical facts like Elizabeth's barrenness and James's being the son of a murdered woman, just as Malcolm is the son of a murdered man. Hanns Sachs carries this idea forward. Noting that the problem of childlessness runs through the play, he writes:

> In this complex the old nature myth personified in the tragedy, namely the victory of spring coming with green branches over the sterile winter, coincides with the actual event, the accession of James I as successor of the sterile Elizabeth who had beheaded his mother. Freud makes it probable also that the night-wandering of Lady Macbeth goes back directly to the last weeks spent in sleepless disquietude of the virgin queen who once called herself in grief a fruitless stock.[85]

Roy Walker and Honor Matthews have also seen Simrock's nature myth in the play, but they have Christianized it. Roy Walker writes that the murder of Duncan and its consequences are 'profoundly impregnated with the central tragedy of the Christian myth'. Duncan, he suggests, is like Christ, and Macbeth like Judas or Satan. Walker suggests that the third murderer of Banquo is Macbeth himself and that he is there in order to suggest that the three together make a kind of unholy trinity. In brief, according to Walker, 'Shakespeare has taken a religious myth and Christianized it'. Honor Matthews also discusses the fertility theme in the play and in fact suggests that 'men's ancient faith in the recurrent miracle of Spring is given *direct* presentation in English literary drama for the first time'. But this 'pagan symbol of fertility', according to Miss Matthews, is combined with 'Shakespeare's strongest dramatization of the Christian Doomsday theme'. *Macbeth*, in short, is 'Shakespeare's Christmas play'. Miss Matthews refers here to the well-known stage direction in the Coventry Nativity pageant: 'Mary and Joseph goeth clean away' and relates it to 'Fleance is 'scaped' in *Macbeth*. Mention has already been made of her observation that Shakespeare has split the hero-figure into Macduff and Malcolm, so that while one of them does the slaying, the other takes over the reign of Scotland.[86]

H. C. Goddard describes the play as Shakespeare's 'Descent into Hell', refers to the Grünewald myth and remarks that the Delphic prophecies are a symbol of the unconscious. Norman Holland relates the nature myth discovered by Simrock to the imagery of the play, noting that *Macbeth* 'fairly bristles with images of vegetation'. He also suggests that Shakespeare may have come to the primitive ritual and myth pattern through the mediation of Elizabethan folk customs. Finally, Harry Morris (1961) applies the fourfold method of interpretation to the play and comes to the expected conclusion that the Porter in Dante's anagogical sense becomes the 'warder of hell itself', that Macbeth and Lady Macbeth represent the experience of being in Cocytus, and that Seyton is meant to recall his more famous counterpart, Satan.[87]

The discovery of the mythic pattern in the play raises, I think, one of the major problems in our approach to Shakespeare. The motifs or patterns are undoubtedly there: spring *versus* winter; sterility *versus* fertility; the immaculately conceived hero, his exile and return; riddling prophecy; the conflict between generations; and so on. But at the same time one feels that the central preoccupation of the play is not explained in terms of these mythic patterns for, after all, the play deals primarily with Macbeth and Lady Macbeth. To consider Macduff (together, I should think, with Malcolm) as the hero might be justified with reference to the pattern of the hero myths, but the fact remains that the central characters are not these two but Macbeth and Lady Macbeth. Northrop Frye takes the extreme view that the play makes sense only if one considers it as dealing with the ritualistic theme of killing the king rather than with the moral crime of murder.[88] What makes this description too simplistic and partial is the important fact that we are made to see so much in the play through Macbeth's consciousness. The mythic pattern is there, no doubt, but what makes it, in a sense, irrelevant is the presence of Macbeth as a thinking subject rather than as a mere function of the ritual plot. It has been the fashion in the criticism of the play since Bradley, in reaction against his kind of character analysis, to emphasize as key passages things like the image of the temple-haunting martlet, the description of the King's Evil, and so on. But surely the most memorable passages in the play are not these but those dealing with Macbeth's and Lady Macbeth's responses before and after the murder, passages evoking with such psychological acuteness the feelings of apprehension, guilt, futility and despair? This is irrelevant, it sems to me, to the mythic pattern (unless its intention is to subvert that pattern) just as the mythic pattern is irrelevant to it.

Antony and Cleopatra

The Roman tragedies have not attracted the myth-prone critic as much as the other tragedies and comedies. Nevertheless, there are a few interpretations that come within the scope of this study. Alan Warner (1957) suggests that the universal appeal of this play is due to the fact that 'Shakespeare has dramatized a variation of a theme that is deeply rooted in myth and legend, the ruin of the strong man by his sexual weakness'. The conflict in the play links it to the legends of Tammuz and Ishtar, Adam and Eve, Samson and Delilah, and Hercules and Omphale. All these, Warner suggests, are variations on what Maud Bodkin would call the archetype of 'woman as the betrayer and enslaver of man'. Warner warns, however, that it would be wrong to read the play as a simple moral lesson against lust. Raymond Waddington (1966), employing the typological method of mythography, suggests that the play is really about the 'mythical and cosmological affairs of Mars and Venus' rather than about Hercules and Omphale or Isis, as has been suggested by others. But, Waddington points out, these latter figures are subsumed typologically under the figures of Mars and Venus. This implies a different view of the love affair than the moral condemnatory one, and in fact Waddington argues that through this major mythological reference Shakespeare manages to raise his lovers' passions 'to the status of elemental life forces'. Not only that, but the maternal image of 'the baby at the breast' suggests, according to Waddington, 'the fabled progeny, Harmony, that is to be the product of this wedding of spirits'. It is with a shock that one remembers after this that the baby at the breast is only a 'poor worm'! Harold Fisch (1970) suggests that in this play Shakespeare manages to evolve a syncretic myth by blending two groups of mythical figures together: Venus-Mars-Bacchus and Isis-Osiris-Seth. This blending had precedents in Renaissance mythography, Osiris having similarities to Bacchus and Isis being the prototype of Venus and other similar goddesses. But this composite myth is set within a critical perspective by being juxtaposed to 'vigorous Biblical realism' as reflected in the speech of the clown. The play is thus not merely a mythologization of the central characters but mythologization within a critical perspective, or rather the mythologization is not Shakespeare's but the characters', and Shakespeare is concerned to expose the illusory and escapist quality of this mythologizing. Fisch might have said in simpler words that Shakespeare wants us to think that when Antony and Cleopatra are making their grandiose speeches they are merely kidding themselves in a 'dream world of Paganism'.[89] This is a familiar and respectable view of the play which does not, perhaps, require the laborious research into Renaissance mythography that Fisch's approach does.

All the three examples mentioned in this section are rather different from much of the myth criticism surveyed so far. They claim to have greater historical authority since they relate the explicit and oblique mythical references in the plays to Renaissance interpretations of the myths. We must remember however that even Wigston's interpretations of the plays proceeds from a knowledge of Bacon's mythography. The key question is, of course, how central is the mythical allusion in our total response to the play; how long after its occurrence does it continue, in the words of Richard Knowles already quoted, 'to reverberate'? As in the imagery approach, this kind of myth criticism gives the illusion that the metaphorical-mythic structure that is discovered can be attributed to Shakespeare's intention, whereas the only certainty is that this structure is the critic's own construct in his attempt to grasp the play as a unity and can be judged as valuable or useless only on the basis of its unifying function. The usual kind of myth criticism does not, of course, make any claims that it is laying bare Shakespeare's conscious intention, but this does not obscure its similarity to the 'historical' kind of myth criticism. Both are concerned with developing useful analogies that would unify our perception of the plays, though sometimes the only real unity lies in the inner structure of the mythical pattern to which the play is being related.

Timon of Athens
No discussion of this play specifically in terms of myth has been seen, with the exception of an article which argues that Timon is a failed alchemist.[90] Since one of the aims of alchemy was spiritual transformation (= rebirth), the play may be seen as presenting the myth and ritual pattern in reverse.

Coriolanus

I have not seen any myth criticism of this play either, though both Harold Goddard and Otto Rank have cited the image of the state as an organism (I. i. 94ff) as an instance of mythical thought.[91]

THE ROMANCES

The Romances as a group have been thought to be the most amenable to the myth and ritual approach. This is partly because their plots seem to share some of the inconsequentiality of mythical plots. Douglas Bush suggests that in the last plays we can see Shakespeare creating his own myths rather than merely using classical and other myths for ornamental or structural purposes. As pointed out earlier, G. Wilson Knight has called the last plays 'myths of immortality'. D. G. James also suggests that in the last plays Shakespeare was trying to construct his own myths, although, according to James, he did not and could not succeed. In this James is in opposition to the view of Knight. E. M. W. Tillyard relates the plays to the final phase of the archetypal pattern of 'prosperity, destruction, and recreation'. Earlier Janet Spens also suggested that the last plays present a solution to the problems of the tragedies. These plays present, according to her, a reconciliation of man with nature, and it is only through such reconciliation that the problem of the individual's death can be solved. The death of the individual is tragic; only when all life is regarded as one is consolation possible. Richard Wincor describes the romances as Shakespeare's 'Festival Plays' and relates them to the drama of seasonal rituals. But he suggests that it is the broad themes of the rituals rather than their ceremonial details that are usually presented in these plays. The implications of such drama, according to Wincor, are what he terms 'Dream', 'Hope of Immortality', and 'Reconciliation'.[92] But, as far as I am aware, Wigston is the first critic to take the last plays as a group, to defend the integrity of their texts, and to interpret them as myths of immortality, reconciliation, rebirth, or the seasonal cycle. The broad outline of the picture of Shakespeare's development in which the last plays are seen as dramas which reconcile all the tensions of the tragedies and the problem plays, was also anticipated, as has been pointed out, by Dowden, who described this last period as one of serenity that comes from being 'on the Heights'.[93] The biographical extension of this that we find in Dowden has not found favour in the twentieth century, but this does not hide the basic similarity between the maps of Shakespeare's development drawn by Dowden and by twentieth-century 'myth and ritual critics' like G. Wilson Knight and others. Wigston and Dowden can therefore be said to anticipate the major themes of twentieth-century myth and ritual criticism.

There is, of course, no unanimity in the interpretation of the last plays even among the myth critics themselves. I have already referred to D. G. James's argument that in the last plays Shakespeare inevitably failed to create a new mythology. Herbert Weisinger (who has written more about the myth and ritual approach than practical criticism applying this approach, and who is subject to periods of doubt regarding its usefulness) argues:

> On the basis of a comparison between the myth and ritual pattern as I have described it in *Tragedy and the Paradox of the Fortunate Fall* and the tragedies, I think that Shakespeare's tragic vision, which he was able to sustain but tentatively in *Hamlet*, most fully in *Othello*, barely in *King Lear*, and hardly at all in *Macbeth*, failed him altogether in the last plays, that his failure is manifested by the use of the elements of the myth and ritual pattern as mere machinery, virtually in burlesque fashion, and not as their informing and sustaining spirit.

The idea of the last plays as 'fables of reconciliation' has also come under attack from different quarters. F. R. Leavis, in a caveat on the criticism of the last plays, suggests that *The Tempest* at least is realistic in tone. Frank Kermode has found in the same play a certain 'coldness of tone' which would be the very opposite of reconciliation. Jan Kott has gone even further and described the play as 'a great Renaissance tragedy of lost illusions'. It is also possible to emphasize without distortion the realistic elements in *The Winter's Tale* and *Cymbeline*. Discussing the symbolic-mythic interpretations of the last plays, Philip Edwards argues:

> A 'balanced view of life' becomes the mist-hidden crag which is the goal of human striving....
> The reduction of the complexity of Shakespeare to a striving towards a balanced view of life seems to me typical of the pallidness of all interpretations of the last plays which insist that they are symbolic utterances. There is an appearance (there is certainly a claim) that depths are being opened, riches are being revealed. But it is an appearance only.

The ideas discovered, Edwards goes on to say, are 'banal, trite, and colourless'. More recently, G. K. Hunter has also criticized the idea that the last plays are merely about reconciliation: 'Their relation to the later tragedies suggests a different view; the capacity to accept the world-as-it-is has had to be bought by a sacrifice of heroic pretensions, by a loss of confidence in the heroic individual. In reading the Last Plays we should feel the sense of this loss even as we rejoice in the sweetness of their reconciliation.'[94]

It is important, I think, to bear these dissenting opinions (assuming that the contrary view is the orthodoxy) in mind in the survey that follows of interpretations of these plays in terms of mythic patterns.

Pericles

Wigston considers this play an 'early attempt to embody the same subject matter as forms the main element of *The Winter's Tale*' This subject matter is described as that of separation, lost child and the harmony of rediscovery. Marina is compared to Persephone, and the detail of Marina appearing with a basket of flowers (IV. i.) shortly before the attempted murder and the kidnapping of her by the pirates is made to fit in nicely with the rape of Persephone 'picking flowers'. Thaisa is, of course, explicitly associated with Diana in the play, but Wigston goes on to actually identify her with that deity and remarks that Ephesus, where she is washed ashore, was a centre of 'all the secret knowledge of the Gnostics', whose teachings were passed on to the Rosicrucians and the Hermetic Brethren of the sixteenth and seventeenth centuries (pp. 7, 23–4, 37–8).

The play occupies an important position in G. Wilson Knight's criticism. His first important critical work was entitled 'Thaisa: An Essay on Myth and Allegory in Shakespeare's Final Plays' (1928). It was not published, but T. S. Eliot may have read it, and his 'Marina' seems to have been influenced by Knight's criticism of the final plays. He in fact sent a copy of the poem to Wilson Knight with the inscription: 'To G. Wilson Knight with, I hope, some appropriateness.' Knight believes that one of his two major contributions to Shakespeare criticism is 'the recognition of the death-reversals in *Pericles* and *The Winter's Tale* as dramatic equivalents to a truth beyond tragedy', the other contribution being his theory of the 'spatial' form of the plays. But in spite of this claim his comments on the plays are rather predictable if one keeps Wigston in mind. In *Myth and Miracle* he points out motifs common to this play and *The Winter's Tale* and writes that 'a reader sensitive to poetic atmosphere must necessarily feel the awakening light of some religious or metaphysical truth symbolized in the plot and attendant machinery of these two plays'. He further describes *Pericles* as a 'myth in the Platonic sense', dealing with 'some mystic apprehension of a life that conquers death'.[95]

Cymbeline

Folk-tale and mythic elements are quite prominent in this play. Simrock remarks on the parallel between this play and the story of Snow White in that in both there is apparent death from poison contrived by an evil step-mother.[96] The Indian reader is likely to see a parallel between Guiderius and Arviragus, and Lava and Kusha, the twin sons of Rama and Sita. Wigston, in his rather exuberant fashion, comes up with several mythical analogies and hidden themes in the play. (He also defends the authenticity of the vision of Jupiter as Shakespeare's 'oracle'—a defence not very different in its broad argument from Wilson Knight's in his chapter on the play in *The Crown of Life*.) Wigston (pp. 335ff.) suggests that Iachimo (= Iacchus) is Dionysos Chthonios, a divinity of the underworld for a season, who 'sleeps in the sacred abode of Persephone'. Persephone is, of course, Imogen, to whom Iachimo goes in a chest in the manner of Dionysus and Adonis, who were both 'Chested Gods'. Imogen is also compared with Diana, who is only another form of Persephone. In a passage already cited Wigston writes: 'In *Cymbeline* we have Imogen, seeking her husband, with text allusions to a monument and to Diana's deer. Diana, as Proserpine, typified *the sleeping power of the earth during winter*. She is, therefore, closely connected *with death*. Her reconciling power is the reconciliation that belongs to the immortality of Nature, that gives back what it takes away, through the grave.' Wigston makes other mythic identifications which are rather difficult to follow, but the important point about his interpretation is the idea, often repeated, of the theme of rebirth and reconciliation associated with seasonal myths, especially the myths of Dionysus and Persephone.

Beryl Pogson interprets the play as presenting the theme of initiation or spiritual rebirth, Imogen being a symbol of 'the

Spiritual Consciousness attainable by Man' and Posthumus of the final or 'Ultimate Man'. The phrase 'Widow's Son' applied to Posthumus is, according to Pogson, 'a recognized term for a candidate for Initiation or spiritual Re-birth'. 'Thus,' she writes, 'he follows in the train of Perceval and a long line of Initiates in Esoteric Legend in the tradition of the Son of Isis. The surname Leonatus implies that his father had reached the Lion Degree of Mithraism—and this fits in with the traces of Mithraism which are in harmony with the characteristics of Roman Britain suggested in the background of the play.' Pogson also mentions with approval the equation of Imogen with the story of Snow-White, which she describes as the 'old esoteric fairy tale' in which the phrase 'living happily ever after' is full of esoteric meaning.[97]

Finally, William Barry Thorne relates the drama to the mummers' play and other folk rituals of *renouveau* and suggests that the primary objective of the plot is to point out 'love's regenerative quality', which is here distributed, in contrast with the early comedies, 'ritualistically to the community at large'.[98]

The Winter's Tale

Several mythic and folk-tale analogues of the play have been discovered, including the Alcestis myth and the story of Patient Griselda. The play is Wigston's most important text, many of his ideas being illustrated from it. He remarks that no one till then (1884) had noticed the 'extraordinary parallel presented between Perdita and Persephone (or Proserpine), and between Hermione and Demeter (or Ceres)' which is reflected in the very title of the play. In this connection he quotes from George Cox's *Mythology of the Aryan Nations* the statement that the story of Persephone 'is naturally found in all lands where the difference between Summer and Winter is sufficiently marked to leave on the mind the impression of death and resurrection'. Wigston also relates the play to the Eleusinian mysteries, observing that the Persephone myth is central to both. In fact, he suggests, the myth *is* a 'Winter's Tale'. Wigston's mythological ideas are derived from nineteenth-century comparative mythographers like Bochart, Creuzer and Cox, though he also refers to Francis Bacon's interpretation of the Persephone myth in *The Wisdom of the Ancients*. Like some of them, notably Cox, Wigston discovers the 'key to all mythology' in the theme of the conflict between summer and winter, which in turn is seen as a symbolic presentation of the more fundamental theme of death and rebirth. Like the mythographers, he takes up the task of identifying figures from myth, literature, folk tale and fairy tale with great enthusiasm. Though these identifications are not always easy to follow, they are roughly as follows: Leontes = Cadmus because Cadmus is a sun god and Leontes is associated with the lion sign of the Zodiac. Cadmus in turn is identified with Osiris, and Hermione with Harmonia, wife of Cadmus. Camillo is held to be a subordinate deity associated with Cadmus and Harmonia, and Polixenes is equated with Polyneices. The quarrel between Leontes and Polixenes is interpreted as the antinomy of light and darkness, mind and matter, truth and error, though the equation here is rather confusing. Finally, the analogy with the Eleusinian mysteries is further elaborated in a comparison of the final scene of the play to the revelation of the statue of Demeter to the initiates in a burst of light as the crowning ceremony of the rites of Eleusis (pp. 7-8, *passim*). Similar interpretations of the play in terms of esoteric doctrine are given by Beryl Pogson and Paul Arnold. Pogson takes up the idea of rebirth and relates it to spiritual initiation, especially as it was practised in the ancient mysteries. In referring to Bacon and to Rosicrucian and Cabbalistic lore Arnold is even closer to Wigston. According to him, in the play, 'le drame cosmique du rachat par la Vierge est accompli en sa forme gnostique'.[99] The myth of Persephone is central in both these interpretations.

E. A. J. Honigmann, in an article already referred to, draws attention to the fact that Wigston attempted to show that the Elizabethans understood the Persephone myth much as we do today. He himself mentions one such interpretation of the myth that appears in the preface to Leonard Digges's translation of Claudian's *Rape of Proserpine* (1617) and points out that Digges was a close associate of Shakespeare. Honigmann concludes that insofar as *The Winter's Tale* (along with *The Tempest*) attempts 'the sophistication of myth' (as in Lyly's *Endimion*), 'Wigston's views fit into the framework of the most modern speculation about Shakespeare's artistic purpose at the end of his career'. William O. Scott follows Honigmann's suggestion (although he does not refer to him) in trying to examine the seasonal and floral motifs associated with the Persephone myth from a 'pre-Frazerian viewpoint to see what Shakespeare's contemporaries would have made of a tale about winter and spring garnished out with a pastoral bouquet'. His conclusion is that Shakespeare was aware of the symbolic import of these motifs as such ideas were fairly commonplace during the Renaissance. The play therefore 'owes its symbolic values to Shakespeare, and our discovery of them is a rediscovery'.[100]

David Hoeniger claims that the play is explicable only as an allegory, the reason given being exactly the same as that given by the allegorical exegetes of the Bible and the classical myths, namely that 'such blatant improbabilities may well be a hint that the meaning of the play is symbolic rather than literal'. (Are the improbabilities any more glaring, one wonders, than those in a tragedy like *King Lear*?) Hoeniger then goes on to make some interesting remarks on the themes of the play, which include, in his view, the theme of summer and winter or the rebirth of nature, and the theme of youth, age, death and resurrection. J. A. Bryant, proceeding from the assumption (which he presents as the conclusion) that Shakespeare's plays are 'explorations of mythic fragments' whereby the 'fable at hand' is revealed as 'participating by analogy in an action which, from the poet's point of view, is Christian, divine, and eternal', argues that Hermione is a type of Christ, Leontes the Jew, Mamillius the Jewish Church, and Perdita the True Church. Bryant admits that absolute correspondence is not possible, but suggests that looking for such perfect correspondence is not really 'respectable'. This is presumably a confession that there is a limit to the exegete's ingenuity. He concludes that the allegory 'is most assuredly there', whether Shakespeare saw it or not. Finally, William Barry Thorne (1968) recapitulates most of the themes mentioned above. '*The Winter's Tale*,' he writes, paraphrasing G. Wilson Knight, 'explores concepts of immortality and fertility in what might be deemed a seasonal myth.' It was rather late in the day, one would have thought, to arrive at *that* conclusion.[101]

The Tempest

Perhaps the earliest 'myth criticism' of the play is Victor Hugo's (1865) interpretation of it in terms of the myth of Cain and Abel, the denouement being, according to him, a presentation of Paradise Regained. Sivori Levey (1921) sees the play as a nature myth, suggesting that Prospero represents the influence of the sun which ensures *prosperity*, Sycorax the evil influence of the

ALLEGORICAL MYTHOGRAPHY

moon, Juno the moon of good influence, Ariel the benevolent south wind, and Caliban the baleful south-west wind.[102]

Among the numerous studies of the sources and analogues of the play is a (misleading) comparison (1864) between Prospero's exile and Rama's in the *Ramayana*. The anonymous writer also suggests that Caliban is derived from 'Kalee-ban' or the 'satyr of Kalee, the Hindu Proserpine', and mentions Hanuman the monkey-god as another possible source. Hermann Grimm (1875) compares the episode in which Ferdinand is assigned tasks by Prospero to several Greek and Indian stories, and W. W. Newell (1903) relates it to the folk tale of the 'bird-wife' and to stories from *The Arabian Nights*, the Argonautic myth, the story of Cupid and Psyche, and two Indian tales—the mythical story of Urvashi and Purūravas and the tale of 'Sudhana and Manohara' (*sic*) from the *Kathā-Saritā-Sāgara*. Don Cameron Allen (1960) notes that coming to a magic island across broad waters in a helpless boat is a common motif in heroic literature (e.g. the Argonauts, Ceyx, Aeneas's arrival at Carthage, and the voyage of Odysseus), and points out that allegorical interpretations of this motif, which go back to the time of Heraclitus, were still common during the Renaissance. Allen thus relates the play to the allegorical tradition of mythography.[103]

Wigston's comments on the play are along expected lines. Miranda is the daughter of Ceres and Jupiter, who is *Prospero*; hence she is *Proserpine*. More importantly, Wigston relates the play to the sixth book of the *Aeneid*, especially with respect to the doctrine of idealism, which, he points out, was taught in the Eleusinian mysteries. He also relates the reference to Dido in the play to the idea of rebirth by arguing that Tunis = Carthage = Libya = the land of the Phoenix (compare 'She came from Libya', *The Winter's Tale*, v. i. 156, which refers to Perdita). Wigston further suggests that the word 'release' in the epilogue means interpretation and is thus associated with the idea of rebirth since the true interpretation of the play is, in a way, a bringing it back to life after a period during which its significance was lying dead or dormant: interpretation becomes an act like the raising of the dead, a miniature creation (p. 326).

This idea, along with several other ideas of Wigston, is echoed by Colin Still in his study of the play which has been referred to earlier. Still's basic idea that *The Tempest*, like all great art which approaches the status of myth, presents the theme of the mystery of redemption would hardly strike the reader as a novel one at this stage of this survey. His comparison of the play with the Eleusinian mysteries should also not come as a novelty after Wigston, though it must be granted that he argues his case with greater intellectual discipline. Still also makes the original suggestion that the play presents two kinds of initiation, the lesser initiation for the members of Alonso's party and the higher initiation for Ferdinand. Further, in basing his interpretation on the archetypal imagery of the four elements and the three intermediate compounds, each with its corresponding 'mythical region' and 'plane of consciousness', Still does carry it beyond Wigston's, though the idea of the correspondence between the microcosm and the macrocosm is, of course, very ancient.[104]

Richard Rosenheim also interprets the play as an initiation myth, pointing out the following features of the mysteries in the play: test of memory (Miranda's I. ii); 'the pious outlook for a Golden Age to come'; and the Rebirth of the Beloved Disciples, Fernando (*sic*) and Miranda. Ferdinand is described as the New Adam who undergoes the Test of Water and the Test of Fire. Shakespeare surveys, in brief, 'the entire previous occult history of man on earth, from the destruction of the fire-world of Old Lemuria to the rebirth of the sunken continent as air-and-waterborne Atlantis'.[105]

THE POEMS

Venus and Adonis

The rebirth motif is very obvious in 'The Phoenix and the Turtle'. *Venus and Adonis* is related to solar mythology by Christopher Butler and Alastair Fowler, who illustrate from Renaissance sources the common solar interpretation of the myth in Renaissance mythography. They quote George Sandys's comment that 'Adonis was no other than the Sun, adored under that name by the Phoenicians; as Venus by the name of Astarten', and suggest that the poem also is based upon a similar reading of the myth.[106]

The Sonnets

Wigston relates the dark lady of the sonnets to Diana of Ephesus, Isis, and the Indian goddess Bhavani. He also suggests that the sonnets represent the 'antinomy of love and hate, and masculine and feminine principles, as Androgynous unity'. There is a similar idea in G. Wilson Knight's theory of Shakespeare's (and other great artists') 'bisexuality'. Leslie Fiedler has referred to 'the myth of the Beardless Beloved', though with reference not merely to the young man in the sonnets but also to the frequent appearance of the heroines in male attire. Northrop Frye has also studied the sonnets in terms of the myths of Eros and the 'white goddess' in her destructive aspect.[107]

IV

The concept of myth whose application in Shakespeare criticism we have been examining so far has been less influential in theory than in practice. It has been pointed out, rightly I believe, that the idea of myth is far more important than the application of specific myths to works of art ('myth' here being understood generally as a mode of thought antithetical to the scientific, rational, and historical; a mode of thought, moreover, which reflects a way of life in far greater harmony with nature and with other men than is possible in a secular or individualistic and materialistic culture). But this is true only as far as theory is concerned; there are indeed numerous essays and books on the idea of myth, far more than there are applications of the idea to works of art. But where actual applications are concerned, it is not so much the concept of myth as a special mode of thought that has been most operative, though implicitly it may be present behind some studies, but rather the concept of myth as a story embodying certain timeless, universal and even sacred truths, usually in the form of an allegory which helps to protect this truth from profanation. This concept, as has been shown above, owes little to the theories of Frazer and other anthropologists, and is rather to be seen as a continuation of the allegorical tradition of mythography and Biblical exegesis. Myth criticism (at least the larger part of it) is an extension of this mode of interpretation to literary works, usually with the intention of giving a mythical or quasi-religious status to the object, and generally involves not merely comparison with specific myths but the reduction of various myths, folk tales, rituals, and works of literature to a common archetypal pattern.

Not all the examples of myth criticism included in the foregoing survey are, of course, of this kind. There are many source studies which merely seek to relate the particular work to some specific myths, folk tales, fairy tales or other literary works, but the cumulative effect of such studies too is to highlight those elements in Shakespeare which are not unique to him but which he shares with a large variety of other works. Northrop Frye's image of a 'primitive', 'popular' and 'conventional' Shakespeare, for example, is built upon the extensive study of Shakespeare's sources in the nineteenth and the early-twentieth century. While such an image is welcome after the excesses of the Bradleyan and formalist approaches, it too involves distortions, especially the exaggeration of those elements in the works which are only incidental or marginal or the highlighting of some aspects at the expense of others equally or more important. The point is clearly illustrated by some of the studies included in the section on *Macbeth*.

There is an important aspect of myth criticism which cannot be explained solely in terms of the allegorical tradition. For though analogy is the main tool employed by such criticism, it is analogy of a special kind. The fact that it is myth or primitive ritual with which the work is compared assumes great importance from this point of view, for the myths and rituals are conceived not only as embodiments of universal or archetypal themes, but also as the *earliest* of these embodiments. It has sometimes been argued that the term 'archetype' should not be taken in a temporal sense but rather as referring to the 'arche' or first principle. This is true as far as the content of myth criticism is concerned, namely the themes that are discovered beneath the surface meaning of the particular work, for they could be described equally appropriately by words like 'universal' or 'fundamental' which do not have the temporal connotation of the terms favoured by the myth critics, terms like 'archetypal', 'primitive', 'primordial' or 'primal'. However, it is the aura of mystery evoked by these latter terms that gives to successful myth criticism its distinctive quality. It is an empirical fact that what Freud has termed the 'return to the original' arouses far greater emotional response than a relating to universal archetypes conceived 'essentially' rather than temporally. In many primitive societies the 'valorization of existence' is achieved through this return to origins (*in illo tempore, ab origine*).[108] Objects and events are given value, mana, mystery, sanctity, by being related to the time of beginnings. Similarly, literary objects are given value or resonance by being returned to their origins in primitive myth and ritual. Successful myth criticism is one which achieves this valorization of the work of art and makes it numinous and resonant, though in most cases this is made possible only by begging the question of literary evaluation.

Norman Holland relates the resonance experienced while reading a mythical work to religious experience of a certain kind:

> Myth-in-literature... 'proves' the existence of the kind of religious emotions proclaimed by Tillich and other neo-orthodox theologians. In this sense, myth criticism becomes just one more phase in Arnold's strategy of claiming for religion a poetic validity or for literature a religious sanction. Myth criticism thus paves a way for the rather vague theism so much in vogue now—on the basis of our subjective experience of resonance.

Holland then goes on to relate this resonance to Freud's 'oceanic feeling': when the reader has awareness (but no certain knowledge) of the myth submerged in a work of art, this awareness gives him the feeling of being assimilated to a larger entity which is related to the 'primal matrix' from which the infant emerges with the development of the individual ego. Holland therefore suggests that mythic works, or rather those works in which the presence of a myth evokes a sense of resonance, usually have a predominance of oral elements reminiscent of the infant's Edenic maternal matrix during the oral stage of his development.[109]

It would be difficult and unwise to comment on this hypothesis without extensive statistical analysis of a wide variety of writings, but Holland's formulation of the factor essential for the experience of mythic resonance in a work—an awareness but not certain knowledge of the myth embedded in it—seems to be accurate. It helps to explain that feeling of the *déjà vu*, if one may use the term without any pejorative connotation, which many readers experience while reading a work of this kind, the feeling that one has read something similar before, combined with an obscure sense of the significance of such half-realized parallelisms. In most cases, of course, the source of this feeling may be traced to tales and stories heard in childhood. But *deja vu* is a rather tricky experience. It is an aspect of the 'uncanny', which Freud relates to the sudden emergence of repressed desires under the impact of some external stimulus. W. J. Dunne in *An Experiment with Time* (1927) suggests a very different explanation, namely that the feeling arises because one *has* seen something similar before, in dreams. Perhaps the final explanation will be provided by neurology and cybernetics. But one thing seems to be certain—that the feeling, partly because it is so vague, can often be *induced* even where it does not arise spontaneously. And this suggests a point about myth *criticism* of the kind studied here. When it is at its best, as in Freud (and some other psychoanalysts), Gilbert Murray, Maud Bodkin, its function seems to be to induce this feeling of the *déjà vu* even in respect of those works which do not find any mythic echoes in the mind of the unaided reader. Once the parallel with myths and fairy tales has been suggested by the critic, one is struck by the rightness of it. It is in this aspect that myth criticism differs from mere allegorical interpretation. For without the comparison with myths and fairy tales this element of recognition would not be there. Freud could have interpreted the theme of the three caskets simply as an allegorical presentation of man's need to come to terms with death without invoking any of the suggestive parallels with myth and folk tale, but without these parallels this 'truth' would not have had the same power to convince. In this respect, it would seem, the role of myth criticism in literature corresponds to that of ritual in the realm of religion. For the purpose of ritual is to sanctify, with reference to the time of origins, the object of worship or veneration. Myth criticism similarly sanctifies, with reference to collective and individual origins, the individual work and the doctrine that this work or the myth critic himself seeks to project. Insofar as this is a characteristic of the mythical mode of thought, myth criticism itself is an example of it.

A certain kind of allegorical criticism also serves to sanctify the work of art, to give it, as it were, a scriptural status. Some Christian interpretations of Shakespeare seem to be examples of such 'mythologizing', for by interpreting Shakespeare allegorically they seek to assimilate him to Christian myth and doctrine. They seem to imply not merely that there are unconscious allegorical elements in the plays, but that they contain hidden wisdom in the manner of the scriptures. The growth of bardolatry is, of course, a well-documented subject and there is little point in rehearsing it here, but the account may be usefully supplemented from a different angle. Some of the earliest references to 'myth' in connection with Shakespeare in the nineteenth century occur, surprisingly enough, in 'Baconian' books and pamphlets.[110] There 'myth' in a phrase like 'the myth of Shakespeare' is used to signify a false or erroneous idea rather than something sacred and profound. But it is usually the case that where one myth is sought to be destroyed another one is seeking to assume its place. Indeed the whole controversy about the real author of the plays follows a mythical pattern. Apart from the fact that many Baconians, including Wigston, were interested in esoteric myths and rituals, there is the fact that this whole insistence on the mysterious origin of the writer of the plays follows the well-known pattern of the lives of mythical heroes of mysterious birth. 'Shakespeare' was obviously such a culture-hero for the Baconians. Whether the Oedipal explanation given by Freud and Otto Rank for this feature of the hero myths applies to these critics, as Alfred Harbage suggests it does, may be a matter of dispute.[111] What is not disputable is the mythical status of the writer of the plays. Thus, myth criticism ultimately helps perpetuate the 'myth of Shakespeare'.

CHAPTER 2

Ritual in Drama: Drama as Ritual

One of the most influential theories relating to myth has been the theory that both myth and drama have their origins in primitive ritual. Although Robertson Smith argued the primacy of ritual over myth,[1] it was through the writings of Sir James Frazer and Jane Harrison that the theory gained wide currency. The more specifically literary applications of the theory were made by Gilbert Murray to Greek tragedy, by F. M. Cornford to Greek comedy and by Jessie Weston to the Arthurian romances. Sir E. K. Chambers and R. J. E. Tiddy studied primitive ritual patterns in English folk drama, and Gilbert Murray and Janet Spens applied the theory to Shakespeare. Most of these works appeared in the first two decades of the twentieth century and had considerable influence on writers like Yeats, Eliot and Lawrence. Through them the theories of Frazer and others, especially the derivation of myths and works of art from ancient ritual—and the interpretation of these rituals as variants or different phases of an 'ur-ritual' celebrating the death and rebirth of a divine king as sacrificial victim—had a profound influence on twentieth-century literature.[2]

Insofar as Frazer popularized the idea of the dying god and divine scapegoat, his contribution to literary theory and practice has been seminal. However, it must be said that his direct contribution to aesthetic theory has been negligible, and his contribution to anthropological theory too has not been rated highly. Very briefly, the relevant part of Frazer's theory is as follows. In primitive societies it was a widespread custom to kill the divine king (who must be considered as one of the later forms of an original 'Vegetation Spirit') in order that his powers be not weakened by the inroads of age. In later times an animal or human substitute was killed instead of the king himself. There was another widespread ritual in which evils and sins were sought to be expelled by being transferred on to a human victim who was then killed or expelled.

It occurred to people later, according to Frazer's rather casual historical hypothesis, to combine these two rituals. Since the divine king (or his representative) had to be killed, it was economical to make him the scapegoat also. In the case of the divine scapegoat, therefore, two rituals which were originally separate were combined.[3] Whatever the intrinsic merits of this hypothesis and of the central point of Frazer's theory, namely the explanation of the curious rule of succession to the priesthood at Nemi in terms of this ritual regicide, in their actual application to the plays of Shakespeare, as I shall try to show later, the idea of the divine sacrifice and that of the divine scapegoat tend to be used without sufficient regard for the very different *feel* of the different, though related, rituals that are involved.

Discussion of the theoretical implications of anthropology for art and literature is to be found not in the writings of Frazer but in those of Jane Harrison. According to her, ritual is prior to myth, myth being 'the spoken correlative of the acted rite, the thing done'. A ritual is 'a collective representation' of the needs and desires of life. The Greek word for ritual, 'dromenon', is related to the word drama, both implying something done or acted. But ritual is rather something either 're-done' or 'pre-done', in other words 're-presented', and this re-presentation, or imitation, springs from unfulfilled desire, which is the source of art and religion alike. Ritual is thus the first stage in the symbolic reconstruction of reality, but it is still tied to practical ends. It is thus 'a frequent and perhaps universal transition stage between actual life and that peculiar contemplation of or emotion towards life which we call art'. The transition from ritual to art is described as follows: 'By the long discipline of ritual man accustomed himself to slacken his hold on action, and be content with a shadowy counterfeit practice. Then last, when through knowledge he was relieved from the need of immediate reaction to imminent realities, he loosed hold for a moment altogether, and was free to look, and art was born.' Using a concept formulated by Edward Bullough she sums up the difference between 'dromenon' and drama as one of 'Psychical Distance'.[4]

At the same time, Jane Harrison insists upon the necessity of *identification* for drama. She observes that primitive religions usually have 'dromena', but drama sprang only from the religion of

Dionysus. The cults of Athene, Zeus and Poseidon in Ancient Greece had dromena but no drama. She offers the following explanation for this:

> Surely it is at least possible that the real impulse to the drama lay not wholly in 'goat-songs' and 'circular dancing places' but also in the cardinal, the essentially dramatic conviction of the religion of Dionysos, that the worshipper can not only worship, but can become, can *be* his god.... It is only in the orgiastic religions that these splendid moments of conviction could come, and, for Greece at least, only in an orgiastic religion did the drama take its rise.[5]

The nature of drama is thus paradoxical, involving both identification and psychical distance.

In *Themis* Jane Harrison discusses the development of Attic drama from the dromena of an Eniautos-daimon (year-spirit), of whom Dionysus is considered to be merely one manifestation. The rituals related to this daimon gave rise to myths which usually followed the pattern of a *contest*, a *pathos* formally announced by a *messenger* and followed by a lamentation (*threnos*), and a final triumphant *epiphany*. This was also the pattern of the things done, and the myth could therefore be described as 'the plot of the *dromenon*' or, as Aristotle defined the term plot, 'the arrangement of the incidents'. Drama, however, required more flexible material than myths tied to rituals:

> The *mythos*, the plot which is the life-history of an Eniautos-daimon, whether performed in winter, spring, summer or autumn, is... doomed by its monotony to sterility. What is wanted is material cast in a less rigid mould; in a word *legomena* not bound by *dromena*, plots that have cut themselves loose from rites. The dithyramb, which was but the periodic festival of the spring *renouveau*, broke and blossomed so swiftly into Attic drama because it found such plots ready to hand; in a word—*the forms of Attic drama are the forms of the life-history of an Eniautos-daimon; the content is the infinite variety of free and individualized heroic saga*—in the largest sense of the word 'Homer'.[6]

The argument is carried further by Gilbert Murray and F. M. Cornford, who try to show that both tragedy and comedy arise from the seasonal rituals of renewal, each genre representing a particular phase in the life of the Year-daimon: comedy celebrating his marriage and the subsequent feast and tragedy representing his death and its lamentation.[7] Both Murray and Cornford support their arguments with analogies between the ancient rituals and such survivals as the English mummers' plays and similar folk drama found in northern Greece and in other parts of Europe, thus suggesting the possible intermediate stage through which the ancient ritual pattern could have got into the plays of Shakespeare.

Another 'ritual' theory of the origin of drama has specific application to modern as opposed to ancient drama. This is the theory that traces the origin of secular Renaissance drama to the liturgical rites of the medieval church and its development in the mystery cycles. Any discussion of Christian rites in Shakespearean drama would, in the light of this theory, be an instance of myth and ritual criticism. Since the liturgy was organized around the crucifixion, the idea of sacrifice had a special place in the Elizabethan consciousness. Through the Bible and the works of the Roman historians the Elizabethans knew a great deal about the sacrificial rites of the ancient Greeks, Romans and Jews. They also had access to information about the rites of primitive tribal peoples through contemporary travel literature. While, for the most part, they considered the non-Christian rites as providing a contrast to the crucifixion, they also looked upon the sacrificial rites described in the Old Testament, especially the sacrifice of the scapegoat, as prefiguring the sacrifice of Christ. It is not surprising, therefore, that we should find in Elizabethan, particularly Shakespearean, drama a good deal of explicit interest in the subject of sacrifice—in *Titus Andronicus, Julius Caesar* and *Macbeth*, for example.[8] There is also a sense of continuity between the Christian and the pre-Christian ritual patterns. O. B. Hardison has therefore suggested that Gilbert Murray's formulation of the ritual pattern of Greek tragedy can be applied to medieval and Shakespearean drama with some modifications. Instead of the six-part structure suggested by Murray (agon, pathos, messenger, threnos, anagnorisis and peripety, and theophany), Hardison suggests a pattern consisting of three parts: pathos, peripety and theophany. Because this pattern is 'comic' in terms of its conclusion, he makes the further point that many of Shakespeare's tragedies can be described as 'comic in structure and tragic in tonality'.[9]

There are several types of primitive and other rituals which do not seem to conform to Frazer's and Jane Harrison's dying-god paradigm. Foremost among these are the 'rites of passage' which were the subject of Arnold van Gennep's classic study. Rites of passage are performed at those critical moments in an individual's life when there is a transition from one social identity or status to another. Such are the rites of birth, initiation (i.e. transition from adolescence to adulthood), marriage and death. Van Gennep showed that these rites are marked by three phases: separation, margin or threshold (limen), and aggregation or incorporation. In the first phase the individual is separated from his usual social or familial environment; in the second or liminal phase he is made to go through various ordeals and tests which often involve a radical disorientation of his normal self; in the third phase he acquires a new, stable social identity.

The major differences between the two types of rites are that Frazer's rites are collective and seasonal or calendrical, repeated every year at fixed points in the calendar, whereas van Gennep's initiatory rites are generally individual and 'life-crisis' rites, each rite being performed only once during the lifetime of the individual. Further, though both kinds of rites are marked by the occurrence of a transitional phase, the liminal experience in a rite of passage is often more radical and more painful than the period of festive misrule associated with the transition from one season to another. However, as the foregoing sentence indicates, there is a common pattern behind the two kinds of rites. This has been described by van Gennep himself thus:

For groups, as well as for individuals, life itself means to separate and to be reunited, to change form and condition, to die and to be reborn. It is to act and to cease, to wait and rest, and then to begin acting again, but in a different way. And there are always new thresholds to cross: the thresholds of summer and winter, of a season or a year, of a month or a night; the thresholds of birth, adolescence, maturity, and old age; the threshold of death and that of afterlife—for those who believe in it.

Both seasonal group rites and individual life-crisis rites are thus seen as basically passage rites intended to facilitate the transition from one state to another, and the pattern of these rites is not unlike the death-rebirth pattern of Frazer's fertility rites. In both groups of rites, moreover, there is a liminal or threshold phase which involves a disorientation of the normal life or of the normal self.[10]

The liminal phase in seasonal group rites usually takes the form of a period of saturnalian misrule or carnival in which all social relations are turned topsy-turvy. The idea of festive misrule or carnival has been an extremely influential one in literary criticism, especially in the criticism of Shakespeare. Frazer linked the carnival with such other figures as the King of Beans associated with Twelfth Night, the medieval Bishop of Fools or Lord of Misrule, and the ancient Roman King of the Saturnalia, as surrogates of the dying god (ch. 58, p. 768). While this explanation may have some plausibility with respect to the rites of primitive societies, its inadequacy becomes apparent in relation to such later developments as carnival and the Feast of Fools, for much more complex social dynamics seem to be at work behind these festive practices. In *Shakespeare's Festive Comedy* (1959), C. L. Barber gives a broadly functionalist account of the role of such festivals in Elizabethan society. According to him, these festivals had the basically conservative function of reinforcing social structure and social cohesion by providing controlled 'release' from the routines and rules of a hierarchical society. The release led to 'clarification', 'a heightened awareness of the relation between man and "nature"' and the ability to see 'holiday' (or the life of nature) in proper perspective in relation to life as whole (including life in society).[11] Social structure was thus reinforced through a temporary release from it.

A very different view of carnival and other popular festive forms is presented in Mikhail Bakhtin's *Rabelais and His World*, which was written around 1940 but first published in Russian in 1965. In a brilliant extension of the idea of carnival, Bakhtin defines it as 'the people's second life, organized on the basis of laughter'. In addition to carnivalesque festivities, the manifestations of this second life include comic compositions, both written and oral, and various kinds of comic parodies, 'flytings', invectives, curses and abuses. Bakhtin rejects the narrow concept of folk culture and folklore found in Herder and the Romantics because the culture of the marketplace and of folk laughter has no place in it. In primitive pre-class and pre-political societies the expressions of this popular culture were as sacred and 'official' as the more serious expressions. Bakhtin points out that even in the early period of the Roman state the ceremonial of the triumphal procession included 'on almost equal terms the glorifying and the deriding of the victor', but with the increasing differentiation of society on the basis of power and class the culture of the marketplace became quite distinct from the official and dominant culture and often assumed an adversarial or subversive role. Thus in the Middle Ages carnival offered 'a completely different, nonofficial, extra-ecclesiastical and extrapolitical aspect of the world, of man, and of human relations', building 'a second world and a second life outside officialdom, a world in which all medieval people participated more or less, in which they lived during a given time of the year'.[12]

Bakhtin uses the term 'grotesque realism' for the aesthetic concept characteristic of folk culture and defines its essential principle as one of 'degradation' or the 'lowering of all that is high, spiritual, ideal, abstract'. Thus, in grotesque realism 'the material bodily principle', i.e. the human body with its food, drink, defecation and sexual life, plays a predominant role. Bakhtin goes on to suggest that although the influence of carnival is to be seen in all periods of literature, during the Renaissance this influence was exceptionally strong and direct. In fact, according to Bakhtin, the Renaissance may be described as 'a direct "carnivalization" of human consciousness, philosophy, and literature'. Bakhtin includes Shakespeare, along with Rabelais, Boceaccio and Cervantes, among carnivalesque writers, though he does not discuss him in detail.[13]

The difference between Bakhtin's 'carnival' and Barber's 'holiday' is not, however, as absolute as it might appear at first sight, for Bakhtin too points out the temporary and transitional nature of carnival, thus implying that at the end of the festivities the participants return from the 'second world' of carnival to the normal social world of hierarchy and class distinctions. It may also be pointed out that Bakhtin's concept of the carnival anticipates to a remarkable degree the concept of 'communitas' put forward by the anthropologist Victor Turner. Turner suggests 'two major "models" for human interrelatedness'. In the first, society is seen as a 'structured, differentiated, and often hierarchical system of politico-legal-economic positions with many types of evaluation, separating men in terms of "more" or "less"'. In the second model, which becomes recognizable especially during liminal periods, society is seen as an 'unstructured or rudimentarily structured and relatively undifferentiated *comitatus*, community, or even communion of equal individuals'. It is this kind of society, which strongly resembles Bakhtin's 'second world', that Turner calls 'communitas'. In communitas the normal distinctions between high and low, strong and weak, normal and marginal are obliterated. The high become low; the 'powers of the weak' are celebrated; and marginal characters (such as the clowns and jesters of medieval and Renaissance Europe) come into their own, for, essentially, 'communitas is a relationship between concrete, historical, idiosyncratic individuals. These individuals are not segmentalized into roles and statuses but confront one another rather in the manner of Martin Buber's "I and Thou".' Among the wide variety of manifestations of communitas cited by Turner are medieval monasticism, millenarian religious movements and such recent phenomena as the hippy culture. Communitas is also seen in ideological forms in a variety of utopian models of society, and Turner cites Gonzalo's commonwealth in *The Tempest* (II. i. 141–63) as an example. Like Barber's 'holiday' and Bakhtin's 'carnival', communitas also is not a permanent state, for though it is an escape from the rigidities of social structure, it itself tends to develop into a rigid and even despotic system over a period of time. Turner sees a dialectic at work whereby 'men are released from structure into communitas only to return to structure revitalized by their experience of communitas', and suggests that no society can function adequately without this dialectic.[14]

The resemblance of this dialectic to van Gennep's three phases of passage rites is obvious, Turner's concepts of liminality and communitas representing a development and extension of van Gennep's ideas. The resemblance to Barber's formula 'through release to clarification' is also a close one since 'release' comprises the two phases of separation and liminality in van Gennep's paradigm. Behind these various formulations of the pattern of festive or initiatory rites lie the 'myth and ritual patterns' mentioned in the previous chapter: order-disorder-higher order, unity-discord-harmony, or death-rebirth, the connection with the last of these being indicated by van Gennep himself in a passage already cited. What these congruities suggest is that these patterns are variants of a common triadic pattern which is deeply embedded in the human psyche and is perhaps ultimately biological in origin. The majority of the myth and ritual criticism of Shakespeare is concerned with demonstrating the presence of one of the variants of this pattern in the plays, these variants being taken as psychological-spiritual universals. There are some critics, however, who have tried to show that these patterns come into the plays through the mediation of Elizabethan life and customs, particularly Elizabethan folk culture. This approach has been especially useful when applied to the comedies, where the analogy with Elizabethan festivity and ritual has proved to be an extremely rich and suggestive one. Indeed the idea of festive comedy, along with the concept of the tragic hero as scapegoat, constitutes the most significant contribution of the myth and ritual approach to the criticism of Shakespeare.

II

The majority of the ritual criticism of Shakespeare and others is concerned with tracing in the work the presence of someone or the other of the specific patterns of ritual discussed so far (dying god, scapegoat, rites of passage, festive rites, sacrifice). There is, however, a kind of criticism which is concerned with analysing the relation of a work to ritual as such. There are two aspects of this approach. One could either concentrate on specific 'ritual' elements within a particular work, or one could think of the work as a whole *as* ritual. 'Ritual' in such usage usually means any 'formal' or 'ceremonial' action, though a sense of the stricter meaning of the term as 'action in relation to sacred things' (Durkheim) is also usually present.

A different approach to the question of the relation of ritual to drama is proposed by Richard Schechner. Schechner suggests that ritual is merely one of a range of activities related to the theatre, the others being play, games and sports. Together, these five comprise the 'the public performance activities of men', all of which are equally primeval. Therefore, while there may be variations and an intermingling of these forms, there is no long-term evolution from a 'primitive' form to a 'sophisticated' one. Play and ritual, according to Schechner, are the two poles of these performance activities. In play the rules are purely inner and subjective, whereas in ritual they are given and objective; play is free and corresponds to the pleasure-principle, but ritual is 'programmed' and corresponds to the reality-principle. The other three activities take place between these two poles. All of them have rules, but these are neither entirely inner nor entirely outer; rather, these rules are like 'frames' within which there is considerable scope for improvization. The three groups—play; games, sports and theatre;

and ritual—thus correspond to egocentric, social and religious awareness. Of course, these categories are not to be taken as mutually exclusive but as overlapping, with the possibility of each of the activities intermingling more or less with the others. Ritual and theatre are particularly close to each other in respect of their actual or intended function; both serve to intensify social solidarity and give a sense of renewed vitality to the life of the individual and the community. According to Richard Schechner, even politically radical theatre is close to ritual. 'The ambition to make theatre into ritual,' he writes, 'is nothing other than a wish to make performance efficacious, to use events to change people.'[15]

The theory of the 'Cambridge School' about the origin of Greek drama in the dromena of an Eniautos-daimon has been the subject of much controversy, one of the major arguments being that there is no compelling evidence in its support.[16] But even though it may not be possible to prove the priority of these specific rituals over the myths and the drama, there is a significant general sense in which ritual *is* prior. The essence of ritual is action rather than words and concepts, and as action may be thought to be prior to concepts and language, and as both myth and drama depend upon these, ritual could indeed be said to be prior to them. Ritual here is to be thought of as a special case of imitative action. The importance of imitation in the process of learning has been known from early times. In recent times Jean Piaget has shown how imitation and play both fit into 'the general framework of the sensory-motor adaptations which characterize the construction of intelligence' In the beginning imitation is a function of perception itself; the imitative action is not merely 'associated' with perception but is 'inherent in the perceptive schema itself'. Piaget traces in detail the development of imitation through childhood from this initial stage to later symbolic and representational functions, showing clearly that not only is imitation prior to language but that it is also instrumental in the acquisition of it.[17] Extrapolating this phylogenetically, one could say that imitative action must have preceded speech and concepts, and that ritual as a special class of imitative actions must have preceded religious concepts and myths.[18] In fact, it must not only have preceded them but also been directly instrumental in their formation. This is precisely what Jane Harrison has argued.

Drama differs from other art forms in that it uses direct imitation.

Imitative action can thus be said to be its very essence. The ritual theory of drama may be critically irrelevant insofar as it is concerned merely with the *origin* of drama; but its concern with origins at least helps to bring out the centrality of imitative action as the *arche*, the first principle of drama. Drama may also be considered as utilizing a more 'primitive' form of perception than the other arts, a mode of perception that is prior to language and concepts and, insofar as it is the business of art to win back some of the concreteness of perception that is gradually attenuated with the development of abstract thought, a mode to be greatly valued. It is this mode of perception that Francis Fergusson has described by the terms 'the histrionic sensibility' and 'the mimetic perception of action'.[19] One of the most important consequences of the ritual theory of drama is thus the understanding that the essence of drama is not something that can be grasped merely through a study of its 'meaning' in the study, but something that has to be experienced as an action which we may either participate in or be spectators of. The emphasis on the importance of seeing Shakespeare's drama in its proper setting, in the theatre, that we find in a number of recent critics can certainly be said to owe a great deal to the ritual theory of the Cambridge anthropologists.

III

As in the case of the myth criticism surveyed in the previous chapter, a good deal of the criticism of Shakespeare in terms of the concept of ritual predates Frazer and the Cambridge anthropologists. This is, of course, as was to be expected, considering that the myth and ritual patterns mentioned earlier were conceived as patterns of primitive myth as well as of primitive ritual: Wigston, for example, was as interested in the rituals of the ancient mystery cults as in their myths. Another kind of ritual criticism of Shakespeare which predates Frazer is the criticism concerned with Christian rites as sources or analogues of the plays or of specific elements in them. We also come across some instances in Shakespeare criticism of the nineteenth century where parallels are drawn between the plays and some specific European folk festival or folk rite, as in Simrock's comments on *Macbeth* cited earlier. But the majority of the criticism of the plays in terms of ritual does derive from Frazer's concept of the dying god and the divine scapegoat, as the play-by-play survey that follows brings out quite clearly. Before we go on to that survey, however, a few general points may be made and some general studies of Shakespeare in the light of ritual briefly mentioned.

Two of the earliest examples of criticism of Shakespeare in terms of Frazer's ideas are Gilbert Murray's essay on Hamlet and Orestes (1914) and Janet Spens's little book *An Essay on Shakespeare's Relation to Tradition* (1916). In spite of their common derivation from Frazer, however, the two can be taken almost as paradigms of two different approaches to the question of ritual in Shakespeare's plays. Murray, as pointed out in Chapter 1, provides a link between Frazerian anthropology and the tradition of allegorical mythography. He also sets the major trend in the ritual approach, which is to relate the particular work to the universal pattern of symbolic actions embodied in the primitive rituals, though it must be said that it is often a fine point to distinguish such criticism from plain allegorical commentary. Janet Spens too is concerned with the presence of the universal pattern in the plays, but she gives the further argument (hinted at but not developed by Murray) that this pattern came to Shakespeare through medieval and Elizabethan folk plays and festive rites. As indicated earlier, this has been the source of several important studies, including C. L. Barber's, of Shakespearean drama in relation to Elizabethan popular culture.

In addition to these two types of ritual criticism, there have been in recent years some very interesting applications of van Gennep's paradigm of initiation rituals to the plays, particularly the comedies. One such study is Marjorie Garber's *Coming of Age in Shakespeare* (1981), which argues that one of the recurrent themes in Shakespeare is the process by which an individual grows into a mature adult, and that this process is conceived as a series of transitions or crossings of thresholds which bear a significant analogy to the passage rites studied by anthropologists. One such transition which an individual must negotiate successfully in order to attain true selfhood is the separation, as in a rite of passage, from persons who are literally or symbolically in the position of parent or sibling so as to establish a new bond with lover or spouse. In the specific case of women, to take another example, Shakespeare seems to believe that mature selfhood involves the giving up of virginity in favour of sexuality, marriage and motherhood, each stage of this process being presented as a rite of passage. Professor Garber sees this ritual analogy reflected in recurrent themes, incidents, motifs and images (especially images of thresholds) in Shakespeare's presentation of several other aspects of the process of maturation. The plays thus offer 'a cumulative portrait of what it means to be a successful adult in a Shakespearean world—and, just possibly, in our own'.[20]

As mentioned earlier, Bakhtin does not offer any detailed study of Shakespeare, but he does make a pregnant though brief remark which suggests how the concept of carnival applies to Shakespearean drama. Bakhtin argues that carnival in the plays is not confined to such obviously carnivalesque elements as clowning, obscenities and references to the grosser bodily functions; rather, as 'the logic of crownings and uncrownings', it directly or indirectly 'organizes the serious elements also'. This idea has been developed by Michael D. Bristol in a recent book in which he tries to demonstrate this logic as it is reflected in three carnivalesque features in Shakespearean and other Renaissance literature. These features—charivari or the burlesque of marriage ceremonies, treating death as a laughing matter, and the festive agon or battle between Carnival and Lent—reflect the resistance found in plebeian culture to any tendency to make authority absolute. In *A Midsummer-Night's Dream*, for example, Bottom's 'translation' and the interlude of Pyramus and Thisby present carnivalesque parodies of the model of 'reconciliation and accommodation' presented in the official wedding feast of Theseus and Hippolyta. Similarly, episodes where death is treated as a laughing matter, as in the Porter scene in *Macbeth*, represent 'festive uncrowning, debasement and renewal', for death is seen as a 'constantly recurring event, linked always to images of the fecundating processes of eating and sexuality that bring forth new life'. The festive agon between Carnival and Lent, in which both are tried and expelled in turn, forms the structural principle of several plays. In *Henry IV*, for example, Falstaff represents Carnival, and Hal Lenten civil policy, though this play breaks the normal festive rhythm that requires that Hal too be thrashed and expelled. Bristol sees the action of *Hamlet* too as built upon the battle between Carnival and Lent, represented by Claudius and Hamlet respectively. The effect of this festive agon, Bristol suggests, is to diminish the struggle in the Danish court and to give it a touch of ephemerality. He goes on to argue that from the standpoint of plebeian culture all struggles for succession are ephemeral, recurrent events. However, following Bakhtin, Bristol emphasizes the point that the carnival undercutting of official ceremonies and attitudes does not reflect a negative, absurdist world-view but rather the people's festive laughter directed at everyone, including the participants in the carnival.[21]

Another line of criticism has been the study not of specific ritual or festive patterns as sources or analogues of the plays but of ritual or ceremonial acts or gestures and of the attitudes associated with them as conscious thematic concerns in the plays. The ritual or ceremonial elements in the plays, such as coronations, triumphal entries and processions, obeisances and other formal gestures, are considered to be, as in primitive society, an expression of a sacramental view of the world and of kingship. The clearest expression of such a view is provided by G. Wilson Knight, who argues that we must approach the history plays in particular with 'a sense of the sacramental'. Knight goes on:

Kingship is closely related to the essence of poetic drama, which seems never properly to have recovered from the execution of Charles I.... How many plays of Shakespeare are without their king or duke? Even the fairies are a royalistic community. Kingship is central to Shakespeare's life-pattern and whatever our political philosophy we must receive such significance correctly and unfold them on the stage with due ceremonial and a willing suspension of disrespect. They are grand plays. In them surges the tumultuous energy of the soul of a nation; they are rich in the pride, pomp and circumstance of earthly power.

Francis Fergusson too suggests (with reference to *Hamlet* but clearly with a sense of its wider application) that the role of the monarch in Shakespeare's time was similar to that of Sophocles's Oedipus and Creon: the king was 'at once ruler, high priest, and father of the community'. He further argues that Shakespearean drama is analogous to ritual not only because it embodies a specific ritual pattern but because it performs for the Elizabethan age a function similar to that of the ritual theatre of Sophocles in ancient Greece, namely 'the "celebration of the mystery" of human life'. Similarly, John Holloway has argued that Elizabethan theatre could, like myth and ritual, be 'a source of power, of sustained, renewed or enhanced vitality, in the life of the community or the individual'.[22]

While emphasizing the ritualistic power of Shakespearean and Elizabethan drama, however, Fergusson also stresses the point that Shakespeare presents ritual in an ironic or tragic light, as hollow or inverted or interrupted—in any case as no longer efficacious. A number of critics, as will be seen from the following survey, have taken up this suggestion to study the failure of ritual in Shakespearean drama, the general trend being to consider this failure as reflecting a tragic rather than an absurdist or politically subversive viewpoint. In recent years, however, the view has gained ground that the presentation of 'maimed rites', especially in connection with royalty, reflects a popular subversion of the hierarchical Elizabethan world order and its mystique of kingship.

THE COMEDIES

As noted earlier, the idea of festive comedy has been a richly suggestive one. It can be traced back to Janet Spens, who first argued that beginning with *The Two Gentlemen of Verona* Shakespeare used a folk play habitually as the nucleus of his comedies. In some of these folk plays, such as those dealing with Robin Hood, there is a suggestion of 'the free life of the forest' in which 'all the restraints of conventional life are necessarily broken and human passions take their natural course'. This idea becomes central to Shakespeare's comedies. Though Spens herself failed to make much of her insight, it may be said to be the foundation of C. L. Barber's classic study, for his contrast between everyday and holiday presents in temporal terms the polarity seen spatially by Spens as that between the ordinary world and the world of the forest. Northrop Frye's idea of the 'green world' is another version of the same theme, as also, in a way, is the traditional pastoral contrast between the court and the country.[23] The strength of Barber's approach lies in his attempt to locate this contrast within the specific cultural context of Elizabethan folk rites and festive practices.

Barber sees Shakespeare's comedies as built on the model of games and pastimes such as the May Game and the Lord of Misrule. The basic common rhythm underlying the comedies and the festive rites and practices is expressed by the formula 'through release to clarification'. Holiday provides a necessary release from the routines of everyday life and gives an opportunity for a revitalizing contact with nature without which no cultural order can survive for very long. Similarly, the comedies present a period of release from social constraints or oppressive rule which finally leads to a better mutual adjustment between the individual and the community. Shakespearean comedy is, however, to be distinguished from the more obviously saturnalian comedy of Aristophanes. These present experience 'entirely polarized by saturnalia; there is little *within* the play to qualify that perspective'. What qualifies the perspective is the external factor that the comedy has an accepted place in the festival of Dionysia; it is thus only a *part* of the festival and as such it need not incorporate the everyday pole of experience. But in the case of Shakespeare, 'because no such clear-cut role for saturnalia or saturnalian comedy existed within Shakespeare's culture, the play itself had to place that pole of life in relation to life as a whole'. In other words, the festival is in this case only a *part* or the comedy, and its misrule works 'to consolidate rule'.[24] In his detailed study of six comedies (*A Midsummer-Night's Dream, Love's Labour's Lost, As You Like It, The Merchant of Venice, Twelfth Night* and *Henry IV*), Barber applies his formula with great flexibility and delicacy to identify in each case the nature of the release and the clarification. The idea of saturnalian or festive comedy thus helps to distinguish this group of comedies from the satiric comedies of Ben Jonson or from the other comedies of Shakespeare himself, as well as to indicate the distinctive feature of each play within the group.

An important recent development of Barber's approach is seen in Edward Berry's *Shakespeare's Comic Rites* (1984), which studies the structure of the comedies in the light of van Gennep's passage rites. Berry argues that the passage-rite paradigm is more applicable to the comedies than the pattern of festive or seasonal rites for the following reasons: in rites of passage the focus is primarily on the individual's progress from one state or status to another; this is also the case in Shakespeare's comedies, whose main theme is love as the way to marriage and happiness; secondly, the middle phase of Shakespeare's comedies, with its radical disorientations and confusions, is more like the liminal phase of passage rites than like holiday; and finally, like passage rites, the comedies mark more or less permanent changes in the characters' attitudes and social status. Berry then goes on to relate the different parts and elements of the comedies to the three phases of the passage rites. Most of the comedies, for example, begin with a literal or metaphorical separation; this is followed by a period of confusion or misrule, including emotional confusion and confusion of identity; the final phase of the comedies, which presents the reintegration into society of the central characters, corresponds to the final phase of the passage rites. Like Barber, Berry too ties his analysis of the comic structure to the specificities of Elizabethan culture by showing the recurrence of this structure in Elizabethan rites and customs relating to adolescence, courtship and marriage.[25]

The Comedy of Errors

I have not come across any discussion of this play in terms of ritual, but its relation to rituals of initiation can be inferred from the commentaries mentioned in the previous chapter.

The Taming of the Shrew

William Barry Thorne (1968) discusses the presence of elements of 'the folk-drama, the ritual, and the pastime of the sixteenth century'. He argues that the Induction prepares for the 'misrule' action of the main plot because Sly is, in a way, a King of Misrule in a saturnalian pattern of festivity, in which the real king is replaced by a mock king and the social order turned topsy-turvy. This is reflected in the main plot in the exchanging of roles between Tranio and Lucentio, in the fantastic marriage dress of Petruchio, in the theme of disguise, and in the scene of 'mad mistaking', in which, for Katherina, night becomes day and day night, 'just as it is supposed to happen during periods of misrule'. Thorne also indicates parallels between episodes in the play and traditional folk drama and ritual, such as the Maying festival and the mummers' wooing play. Petruchio's boasting, for example, is related to that of the fool in the wooing play, and the expression of rivalry between the suitors (Gremio and Tranio), to the contest between the old and the young suitors in the same play. The struggle between the old and the young is, according to Thorne, not only the theme of the mummers' plays and of 'the primitive ritual underlying the May flight to the woods and all the many forms of Saturnalia or misrule', but also of nearly all the comedies of Shakespeare. Young men defeat the anticomic elements, the harsh laws imposed by the old men, and restore the fertility and well-being of the community represented by the women. Thorne observes that the finding of a husband for Kate and the freeing of Bianca from captivity resolve 'an unhealthy situation in the family and also, symbolically, in the community itself'. *The Taming of the Shrew* thus illustrates the deep roots in folk tradition of Shakespeare's earlier comedies.[26]

The Two Gentlemen of Verona

Janet Spens's comment on 'the free life of the forest' has already been cited. It is the presentation of this free life that gives reality and depth of meaning to *The Two Gentlemen of Verona*. Spens goes on to relate the Robin Hood plays and other folk plays and rituals to the primitive rituals of *renouveau* studied by Frazer and others.

Love's Labour's Lost

C. L. Barber (Chapter 5) argues that the play begins with the 'folly of resistance' (i.e. the men's vow to shun women) which soon gives way to the 'folly of release', a festive release not of love but of the witty expressions of love, and the clarification achieved through this release is 'the recognition that love is not wooing games or love talk'. That is why there is no marriage at the end. And yet 'these sports are not written off or ruled out; on the contrary the play offers their delights for our enjoyment while humorously putting them in their place'. The songs of spring and winter with which the play concludes evoke the daily life of the community which provides the backdrop for the festive occasions. They thus provide for the conclusion of the play what is usually suggested through marriage, namely 'an expression of the going-on power of life'.

A Midsummer-Night's Dream

A ritual analogue of the play in the Germanic custom of the *trinoctium*, of waiting before consummation of marriage, was suggested in 1897.[27] Janet Spens (pp. 43–4) points out the more obvious parallel between the play and the May Day festival. She also cites the ancient Greek custom of ritual matings at night in a forest.

According to C. L. Barber (Chapter 6), the folly that this play is concerned with is 'delusive fantasy', and its release leads to 'clarification' about the role of imagination in life. Peter F. Fisher argues that the play presents 'the irrational force of sublunary passion' in conflict with 'the rationally ordered world of the Athenian court in the heroic age of Theseus'. This conflict is resolved by placing the action of the play within the larger context of nature. The May Day or Midsummer festivity corresponds to the Saturnalia of the winter solstice and symbolizes the release of passion. This is, of course, similar to Spens's idea of the release provided by the 'free life of the forest', but Fisher considers this world of the 'elemental power of nature' to be only one of three 'spheres of influence' working on the lovers, the other two being 'the classical heritage of reason' and the 'workaday world of common and uncommon sense'. James E. Robinson sees the play as fusing 'comedy as ritual' with 'comedy as argument or rhetoric'. The ritual aspect of the comedy consists in the magical elements, the fairies, the moonlit wood, and so on. It is an expression, in Robinson's view, of the desire to be at one with nature within a universe conceived as sacramental. The rhetorical aspect, on the other hand, expresses the desire to be at one with the law. In the play these two desires, initially at conflict with each other, are finally reconciled in marriage. All the three critics thus come to the conclusion that the play manages a very unique and successful synthesis or balance between divergent and opposing elements and attitudes: festivity and ordinary life (Barber), passion and reason (Fisher), and ritual and rhetoric, nature and law (Robinson). They all agree, moreover, that the ritual or festive element, however conspicuous, is not to be taken by itself, but to be seen in the larger perspective within which Shakespeare places it.

The Merchant of Venice

Janet Spens suggests that Antonio is the scapegoat. C. L. Barber has criticized this, arguing that it is Shylock who presents analogies with the scapegoat. According to him, this play as a whole 'is not shaped by festivity in the relatively direct way' that he traced in *Love's Labour's Lost* and *A Midsummer-Night's Dream*. He argues, nevertheless, that there are 'analogies to social occasions and rituals' which can be useful in understanding the symbolic action of the play. One such analogy that Barber points out is between the role of Shylock and that of the scapegoat in primitive rituals. The scapegoat is defined as 'a figure in whom the evils potential in a social organization are embodied, recognized and enjoyed during a period of licence, and then in due course abused, ridiculed, and expelled'. A little earlier, Barber equates Shylock with the killjoy figures who, along with butts and intruders, provide the complementary and antagonistic roles to those of the revellers, wits and insiders respectively within the festive framework of the action of the play.[28] However, it is difficult to see how the roles of the killjoy and the scapegoat can be easily reconciled: Shylock cannot be both a Puritan and a Carnival King, a Malvolio and a Falstaff. This difficulty, along with the disagreement regarding the very identity of the scapegoat figure in the play, points to a certain vagueness in the use of the concept of the scapegoat.

Paula Brody, in the article referred to in the previous chapter, relates the role of Shylock not only to that of the scapegoat figure, but also to the totemic practice of *omophagia* or the ritual eating of raw flesh. She writes: 'Shylock wants omophagia; instead he becomes the scapegoat in the ritual of renewal, the object which is both sacrificed and also deified.' The ritual of *omophagia*, according to Brody, explains Shylock's desire for the pound of flesh in a way that his own rationalizations of this desire ('say it is my humour', 'a certain loathing I bear Antonio', and so on) do not. In the *omophagia* the person who eats the flesh is supposed to assimilate the qualities of the victim. Moreover, it is a form of communion with the spirit of the group: by partaking of the flesh of the victim one becomes a socially accepted member of the group. In wanting to take a pound of Antonio's flesh, therefore, Brody argues, Shylock wishes to be assimilated to Venetian society. The absurdity of this view is readily apparent. There is little evidence in the play to warrant the equation of wanting a pound of flesh with wanting to eat it. But even if one were to allow this equation, the parallel with totemic cannibalism would still be rather remote because the essence of such ritual, presumably, is the *communal* sharing of the victim's flesh: a man is assimilated to the totemic group because he has partaken of this flesh and blood with the other members of the group. It is in this sense that he is one with them in flesh and blood. But Shylock explicitly refuses communal sharing of *any* meal with the Christians. He seems to be quite happy with his isolation; it is precisely the assimilation into the Christian group that he fears.

Brody takes up Barber's observation about Shylock's scapegoat function and elaborates upon it a bit further, and with further absurdity. The temporary deification of the scapegoat, which she suggests is essential to the scapegoat ritual, is parallelled in the play by the fact that Shylock has been admitted to Venetian society to the extent of being allowed to lend money and 'to enjoy participation in its feasting, and equality within the ritual of law'. But at the 'peak of his triumph' his fortune changes. However, before he is finally expelled, he must be made, 'at least temporarily, a *full* member of the tribe. . . . Thus, the baptism of Shylock.' Once he has been baptized, Brody suggests, the ritual sacrifice may be completed. By being forced to forfeit half his fortune he is, in ritual terms, destroyed. The fact that Shylock is not actually baptized in the play and that, in any case, the baptism is supposed to follow rather than precede the confiscation of his property (which is supposed to symbolize his ritual death) is completely ignored. Once again we see an uneasy fit of the ritual role on the dramatic character, and a confusion about the outlines of the ritual as well as about the role of the character.

Much Ado About Nothing

I have not found any discussion of this play specifically in terms of ritual.

As You Like It

Janet Spens sees several motifs from folk play and ritual in the play. In particular, she suggests that Shakespeare made use of the mummers' play in the figure of Jaques, who resembles the 'melancholy fool' of these plays. This has been questioned by R. J. E. Tiddy, who points out that there is but one 'melancholy fool' in all the mummers' plays, namely the Fool in the Revesby Plough Monday Play, who says, 'I am the noble Anthony as melancholy as a mantle tree.' This, according to Tiddy, is mere nonsense without any significance. Tiddy admits, however, that the deer-killing in *As You Like It* may be based on 'sights and doings which Shakespeare saw in Arden' and which were strongly tinged with folk ritual. Finally, C. L. Barber relates the play's conventional pastoral contrast between court and country to the one between holiday and everyday seen in the other festive comedies. He argues that the play achieves a balance between seriousness and levity which corresponds to the balance between the festive and everyday attitudes.[29]

Twelfth Night

As early as 1867, E. Montégut pointed out the relation of this play to the Twelfth Night festivity from which it derives its title. Montégut describes the play as a 'masquerade, slightly grotesque, as befits a play whereof the title recalls one of those festivals which were most dear to the jocund humour of our forbears'. He also refers to the crowning of a mock-king for the festival and the general atmosphere of carnival topsy-turvydom. This is also the approach of Janet Spens, who suggests that Sir Toby is a Lord of Misrule. C. L. Barber also considers the play a festive comedy in which Malvolio is the anti-comic figure who must be expelled. More recently, Melvin Seiden (1961) has argued that Malvolio is the 'scapegoat sacrificed to the amoral bacchanalian gods of comedy'. Malvolio, he writes, 'is Shakespeare's comic Coriolanus, a man beset by the wolves who are his enemies and the jackals who are or ought to be his friends. In America no one loves a cop— even when he's called a policeman. In Illyria the natives are apparently no different, and even light-hearted Illyrian comedy turns out to be a cannibalistic affair, at bottom.'[30] Once again we observe the rather loose use of the concept of the scapegoat. Any sacrifice must not be taken to be a scapegoat sacrifice. In any case, expulsion is not the equivalent of sacrifice, nor, for that matter, is killing. To expel a recalcitrant element from a community is an action which does not require Frazer's idea of the divine scapegoat to explain it. The sins and evils of the community are not transferred to Malvolio, and he is in no sense divine or taboo. Even in a psychological sense the concept of the scapegoat in relation to Malvolio does not make sense. For in the scapegoat, it may be argued, we exorcize those desires and impulses within us which we would like to enjoy but dare not, and which are therefore displaced on to another person whose temporary freedom from social or moral restraints we vicariously share, but whom we finally sacrifice in order to make peace with the reality principle. Or, in a more simple way, a scapegoat might be any person or object that we can blame for our misfortunes or accidents (when we kick a stone in anger after stumbling, we are making of the stone a scapegoat). But in neither of these psychological senses either can Malvolio be said to be a scapegoat. One does not know what answer to give, therefore, when Seiden asks: 'If Malvolio is not the perfect mythic scapegoat, where in our literature does one find a figure who can be called a scapegoat?' According to Barber, in the festive action it is the comic (or festive) figure that is ultimately sacrificed. He writes that 'to put Carnival on trial, run him out of town, and burn or bury him is in folk custom a way of limiting, by ritual, the attitudes and impulses set loose by ritual' (p. 213). Seiden, on the other hand (and Barber as well elsewhere) maintains that it is the anti-comic figure that is finally sacrificed. It may be possible to argue that *both* are sacrificed or expelled (as Carnival and Lent) because they represent extreme attitudes to festivity, but little is gained by using the term scapegoat to describe them both.

The Merry Wives of Windsor

The tricks played on Falstaff, especially the pinching and burning when he is disguised as Herne the Hunter, have strong ritual overtones. Northrop Frye describes them as 'an elaborate ritual of the defeat of winter, known to folklorists as "carrying out Death," of which Falstaff is the victim' Frye adds: 'Falstaff must have felt that, after being thrown into the water, dressed up as a witch and beaten out of a house with curses, and finally supplied with a beast's head and singed with candles while he said, "Divide me like a brib'd buck, each a haunch", he had done about all that could reasonably be asked of any fertility spirit.' Sitansu Maitra considers the tricks on Falstaff as variants on the expulsion of Carnival. In a lecture to the English Association, J. A. Bryant suggests that Falstaff is a 'scapegoat for a community afflicted generally by the lust and greed for which some of its members seek to make him solely responsible'.[31]

All's Well that Ends Well

Janet Spens (pp. 38–41) relates the play to the folk plays of Shrovetide or Hocktide. A part of the Hocktide festivities was the struggle for a head or a hood, and she finds a hint of this in the ragging of Parolles (IV. iii). She also suggests that the 'hocking' of men by women in this festival is parallelled in Helena's 'capture' of Bertram. Some of the folk and mythical motifs in the play mentioned in Chapter 1, such as the healing of the king and the fulfilment of the task, may also be considered as ritual motifs, and the bed-trick interpreted as a survival of ritual love-making to ensure fertility of the land.

Measure for Measure

A. D. Nuttall develops some of the rather surprising implications of Roy Battenhouse's idea that the theme of the play is Atonement. Central to the concept of Atonement is the principle of vicarious suffering, of Christ taking on the sins of humanity and suffering for it. If the Duke represents God (as the Father only, as Nuttall argues), then the unavoidable conclusion which is 'both unthinkable and only too plain' is that Christ must be represented by none other than Angelo. The play is thus not a straight but a *critical* version of the doctrine and myth of Atonement, with Angelo, as the victim, taking on the necessary sins that human judgment of other human beings involves and thus reconciling the contradiction between 'the ethic of government and the ethic of refraining from judgment'. Not only is the Christian myth, therefore, present in the play, but behind that myth lies the 'shadowy structure of a disturbingly alien shape'. This structure (later called a 'sub-structure'), Nuttall suggests, is that of the primitive scapegoat rituals: 'Under the pressure of Shakespeare's genius the figure of the atoning sufferer begins to take on the lineaments of his anthropological ancestor, the scapegoat.' Angelo is thus a 'Christ-figure with a difference', being at the same time a 'Devil-figure', at once 'the redeemer and the polluted'. In this way, Nuttall argues, one can account for the mysterious 'resonance' of Angelo's character, 'by showing that the evil he does has its place in a necessary scheme of redemption'.[32]

THE HISTORY PLAYS

In the criticism of the history plays the concept of ritual has been used primarily in the sense of formal actions and ceremonies, most of them associated with the mystique of royalty. G. Wilson Knight, as mentioned above, emphasizes the central role of the rites of royalty in focussing 'the energy of the soul of a nation', in bringing the whole nation together in a sort of mystic communion.

Eric La Guardia takes a different view of the ceremonial nature of these plays. He argues, apparently following Tillyard, that the second tetralogy traces a progress from 'ceremony to history', from 'divinity to mortality', and from a 'golden' to a 'brazen' world. 'Ceremony,' he writes, 'takes a sacramental view of nature; it operates within mythical rather than historical time; it attempts to preserve the order of culture in opposition to the disorderly flow of human experience.' The change from the 'mystical kingship' of Richard II to the rational kingship of Henry V is not presented, according to La Guardia, as either progress or regression but rather as a dramatization of 'man's continuous participation in both the mythical and the historical'. The argument is supported by an analysis of the kinds of language used by Richard and Henry, ritualistic and sacramental in one case and rhetorical and rational in the other. Alvin Kernan comes to a similar conclusion about the second tetralogy, which he terms Shakespeare's *Henriad*. These plays present, according to him, 'a movement from ceremony and ritual to history and drama'. In other words, one can say, Shakespeare's histories dramatize the very process which made it possible for them to be written, namely the change from a mythical, ceremonial world-order, with little sense of historical time, to a historical mode of understanding political reality. Finally, David Bevington suggests that ceremonies of state in the plays can be viewed as 'the rites of passage of the body politic, for they celebrate moments of transition in the social order'. In particular, 'coronation is an awesome ceremony on Shakespeare's stage, one that embodies all the hierarchical values that are visually implicit in the theatre building as *theatrum mundi*'. Usually, however, Shakespeare presents these ceremonies as mere show without any substance, or as disrupted or desecrated, though the effect of such presentations is not to put the value of ceremony as such in doubt but rather to affirm, through the very negation of it, the ideal of a hierarchical order.[33]

Henry VI

J. P. Brockbank suggests, without elaborating, that Henry VI has the dramatic role of sacrificial victim' in these plays. Sigurd Burckhardt, commenting on the scene between the Countess of Auvergne and Talbot (*1 Henry VI*, II. iii), makes a point similar to La Guardia's and Kernan's about the change from a ceremonial to a more functional style of life. The blunt, functional language of Talbot represents, according to him, the new style of life and manners that was to replace the feudal ceremonialism of the warring barons.[34]

Richard III

Brockbank suggests (p. 298) that in the scene in which Richard is cursed by the ghosts of his victims (v. iii) there is a brief hint that he is capable of assuming the role of the sacrificial victim. Norman Holland's comment, cited in the previous chapter, on the mythic pattern of the play is also obviously relevant since the pattern of the good king killing the bad boar-king and making the land fertile once more could also be the pattern of primitive rituals of regicide. A. P. Rossiter, using a distinction proposed by Clifford Leech between 'ritual' and 'document', argues that the play, like ritual, 'conveys homage' to the power of human will embodied in Richard. But at the same time it also reconciles the spectators 'to the destruction of an "admirable" man as an affirmation of a divinely-directed principle of order'. Richard is thus the scapegoat in whom we enjoy our own aggressive impulses before exorcizing them by killing him.[35]

King John

I have not seen any discussion of this play in terms of ritual.

Richard II

The ceremonial aspect of this play has been remarked upon by several writers. John Dover Wilson, following Walter Pater's comparison of the abdication of Richard to an 'inverted rite', compares the whole play to the catholic Mass. The idea of the 'inverted rite', he suggests, goes to the heart of the play, 'since it reveals a sacramental quality in the agony and death of the sacrificial victim, as it were, of the god slain upon the altar, which we to-day can only begin to understand by reading a book like *The Golden Bough*'. E. M. W. Tillyard considers the play to be 'the most formal and ceremonial' of all Shakespeare's plays; William G. McCollom has also commented on the ritual nature of the play. Finally, J. A. Bryant, whose study of the play has already been referred to in Chapter 1, suggests that besides using the Biblical story 'as analogue for his secular fable', Shakespeare in this play, by frequently alluding to 'the symbolic substance of analogous pagan ritual' (sun and ice, summer and winter, etc.), presents a work which has 'ritual analogy with the sacrifice on the cross'. Bryant points out that three of the four rituals of fertility that Cornford finds significant for the development of drama show similarities with the action of *Richard II*. These are, in Cornford's terms, 'The Carrying out of Death', in which the sin of the whole kingdom is sought to be purged with the death of a single sacrificial victim; 'The Fight of Summer and Winter'; and the deposing of the old king or old year by the new. These analogies with primitive and Christian ritual give to Shakespeare's 'secular fable' a significance achieved only rarely in drama.[36]

Henry IV and *Henry V*

In Falstaff several critics have seen the Fool-as-Scapegoat. Lord Raglan argues that he is as mythical a figure as Hecate or Ariel, though more realistically presented, and points to several myths and legends where the hero is accompanied by a buffoon, e.g. Dionysus and Silenus, Akbar and Birbal, Don Quixote and Sancho Panza. The origin of Falstaff, he suggests, lies in the primitive belief in the fool as holy (cf. the image of Falstaff resting in Arthur's bosom), and his drunkenness is related to the frequent association of prophecy with the ritual use of intoxicants and drugs. John Dover Wilson observes that whatever may be his origin, Falstaff has become 'a kind of god in the mythology of modern man', a modern Bacchus or Silenus. Insofar as Falstaff represents, like these gods, the exhilarating freedom from social restraints, he is like Carnival, and like Carnival he is expelled at the end (though this last is not a point that Dover Wilson makes). He does however suggest that the 'English spirit' needs order as well as liberty, and that the play celebrates a 'double coronation': of the 'English Bacchus' as well as the 'English Harry'. For the English spirit, then, mere festivity is not enough and must finally be put in its proper place. This is an argument that anticipates C. L. Barber's idea of festivity as well as Bristol's argument about the festive agon between Carnival and Lent, though their conclusions are different. Barber compares the expulsion of Falstaff to the trial and expulsion of Carnival, but argues that whereas generally suggested through comic irony in order that it may lead to 'clarification', in this play he has recourse to a ritual method of putting Carnival in place rather than an ironic one. To this extent the play represents a failure of irony. In using the ritual method to expel Falstaff, Shakespeare has used the theatre 'as a substitute for ritual, without the commitment to participation and discipline proper to ritual nor the commitment to the fullest understanding proper to comedy or tragedy'.[37]

J. I. M. Stewart explains the rejection of Falstaff as an example of the expulsion of the scapegoat and the ritual killing of the father-king (Falstaff becoming a father-substitute through a process of displacement). Stewart writes:

Falstaff is in the end the dethroned and sacrificed king, the scapegoat as well as the sweet beef. For Falstaff, so Bacchic, so splendidly with the Maenads Doll and Mistress Quickly a creature of the wine-cart and the cymbal, so fit a sacrifice (as Hal early discerns) to lard the lean, the barren earth, is of that primitive and magical world upon which all art, even if with a profound unconsciousness, draws.

Philip Williams comes to a very similar conclusion about the role of Falstaff as father-substitute and scapegoat.[38]

Thus we see that starting from the point that the expulsion of Falstaff resembles an act of ritual, Stewart and Williams on the one hand and Barber and Bristol on the other come to precisely opposite conclusions. The first two 'explain' the expulsion in terms of the ritual and thus justify it aesthetically, whereas Barber and (to a certain extent) Bristol use the ritual analogy to 'explain' the unsatisfactoriness of the expulsion. It would seem, then, that the aesthetic problem of whether the rejection of Falstaff is satisfactory or not must be settled before we go on to explain it as a survival of 'atavic' impulses (to use Stewart's term).

Henry VIII

G. Wilson Knight comments on the ceremonial aspect of the play in *The Crown of Life*, but there is little else that is relevant to the ritual approach.

THE TRAGEDIES

In the criticism of the tragedies, scapegoat and other sacrificial rituals have naturally been referred to most frequently, though references to initiation rites are not uncommon. According to

Robert Hapgood the association of the tragic hero with the scapegoat is 'easily the soundest and most suggestive contribution' made by the myth and ritual critics. The most sustained effort to apply the scapegoat paradigm to the major tragedies, though certainly not in 1961 (the year of its publication) the most original, is John Holloway's *The Story of the Night*. Holloway traces a recurrent pattern in these tragedies, a pattern which fits the later tragedies better than *Hamlet* and *Othello*:

> This pattern has at its centre a very distinctive role pursued by the protagonist over the whole course of the play: a role which takes him from being a cynosure of his society to being estranged from it, and takes him, through a process of increasing alienation, to a point at which what happens to him suggests the expulsion of the scapegoat, or the sacrifice of a victim, or something of both.

> The death of the protagonist is thus not merely the final misfortune he has to suffer, and though in each case it is presented realistically as the outcome of the human situation of the play, it has also, at the same time, 'the quality of stylized and ritual execution', being recognized by protagonist and pursuers alike as 'the stylized act which fitly closes a stylized sequence'.[39]

The other major line of criticism of the tragedies in terms of ritual has been the study of Shakespeare's presentation of ritual and ceremony in the plays. The tragedies, of course, like the history plays, are full of the pomp and circumstance of royalty, though its mystique is subjected here to even sharper and more sceptical scrutiny. Hapgood argues that the mature tragedies present rites 'maimed by reality', i.e. they strike a balance between fulfilling our hopes that the sacrifice of the hero would bring about regeneration of the community, and disappointing them. This balance, essential for the full tragic experience, is lacking in the early tragedies, where the sacrificial ritual is either entirely successful, as in *Titus Andronicus*, *Romeo and Juliet*, and *Richard III*, or a total failure, as in *Richard II* and *Julius Caesar*.[40] However, irrespective of the success or failure of the rituals within the play, a Shakespearean tragedy *as* ritual has been seen (by Fergusson and Holloway, for example) as performing, through the audience's participation in the sacrificial action, a role akin to that of ritual in primitive societies, namely inducing an enhanced sense of life and community.

Titus Andronicus

William H. Desmonde presents the thesis that the plot of *Titus Andronicus* was derived by 'Shakespeare or one of his contemporaries from a Roman play or myth stemming from Greek ritual origins, and ultimately from tribal puberty rites'. He describes the major episodes of the play as follows: 'the struggle between two princes for the kingship, following the death of the old king; a human sacrifice to propitiate the dead soul; a marriage by capture in which a son is killed; a rape near a pit in the ground; and a cannibalistic meal. Furthermore, all of Titus's sons are gradually killed, with the exception of the last, who succeeds to the kingship.' These episodes, according to Desmonde, derive from the myths of Pelops and the rape of Persephone, 'both of which were enacted frequently in antiquity as ritual dramas'. The former myth is related, according to Desmonde, to Oedipal conflicts in the 'primal horde' and to the rituals seeking to assuage the guilt of the primal crime. It is also related to tribal puberty rites, following Theodor Reik, by arguing that these rites are merely re-enactments of the primal crime, but with the son taking the place of the father and atoning for the guilt of the brother-horde. The puberty initiation rites were also, suggests Desmonde, ceremonies portraying the death and rebirth of the neophyte. The Persephone myth, according to Desmonde's hypothesis, represents 'female puberty rites' as opposed to the male initiation rites whose traces can be found in the Pelops and Dionysus myths. The episode in the play which corresponds to the myth and ritual of Persephone is, of course, the rape of Lavinia near a pit, the pit being an important detail since it suggests the disappearance of Persephone under the earth. Thus, Desmonde concludes, '*Titus Andronicus* is the survival of a male and a female puberty rite of primitive origins, which survived in classical Greece in the Eleusinian mysteries.' He admits that the source of Shakespeare's play may be the story of Procne and Philomela in Ovid, but suggests that this in no way invalidates his theory since Ovid himself seems to be aware of the ritual associations of the myth and places the scene of Tereus and Philomela at the time of the Bacchic rites. And when, as Desmonde points out, Procne, like Demeter, went in search of the ravished and hidden virgin, 'she was clad in the ritual attire of the Dionysian revels'. The play, thus, is to be seen as representing the pattern of death and rebirth associated with initiation rituals. In spite of the copious references to anthropologists, however, Desmonde's interpretation of the play really belongs to the tradition of allegorical mythography, with a psychological theory replacing the former theological syncretism. At any rate, there seems to be little difference between comparing the play to the *myth* of Persephone and comparing it to the *ritual* of tribal initiation, since both are interpreted as pointing to the same psychological theme. The point that the myth mediates, as it were, between the ritual and the work of art does not seem to matter very much here, meaning little more than that it occupies a middle position in a purely temporal sense.

Robert Hapgood suggests that the characters in the play are like a great body mutilated and dismembered and waiting to be reborn. Titus purges five enemies, sacrifices the innocent Lavinia and, finally, himself, the 'hero-scapegoat', for the metamorphosis of the whole community. The saviour of this community is Lucius, whose departure and return remind us of Astraea, goddess of Justice. Hapgood also points out that Titus is the first of the tragic heroes to undergo the twin change from cynosure to outcast and from admired nobleman to hunted monster. The hero as scapegoat 'becomes the worst case of the very ills he would purge'.[41]

Romeo and Juliet

As mentioned earlier, Hapgood argues that the deaths of Romeo and Juliet are a case of successful sacrificial rites as they bring about the atonement of the two feuding families. Wigston's discussion of the play, mentioned in Chapter 1, suggested analogies with esoteric rituals as well as myths.

Julius Caesar

Discussions of ritual in this play centre on the theme of sacrifice. Brents Stirling remarks that the theme of 'incantation and ritual' is prominent throughout the play. Brutus, he argues, tries to ritualize the murder of Caesar as a sacrificial act for the good of Rome, whereas Antony tries to invert this ceremonial formula. Hapgood, Marienstras and Peter Anderson have also concentrated on the theme of sacrifice. While the first two share Stirling's interest in the failure of sacrificial ritual, Anderson's concern is with the 'language' of sacrifice. His essay elaborates the statement of Granville-Barker quoted as its epigraph that 'Pompey dead is to Caesar something of what Caesar dead is to be to Brutus and the rest.' Anderson sees the form ('eidos') of the play as 'the mythic pattern of sacrifice in which Caesar is sacralized and victimized by his "sons" as they seek contiguity with the divinity Pompey'. The sacrificial object, according to Lévi-Strauss, is a medium of exchange between the deity and the worshipper. As such it is attached to both. The 'language' of sacrifice is a 'metonymic' language: the sacrificial victim is 'selected from a natural series to represent the series'. The fundamental characteristic of metonymy is 'displacement', which Anderson traces in the language and imagery of the play. Among examples of displacement (which is associated with 'dislocation', 'replacement', and 'exchange') are the following: the tradesmen in the opening scene are 'out of place'; even the scarves on Caesar's statue are considered to be out of place by Flavius and Marullus; Caesar repositions Calphurnia; and 'the battle of Philippi is lost by *position*'. The tradesmen's punning in the first scene is also, according to Anderson, a linguistic counterpart of the metonymic language of sacrifice: 'Pompey has been exchanged for Caesar. And with the tradesmen's *linguistic* chagrin at their chastisement ("they vanish tongue-tied in their guiltiness") punning is punished and guilt is associated with the language of metonymy.' Gestures and images in the play also speak the language of sacrifice, as in the frequent references to genuflection, which is the 'body attitude' of sacrifice. In contrast to the kneeling of the conspirators, Caesar's body attitude is one of fixation, which is important for his position as sacrificial victim: 'it is his significant response to the significance of genuflection'. Anderson also comments on the way in which the sacral quality of Caesar is established and on Brutus's suicide as itself a kind of sacrifice; the spirit of Caesar now resides in his own body, and hence that body must be destroyed. The theme of sacrifice thus permeates the whole play.[42]

Hamlet

Perhaps the most famous study of ritual in the play, apart from Murray's essay, is Francis Fergusson's chapter on the play in *The Idea of a Theater*. The main action of the play, which is seen to be similar to that of *Oedipus* and also to bear strong analogy to scapegoat rituals, is described by Fergusson as 'the attempt to find and destroy the hidden "imposthume" which is poisoning the life of Claudius's Denmark'. This action is realized through the story and characters as well as through a series of ritualistic and improvisational scenes. The rituals in the play (e.g such scenes as the changing of the guards, the ceremonies at the court of Claudius, Ophelia's funeral, and the duel between Hamlet and Laertes) provide moments in which the plot-lines are, as it were, gathered together: 'the issues are held in suspension, and we are reminded of the traditional social values in which all have some sort of stake' They serve, Fergusson continues, 'to focus attention on the Danish body politic and its hidden malady: they are the ceremonious invocations of the well-being of society, and secular or religious devices for securing it'. On the other hand the improvisations (e.g. Hamlet's sermon on drunkenness; his exchanges with Polonius, Rosencrantz and Guildenstern, and the players; the joking with the gravediggers) are 'individualistic actions that throw doubt upon the efficacy of the official magic'. The play within the play is both ritual and improvisational entertainment, 'and shows the Prince as at once clown and ritual head of the state' Fergusson writes:

The rituals, the stories, and the improvisations together make the peculiar rhythm of *Hamlet* as a performance. Denmark is shown as waiting, as it were, in the darkness of its ineffective ceremonies and hollow communal prayer while the infection, 'mining all within', divides every man in secret from every other and bursts forth, from time to time, in savage but brief and ineffective fights.

The mana has departed, as it were, from the ritual acts owing to some desecration. Only the sacrifice of a royal victim can restore it.[43]

Fergusson points out that *Hamlet* is different from *Oedipus* in one important respect: 'Even the ritual process itself is, in *Hamlet*, directly dramatized: i.e., presented in a tragic, ironic light. There are no rituals in *Oedipus*: Oedipus is a ritual. But Hamlet has an extremely modern and skeptical, a Pirandellesque, theatricality as well; Shakespeare plays with the basis of his own make-believe.' But in spite of this Shakespeare never, according to Fergusson, satirizes the values and beliefs associated with the rituals; if they are shown to be ineffective, then their failure is presented as tragic rather than absurd.[44] This idea has been developed by other critics and also applied to other plays. Robert Hapgood, for example, elaborates upon the idea that in *Hamlet* the ritual of kingship is presented as having lost its mana, though there is no questioning in it of the foundation of belief in ritual.

William Montgomerie tries to study ritual and folk elements in the play from the mainly antiquarian point of view of a folklorist, but he does try to draw a parallel between the role of Hamlet and the ritual role of the hero in the Grail legend. He also draws, rather unconvincingly, a parallel between the dumb-show in the play-within-the-play and the mummers' plays. The fact that in the mummers' plays it is medicine which is poured through the ear to revive a dead man, whereas in *Hamlet* it is poison designed to kill, is explained as 'an Italian intrusion in a typically English ritual where the killing was traditionally by the sword'. The pouring of poison in the ear is thus considered to be both a parallel to the mummers' play *and* an Italian intrusion. Montgomerie also mentions some other ritual elements. For example, he maintains that Claudius's flight from Hamlet's play is the survival of a traditional ritual, of which the annual flight of the priest-king at Rome (the *Regifugium*) was the type. F. V. Morley also seeks to explain the play in terms of Elizabethan folk festivals. He argues that in Shakespeare's time the Hocktide festival coincided with the 'mockery of the Danes', which was a ritual play about the defeat of the Danes. In *Hamlet*, he suggests, there are elements of this folk play, or at least of the tribal attitudes that were expressed in such plays. Thus, Hamlet is ineffectual because the stereotype Dane is ineffectual. Hamlet, according to Morley, is merely a traditional character, not a person. And he cannot win because the Hocktide tradition is against him.[45]

Charles W. Eckert undertakes a detailed analysis of the common elements in the Hamlet and Orestes sagas and the Roman legend of Junius Brutus. Examples of these common elements are: a hero whose uncle murders his father and marries his mother; a feigning of madness by the hero (in the Ambales saga the hero goes to the extent of reducing himself to an animal-like state); misogyny; killing of the king's councillor; exile, dangerous voyage, return, and revenge on the usurper. Not all of these motifs, of course, are present in all versions of the legends, and Eckert suggests that they are not all explicable in terms of 'an initiatory or a regicidal or a scapegoat paradigm'. He goes on to argue that a broader paradigm than any of these is needed to explain all the common elements. The paradigm that he suggests is that of 'two of the oldest and most universal bodies of ritual activities—purgative or apotropaic ceremonies (Greek *katharmoi, apotrope*) and initiatory rites (Greek *teletai*)'. The common elements of the stories may be seen, according to Eckert, as the 'mythic corollaries' of these rituals. He writes that the three heroes especially important for his study, 'the Greek Orestes, the Roman Brutus, and the Scandinavian-Christian Hamlet, are all connected with the New Year's festivals, particularly with the purgative and initiatory rituals performed at these times'. Thus, Orestes is associated with the festival of Anthesteria, Brutus with the Regifugium, which was celebrated in February, and Hamlet with the New Year and Christmas festival.[46]

The purgative and initiatory rituals are, according to Eckert, the social and individual aspects, respectively, of the same symbolic action. The elements of the purgative rites are the procession of the 'rhabdos', the 'sphagia', and the 'holocaust'. Both Brutus and Hamlet (in the legend, though not in the play) receive one or two golden staffs during their period of exile; Orestes also carries a 'wool-tufted branch of olive'. All these may be seen as survivals of the rhabdos or purgative wand, and the fact that nearly all the heroes in this tradition carry a wand indicates, Eckert argues, that 'they are engaged in some ritual activity of broader significance than killing a Frazerian king'. The sphagia explains Hamlet's brutal slaying of the king's councillor. This rite, performed during the Greek New Year, has to be distinguished from the 'thusia', the 'meal shared with the gods', by the fact that it was usually performed at night, on a low mound or in a trench, with the victim being totally dismembered or burned and his remains buried or cast in water. The purpose of this ritual was not communion but placation and aversion. In Greece and Babylonia the sphagia was followed by the flight of the officiant. This detail of the plot, Eckert suggests, is easily rationalized, as in the case of Hamlet's exile, which comes so naturally in the sequence of the story that the reader would not suspect any ritual significance 'were the exile not preceded by the brutal *sphagia*'. (In *Hamlet*, one may suppose, the brutality is reflected not in the killing as such, but rather in Hamlet's sentiment towards the dead Polonius.) Finally, the holocaust is reflected in the Hamlet tradition in the burning of the hall with all the courtiers in it. In the play, of course, no such holocaust takes place, but the fact that the term is often used as a metaphor to describe multiple deaths like those at the end of this play may suggest a connection between the play and the ritual tradition (pp. 329–30).

The initiatory rites whose traces can be seen in the stories of this tradition closely parallel the rites of the New Year festival: they 'occur at an individual rather than a social period of crisis, and effect a personal rather than a social death and regeneration'. The initiatory rites of Greece and northern Europe were, as Eckert points out, similar in structure. The chief rites were: removal of boys from their homes; a period of frightening seclusion in a hut or woods where they might be forced to live like wild animals; ordeals; instructions; mock or real tyrannizing of women to symbolize transcendence of feminine ties; the investing of the initiates with adult objects or articles of clothing and return to the social group. This, according to Eckert, is 'the scenario at the most primitive level, and the myths we are considering represent various stages of rationalization'. The Hamlet saga, according to him, is the most conservative, or primitive, and part of this primitiveness is no doubt carried over into the play. One of the elements of these rituals reflected in the play is Hamlet's madness (an example, according to Eckert, of the 'telestic madness' that Plato refers to in the *Phaedrus*), which is otherwise only superficially rationalized as 'feigned'. This madness corresponds to the stage in the initiation ritual when the boys are forced to live like wild animals (beast-like = mad; cf. 'berserk' = [etymologically] warrior or initiate dressed in beast's skin). The tyrannizing of women is reflected in nearly all the variants of the legends; in the play it is quite obviously reflected in Hamlet's misogyny. The voyages undertaken by many of the heroes, including Hamlet, correspond to the ordeals that the initiate must undergo before being finally accepted in his community (pp. 331–5).

In the Hamlet-Orestes tradition, according to Eckert, the initiatory and the purgative rituals are combined, the hero-priest who drives away evil must himself, like an initiate, be purified first. He concludes:

The basis for the purgative-regenerative and initiatory patterns found both in the festivals and in the myths is the universal *gestalten* of death and rebirth. Because the social and the personal rites are superimposed in the myths, the pattern becomes fugal in its complexity, obscuring the essentially simple theme for readers who no longer live intimately with both the myths and rituals. That a hero should undergo initiation (i.e., perfecting, preparation) before accomplishing his destiny answers a psycho-logic that is as operative in modern fiction as in the Hamlet sagas; but the specific initiatory activities in which he engages are no longer initiatory to us, and may impress us as so much 'clumsy supernaturalism'. (p. 336)

Troilus and Cressida

I have not found any discussion of ritual elements in this play.

Othello

Othello, too, has not attracted the attention of the ritualists. Holloway (p. 50) does point out the general ritual movement by which the hero is transformed from the cynosure of all eyes to a victim (in this case, almost a monster), but he suggests that Othello's tragedy remains a purely personal one. There is no sense 'of a society which is swept along with the protagonist and suffers a decline parallel to his own'.

King Lear

Janet Spens (pp. 49–52) connects Lear, along with Jaques, with the Fool in the sword play. Shakespeare realized, she writes, that 'the story of the Summer-King or Fool who is slain, is the story of pitiful human decay and death, of the passing of the generations'. Indeed, according to her, the figure of the 'pharmakos' or scapegoat is the very essence of tragedy. She does not explain, however, how the parallel between the Fool of the sword play and Lear could be meaningful when that Fool, unlike Lear, springs back to life after being slain by his sons.

Sarah Anne Davidson, using the ideas of Frazer, Gilbert Murray, Jane Harrison and Janet Spens, argues that King Lear is a scapegoat figure, a year-daimon who is finally sacrificed. To demonstrate this thesis she tries to find out 'what in the background of the mythological Lear might fit him for such a role'. She relates Lear to the myth of Cecrops and his three daughters and suggests that Cecrops might be a 'year-daimon, a symbol of Reincarnation', since he is associated with a serpent and is himself part serpent. One of the daughters is faithful while the other two are not, which relates them, according to Davidson, to the three daughters of Lear. And as the cult of the daughters of Cecrops was associated with the carrying of dew during the festival of Hersephoria, the daughters themselves may be personifications of dew. This again, in Davidson's view, links the myth with rituals of the year-daimon and May Day festivities.[47]

The more immediate background for the play is in Celtic legend, and Davidson comes to the conclusion that the Celtic legend of Llyr is also based on rituals of the year-daimon. Llyr (to put her argument very briefly) means the sea; the sea is often, in Celtic legend, associated with darkness, hence there must be an implication of a king of light who opposes the king of darkness, a summer king *versus* a winter king. Llyr's wife in some versions of the legend is actually the wife of Lug, the sun god. Llyr is thus associated both with light and darkness. Or, one can say, Llyr and Lug are different aspects of the year-daimon. Also, in another version of the legend, it is said that two men fight every first day of May for the hand of Cordeyella or Creiddylad, the daughter of Leir. Hence she too is associated with the theme of the battle between the seasons. Coming then to discuss *Lear* in particular, Davidson points out that according to Gilbert Murray there are two types of vegetation kings: the summer-king and the winter-king; the latter is in reality the summer-king's slayer grown proud and royal. Lear, she suggests, is of the second type, the old winter-king who is made the scapegoat. Like the primitive scapegoat he is both sacred and taboo, the sacredness being reflected in what Kent calls 'authority' and the sense of the taboo in his madness.[48]

Douglas Hewitt links the idea of the scapegoat function of Lear more directly to the response of the Elizabethan audience than Spens or Davidson manage to do, in spite of their references to the English folk plays. Hewitt suggests that in spite of Christianity old pagan festivals had survived in Elizabethan times—for example: the carrying out of death to ensure a good harvest, the morris and the sword dances, the mummers' plays and the May games. All these, according to Hewitt, were different forms of the worship of the god of fertility, and 'just as Greek Tragedy, which originated in the worship of Dionysos, derived part of its force from its religious associations, so Elizabethan drama, when performed to an audience responsive to the folk ceremonies from which the plays sprang, may have made certain appeals which are now lost'.

The audience's awareness of the folk ceremonies modified their response to the play in two ways in particular. The parallel between the role of Lear in the play and the role of the scapegoat, a parallel of which they could hardly have been unaware, must have given a certain sense of inevitability to Lear's expulsion and death, a point which anticipates Holloway's description of the stylized death of the tragic hero. The ritual role was laid down, given, and the character could improvise upon it only to a limited extent. Hence, the individual character of the scapegoat-king was not important; any conflict within him became not an individual psychological conflict, but a more general conflict of values. Secondly, the hero-as-scapegoat was yet another manifestation of the link between the microcosm and the macrocosm that has been shown by Tillyard and others to have been such a marked feature of the Elizabethan world picture. This linking of the hero-scapegoat with the welfare of the whole community gave to Lear and other tragic heroes their importance and dignity. Already, however, according to Hewitt, this world-picture was fading away, and 'the feeling persists, as one contrasts Shakespeare with later dramatists, that he wrote at the last moment when this background of vague and misunderstood myth could combine with other beliefs and attitudes to produce the sense of inevitability and of the solidarity of the protagonists with their people which the finest tragedy demands'.[49]

William Empson (1949) briefly hints at a different way of looking at the concept of the scapegoat. Lear, he suggests, as the scapegoat 'who has collected all this wisdom for us is viewed at the end with a sort of hushed envy, not . . . really because he has become wise but because the general human desire for experience has been glutted in him; he has been through everything. "We that are young / Shall never see so much, nor live so long".'[50]

William Frost argues that in Elizabethan drama ritual has a function analogous to that of disguise and like it is probably connected with the very nature of drama. Ritual, or 'ceremonial situation', works to free actors and playwrights from the demands of verisimilitude, 'for the participants in a rite are assumed *a priori* to act parts and to speak languages not simply their own or natural to them as individuals, but traditional or appropriate in some way to a publicly acknowledged occasion'. Frost extends the term 'ritual' to include 'any speech or situation which will be felt by participants or spectators to be predictable in important aspects'. The presence of such ritual in drama has its drawbacks. For example, as Frost points out, it blots out the individuality of character, mechanizes the action, and is an 'added temptation to the dramatist to extract an added *frisson* from ritual by interrupting it'. With this preamble, Frost goes on to study the role of ritual in *King Lear*, concentrating on the first scene. This scene, which according to him is the most ritualistic in the play, is appropriate because it is in harmony with the mythic or folk-lore nature of the story and helps to produce, through its 'machine-like quality of ritual', precisely the effect of 'nightmarish inevitability most useful . . . for certain sorts of tragedy'. This ritual is contrasted in the play with a number of other elements, such as the realistic or non-ritualistic prose of Kent and Gloucester in this scene. This provides a bridge between the ritual and the naturalistic drama and also throws the ritual into relief. There is also the contrast between the ritual in this scene and the scenes in Goneril's household and in the storm. The latter scene embodies a parody of all the ritual acts of the first scene. Finally, there is the contrast between the opening and the conclusion, where 'ritual has lost all relevance to the king' and the king and Cordelia have lost all relevance to the new rituals and to the play. Frost concludes: 'We are now in the presence, not of the ceremonies by which human beings encompass their condition, the *rites of passage* of the anthropologists, but of the barest facts of that condition itself. King and daughter, no longer figures in myth or allegory, come before us fragile, irreplaceable, and particular, a pair of jailbirds and losers.' Thus, according to Frost, the play presents not a ritual pattern of events, but rather the *failure* of ritual, in a manner somewhat similar to that in *Hamlet* but with a far more radical questioning of the efficacy of ritual as such. Judah Stampfer also argues that the play presents a failure of ritual, but this time it is held to be a failure of the rituals of penance. Finally, Maynard Mack comments on the play's radical questioning of the efficacy of ritual. Referring to the passage beginning 'Plate sin with gold', he writes:

No one, I suspect, who had responded to the role of the king in Shakespeare's history plays, or the king's role in contemporary drama generally, could miss the shock in these lines, coming as they did from 'the thing itself'. If we suppose, further, that the structural conventions of the Elizabethan theatre, with its 'very solid three-dimensional symbols of order, representing 'home, city, and king', sometimes induced in observers a deeper identification, a sense that they were witnessing in the career of the stage monarch a 'sacred combat' or ritual struggle that enacted the corporate (and individual) quest for well-being and self-knowledge in the person of the king, we may guess that the shock of this reversal was profound indeed.

An ideologically more positive interpretation of the failure of ritual in the play is, however, suggested by M. D. Bristol. Describing the play as a 'violent Carnival mummery', he argues that its carnivalesque inversions and parodies unmask—through the analogy that the conflict between Lear and his antagonists bears to the Battle of Carnival and Lent—both the mystique of royal authority and the cult of practical authority. The play as Carnival thus questions any 'fixed and final allocation' of authority or social wealth.[51]

Finally, mention may be made of the application of a very different concept of ritual to the play. Michael Howard Riley proposes two primitive archetypes of drama, sociodrama and psychodrama. The former involves 'participation of groups of "actors" and attempts to state and resolve a problem or conflict inherent in social relations'. The African 'rituals of rebellion' studied by Max Gluckman and Monica Wilson and the medieval festivals of the 'boy bishop' and the 'lord of misrule' are examples of such sociodrama, and Ben Jonson's *Sejanus* is cited as a literary example. Psychodrama is exemplified, in primitive society, in the solitary trance performance of a shaman or medicine man who acts out, in Riley's words, a 'myth' which is resolutely asocial and otherworldly. *King Lear* is proposed as a literary example of this type of drama which presents the 'ecstatic dramatization of an "inner" state of consciousness', Lear's spiritual journey being, in Riley's view, a literary 'rediscovery' of the 'shaman's mediation between the perceptible world and the mysteries of "nature" as well as the hearts of men'.[52]

The function of the shaman, according to Riley, is like that of myth. Just as myth, in Lévi-Strauss's terms, provides 'a logical model capable of overcoming a contradiction', so also the shaman provides 'a "dramatic" model capable of (momentarily, histrionically) overcoming a contradiction'. The shaman *is* a myth in that 'he bears witness to a spirit world and makes his audience believe in it'. Lear is such a shaman who, in his entranced madness, 'creates an emotion, pity, which is capable of, momentarily, overcoming a basic contradiction in human behaviour'.[53] This contradiction, if I understand Riley, is between the demands of family affection and political necessity. While one may readily accept the idea that tragedy is concerned with overcoming, or at least reconciling, contradictions in human experience, it must be pointed out that the parallel between Levi-Strauss's *logical* model and Riley's *dramatic* (and affective) model is only a loose one.

Macbeth

Many of the interpretations of the play as a nature myth are obviously relevant here since the myth is usually related to actual seasonal rituals, as in Simrock's observation, cited in the previous chapter, that the legend of King Grünewald and the moving forest originated in the German religious custom of May festivals. Janet Spens (pp. 76f) tries to relate the revenge theme in this play as well as in *Hamlet* and some other plays to the annual ritual deposition of one king by another, though this appears to be too great an extension of the concept of the scapegoat ritual. Holloway sees in this play too the tragic movement of the hero from cynosure to outcast, Macbeth being 'a scapegoat, a lord of misrule, who has turned life into riot for his limited time, and is then driven out and destroyed by the forces which embody the fertile vitality and the communal happiness of the social group' (p. 73).

Antony and Cleopatra

John Holloway (p. 120) finds in this play too the pattern of the scapegoat sacrifice, especially in the manner in which Antony and Cleopatra begin to resemble hunted animals before they die.

Timon of Athens

Robert C. Elliott, in a fine essay on the play, argues that Timon is a satirist-curser in the tradition of primitive railers, whose curses against enemies were based on a belief in word magic. But Shakespeare, according to Elliott, is not to be taken to be identifying with the character of Timon, as some critics have supposed, but rather as showing through the action of the play the *failure* of such ritual cursing to achieve practical ends. In this way, then, the play can be linked with the others in which Shakespeare has been shown to have been concerned with the failure of ritual or magic. Elliott writes:

> After his fall from prosperity Timon's language takes on the incantatory tone of a prophet. He tries to preempt the full power of the archaic curse, calling on the gods, the heavens, the earth—and, as it were, the demonic power within himself—to confound the hated creature man. It is as though Timon were reenacting the ancient role, attempting to change the world through the power of language. He is a magician manqué, a primitive satirist ages out of his time. Part of his frustration, part of his ultimate humiliation, is the fact that magic is no longer viable.... Still the awful words affect us; in obscure ways we are moved by Timon's efforts to manipulate atavistic powers.[54]

Commenting on the sacrificial pattern in the play, Holloway (p. 134) suggests that the barmecide feast is like a parody of the Last Supper, and the scene at Timon's cave 'like the baiting of a hunted animal at its den'..

Coriolanus

Holloway (pp. 125, 130) finds the sacrificial pattern more marked in this play and in *Timon of Athens* than in any of the other tragedies. Certainly the killing of Coriolanus is closer to ritual execution than the death of any other tragic hero except Macbeth.

Kenneth Burke (1966) examines Coriolanus's role as a 'cathartic vessel' who forces us (and forced the Jacobean audience) to confront certain social tensions which are finally resolved through his death. Besides, Coriolanus as a railer, like Timon, points to 'the "curative" function of invective as such when thus released under controlled conditions that transform the repressed into the expressed, yet do us no damage'.[55] Burke's interest in the purgation of social tensions through the spectacle of 'vicarious victimage' is a historical one since the tensions are seen as peculiar to Jacobean society. However, as some of these tensions, and tension as such, are almost universal, there is also a trans-historical, psychological dimension to his concern with the cathartic function of ritual.

THE ROMANCES

The romances have not attracted much attention from a specifically ritualistic point of view, although in them ritual and ceremony appear in closer and more direct association with religious feeling cussed in the previous chapter have been almost exclusively the concern of the myth and ritual criticism of these plays. William Barry Thorne does make an attempt to relate these plays to Elizabethan folk plays and rituals, though not in a very original manner. His approach as shown in Chapter 1, consists in pointing out seasonal myths and rituals in the plays (in separate essays on *Cymbeline* and *The Winter's Tale*) interpreting these myths and rituals as embodiments of the theme of rebirth, and then associating them with Elizabethan folk plays, which also, according to him, deal with the same theme. Janet Spens (p. 38) also suggests a parallel between *The Winter's Tale* and the harvest feast play. But this amounts to saying no more than that a harvest-feast scene is actually presented in the play. Spens does not go on to discuss whether this could be related to a broader ritual pattern of which the play as a whole could be considered to be a reflection. F. C. Tinkler has some interesting suggestions to make about the connection of the play with Elizabethan folk culture. He indicates a pattern of death and rebirth and suggests that Mamillius, as a projection of his father, takes on the burden of the scapegoat; he dies in winter, and when we see Perdita and Florizel for the first time it is spring, i.e. the season when the dying god is reborn and the wasteland made fertile once more. The theme of the seasonal cycle, the belief in the 'magical' connection between the individual and society and nature, as well as some other elements—for example, the 'savage humour' of many of the scenes—are related by Tinkler to a predominantly agricultural community and the 'conservatism and the distrust of all excess' that go with it.[56] In thus bringing the theme of the seasonal cycle and of death and rebirth from the realm of religion and metaphysics down almost literally to earth, Tinkler makes, I believe, a valuable point. He also, to a certain extent, anticipates Bakhtin's idea of plebeian culture and folk laughter.

THE POEMS

The poems seem not to have attracted the ritualists at all.

IV

As indicated earlier, and as can be seen from the discussion in the preceding section, there are two major ways in which the concept of ritual is used in the criticism of Shakespeare. First, and most frequently, specific rituals, either in their primitive form or as mediated through Elizabethan folk plays and customs, are seen as sources or analogues of the plays. The rituals most frequently invoked are those connected with the figure of the scapegoat, though references to initiatory and to other sacrificial rituals are not uncommon. In criticism of the comedies, in particular, the use of festive rites and figures as sources or analogues of the dramatic characters or action is also frequent and has produced some truly original and perceptive criticism. Second, the plays are examined in terms of ritual as such. This approach can be subdivided into two: (a) there is criticism which examines ritual elements within a play, 'ritual' being generally defined as any kind of formal, non-utilitarian action. The term is further extended to include such phenomena as the use of formal, stylized speech and dialogue; (b) the play itself is seen *as* ritual, or as analogous to ritual, not because of its structural similarity with specific primitive rituals but because it can be seen as performing, within its own society, a function analogous to that of ritual in a primitive society.

As already stated, the idea of the tragic hero as scapegoat has been described by Hapgood as the soundest and most suggestive contribution of the myth and ritual approach. While the suggestiveness of the concept is undeniable, it goes with a certain vagueness, even confusion, when the concept is applied to specific plays or characters. The source of this confusion can be traced back to Frazer himself, who argued that the scapegoat ritual represents the fusion of two rituals which were originally separate, one dealing with the sacrifice of a spirit of fertility and the other with the expulsion of the scapegoat. This fertility spirit (or Eniautos-daimon) is seen manifested, by Gilbert Murray and others, as both the summer and the winter king, and the expulsion of one by the other interpreted as a symbolic action to ensure fertility. Janet Spens generalizes the idea further when she writes that 'the story of the Summer-king, or Fool who is slain, is the story of pitiful human decay and death, of the passing of generations', and identifies him with the figure of the pharmakos or scapegoat, whom she considers to be the very essence of tragedy (pp. 51–8). But it is difficult to see any necessary connection between the two. If the summer king is slain by the winter king and is subsequently avenged by another summer king, the most obvious analogy is with the actual state of affairs in human and non-human society, where the older ruler is finally deposed by a younger rival, a father by a son. The killing or expulsion of the older figure, either literally or symbolically, may be just a reflection of this law of nature. Very often the combat between the present ruler and his challenger is institutionalized and ritualized; it is arranged to take place at regular intervals rather than arbitrarily at the will of the contestants. This may represent the victory of culture over nature, but usually the cultural phenomenon follows the course of the natural process: the cycle of winter and spring, the rise of phallic aggression in the mating season. The ritual combat at Nemi may have been an attempt to confine within cultural boundaries the anarchic impulses of nature and thereby ensure the cohesion of the community. Periodic expulsions of old rulers, like periodic elections in modern societies, may thus be said to represent culture's compromise with nature. To use the term scapegoat to refer to all such phenomena is to deprive it of any useful meaning.

In the actual criticism of the plays the term is used even more loosely to refer to practically any expulsion, killing or death. Thus all the tragic heroes from Titus to Coriolanus have been seen as scapegoat figures. In addition, Falstaff, Malvolio, Antonio, Shylock, Angelo and even Iago have been seen as scapegoats. In some cases the character as scapegoat is associated with fertility and the forces of good, in others with sterility and evil, and in still others with both. But surely Romeo and Juliet as sacrificial victims are very different from Macbeth; they are sacrificed not because they are guilty but because precisely the opposite is the case. It is because they are young and pure that the mingling of their blood in sacrifice may be thought of as a sacrifice for the atonement of the two feuding families. In contrast, Macbeth is linked to the sterility of the land and must be destroyed in order to restore fertility. Again, Falstaff as carnival or lord of misrule represents the spirit of festivity and fertility, as Stewart suggests, and is thus a very different kind of scapegoat from Shylock or Malvolio, whose anti-comic and anti-festive spirit relates them to the forces of sterility. To make the confusion worse, Holloway, as we have seen, describes Macbeth as the spirit of sterility as well as the lord of misrule, confounding the positive sense of 'misrule' as festive topsy-turvydom with its purely negative moral and political sense. Macbeth thus becomes both Carnival and Lent, the spirit of festivity as well as sterility.

The use of the concept of the scapegoat also generally involves a confusion between the anthropological and psychological senses of the term (which correspond, more or less, to its literal and metaphorical senses respectively). This is seen, for example, in the use of the term to describe such recent phenomena as the Nazi attitude towards the Jews. There *is* a parallel between such phenomena and the primitive ritual, but the difference is even more important. It may be put thus: the primitive ritual, from what accounts we have of it, involves a conscious transference of guilt and responsibility to the scapegoat figure; the primitive, one imagines, knows that the figure is not really guilty to begin with. The modern man, however, who was told that all the problems of Germany were caused by the Jews often did, in fact, really believe it. The transference, in other words, was unconscious and therefore, it is possible to argue, more dangerous. In this respect, one must admit, primitive societies show far more cultural sophistication than some modern societies. They manage to contain within cultural forms impulses of hostility towards minorities and aliens. These impulses, precisely because they remain unconscious, cause considerable havoc in modern societies.

The distinction may be clarified in another way. Frank Kermode makes a distinction between 'myth' and 'fiction': a story or idea one really believes in would be a myth; if, however, it is given only conditional assent or entertained as a hypothesis only, prefaced by an 'as if', then it is a fiction.[57] A fiction is a model of reality and not reality itself. I imagine that myth and fiction in this usage would be associated with primitive and sophisticated attitudes respectively, but as it turns out the real situation is precisely the opposite. It is the primitive who shows the more sophisticated attitude in taking the scapegoat figure only as a fiction, a make-believe, however efficacious and potent, and it is the modern man who has shown himself to be prone to mythical literalness.

The distinction between the two senses of the term scapegoat just described is often obscured in the criticism of the plays discussed in this chapter. Is Shylock, we might ask, a scapegoat because guilt and responsibility is transferred onto him unconsciously? If so, whose guilt? Is Shakespeare presenting in his play the mechanism by which guilt is transferred onto an alien figure by the Venetians? There seems little evidence that Shakespeare shows an awareness that the Venetians are unconsciously making of Shylock a scapegoat. The play is not a study in social prejudice as, it is possible to argue, *Othello* is. But in *Othello* the scapegoat theme is not so evident. To be prejudiced is not necessarily to make of the object of prejudice a scapegoat. But if Shakespeare is not studying in the play the mechanism of 'vicarious victimage', to use Kenneth Burke's phrase, is it the case that he himself, and his audience, are the ones that are making of Shylock a scapegoat, unconsciously? Can one say that Shakespeare, in purging Shylock, is purging himself and his audience, as C. L. Barber argues, of possible guilt associated with their attitude towards money? Because of Shylock's sacrifice, Shakespeare and his audience are, as it were, able to make peace between their conscience and their love of money. But these psychological hypotheses about unconscious projections lead us far away from the usual kind of myth and ritual criticism, which is concerned with the tracing of analogies with actual rituals *within* the plays. In the possible applications of the concept of scapegoat that I have just suggested, this is not so. There the concept is used in a metaphorical sense and extended to include the creative process and the relation between the artist, the audience and the work. Perhaps it is arbitrary to talk of the limits of the ritual approach, but I do want to suggest that in the use of the concept of the scapegoat necessary distinctions are often overlooked, and an anthropological concept confused with a psychological one.

In Barber's discussion of the expulsion of Falstaff there seems to be a similar confusion. Barber does, in fact, suggest that in the play the 'magical' expulsion of Falstaff is to be taken as Shakespeare's private ritual rather than just Hal's (p. 219). It is this magical engineering of the coup against Falstaff that constitutes, in Barber's view, the chief failure of *2 Henry IV*. But one could argue that the failure (if it is that) is due to precisely the opposite reason. The scene represents a failure because it is *not* like a public ritual of scapegoat riddance, but rather a private ritual given the form of a rational act done for reasons of state. The scene is not a ritual literally but only in a metaphorical sense; it is not, to put the matter differently, a ritual *within* the play but one only if we take the whole relational network (artist-work-audience) into account. Within the play it is merely and literally a scene of expulsion, without any suggestion of ritual purgation which many have discerned in the killing of a character like Macbeth.

It would seem then that a more consciously metaphorical use of the concept in a functional and psychological sense would be more useful, as in the criticism of Kenneth Burke, in whose critical theory the figure of the scapegoat features prominently, but in a psychological-cum-sociological sense. In using the concept one must be quite clear whether one is taking the individual character concerned as literally a scapegoat within the play or as one only in relation to the artist's life and his society. One must also have a historical sense of the evils that are being sought to be transferred onto the scapegoat figure and the tensions, social and psychological, that are being purged through it. This would involve a kind of depth-analysis rather different from the usual tracing of the ritual pattern supposed to be hidden below the level of plot and character.

Examples of the second way in which the concept of ritual features in criticism of Shakespeare may be seen in the works of critics like Francis Fergusson, C. L. Barber, Robert Hapgood, and others who are concerned with examining the place of ritual within a play as a whole. This kind of criticism is usually extended to the discussion of the rival attitudes of the major characters towards life as reflected in their attitudes towards ritual, especially the rituals of kingship. The consensus of opinion among such critics is that Shakespeare's drama presents a period of transition from a ritualistic (i.e. involving belief in the practical efficacy of rites—hence, more generally, mythico-religious) to a pragmatic, utilitarian attitude. In Shakespeare's drama the scepticism is as marked as the more primitive belief in ritual, and critics tend to emphasize one or the other depending on their own predilections. Fergusson, for example, while admitting that in *Hamlet* the ritual of kingship is shown to be ineffective, argues nevertheless that this does not imply a loss of faith in ritual as such. Robert Heilman and Philip Wheelwright also feel that although, in Heilman's phrase, the plays generally present 'myth in crisis', the sympathies of Shakespeare lie with the mythical-religious-ritualistic world-view.[58]

To consider the plays *as* ritual, which is the other way in which the idea of ritual as ritual enters the criticism of Shakespearean drama, is to argue for the persistence of belief in ritual, though in a modified sense. It is the play as a whole which is now considered as providing the efficacy of ritual, not for the characters in the play but for the audience and the society at large. This efficacy is not, of course, to be understood in a merely material sense. As Holloway puts it, it is a matter of giving the audience a sense of power and of belonging to a community. The Aristotelian theory of catharsis can also be invoked, as Kenneth Burke has done, to explain the efficacy of tragedy, or drama generally, as ritual. Also to the point is Yeats's famous remark that tragedy is a breaking of the dykes that separate man from man.[59] Tragedy, like the rituals of the dying god, enhances, in this view, the sense of community among its audience through their participation in a spectacle of heroic suffering. A consequence of the ritual criticism of the drama would be a modification of the latter part of Yeats's statement, namely that it is upon these dykes that comedy is built, for Shakespeare's initiatory or festive comedy too can be seen, unlike the satirical comedy of Jonson, as relating man to man and enhancing the sense of community. Broadly speaking, this sense of community relates, in the comedies, to the family and society; in the history plays to a nascent nationalism; in the tragedies to a sense of sharing in the existential condition of man; and in the romances to a religious sense of integration with the superhuman powers that govern human life.

It can, then, be said that drama as ritual reverses the process by which, according to Jane Harrison and Ernst Cassirer, it first evolved from the magico-religious matrix. As Harrison argued, drama arose from 'dromena' when the latter were emancipated from practical ends. In contemporary theory and practice of theatre, however, it is precisely this psychic distance that is sought to be removed. To quote Schechner again, 'the ambition to make theatre into ritual is nothing other than a wish to make performance efficacious, to use events to change people. Cassirer's analysis seems old-fashioned and Artaud's prophetic.'[60] Schechner is speaking of the directly political ends of drama, but even when the ends are defined in a more psychological sense, the strength of the theory of drama as ritual is that it attempts to relate drama to other forms of cultural activity rather than to see it in isolation.

Some qualifications must, however, be made about the theory as formulated by Holloway. He attempts to bring his anthropology up-to-date by suggesting that, after Malinowski and others, myths are no longer thought of as embodiments of truth or expressions of a peculiar mode of thought, but rather as dynamic elements within their culture. The important thing about myth is that it performs an important social function. On this analogy literature too, according to Holloway, may be said to have a function to perform rather than a truth to convey. Similarly a great work of art may be compared to a ritual, which also has a social function to perform. The difference between myth and ritual is said to be analogous to the difference between the story of Lear and the play *King Lear* (pp. 176–7). I think that Holloway is right to insist on the social function of myth and ritual. But the corollary of that view would be to insist on the social function of literature. In order to determine that it would be necessary to place the work of art in its historical setting: just as the meaning of myth or ritual can be understood only in the context of their particular societies, so also the work of art can be understood properly only when seen in its social context. Holloway is no doubt aware of this implication of the extension to literature of the anthropological theory of myth, and he is also aware that a work of art, unlike myth, can sometimes be a subversive force. (So can myth, actually, if we follow Sorel's use of the term.) But whether the work of art is subversive or conservative can only be decided with reference to its social co-ordinates, either of the society of its origin or the reader's own. But Holloway takes a non-historical view of society; he is concerned not with particular societies but with society as such. The distinction is very clearly brought out when we compare his criticism with, say, the criticism of Kenneth Burke. The comparison is appropriate because Burke too is concerned with the function of drama-as-ritual.

In the paragraph above reference has been made to the social function of both myth and ritual, but the distinction between them is perhaps even more important from the specifically literary point of view. Leaving aside the question of the priority of either myth or ritual, it is generally agreed that although myth has a social function, that function is operative only through its enactment or recitation in ritual. Anthropologists have shown how the recitation of myth is an important communal occasion. Similarly, Elizabethan drama has been seen by several critics as providing for its contemporary society what would normally be provided by ritual in more simple societies. (Consider, for example, Francis Fergusson's remarks on the ritual function of the drama in Elizabethan culture in his discussion of *Hamlet*, or the comments of Maynard Mack and Douglas Hewitt on *King Lear*.) This was so, one might argue, because the drama, through its re-enactment of the 'myths' of the age (the 'Tudor myth', the fear of rebellion, the belief in the 'magical' connection between the king and the country or in the supremacy of law and order—to take some random examples) brought these myths within the focus of the collective consciousness and gave them functional potency. We see here a connection between the idea of ritual as giving power to myth and the idea propagated by F. R. Leavis that literature is an *enactment* of values. The equation I am suggesting is: ritual: myth = the particular work of literature: values.

If the point about the ritual function of Elizabethan drama is accepted, then we can see another way in which Shakespeare's drama represents the failure of ritual. In some ways this drama presents the most powerful celebration of the values of order and kingship, as G. Wilson Knight has pointed out. Shakespeare's drama-as-ritual does not merely derive its power from these ideas; rather, it imparts power to them. At the same time, these ideas are subjected to ironic probing or to the carnival logic of crownings and uncrownings. At any rate the efficacy of the ritual celebration of order and kingship was not to last long. The anxieties that lay behind it were soon to be proved to have been well-founded. Within less than thirty years of Shakespeare's death the Civil War broke out. That represents the failure not of the rituals of Shakespeare's dramatic characters within the plays but rather of the ritual drama of Shakespeare himself. In the larger context of history, Shakespeare's drama as 'official' ritual represents as pathetic a failure of belief in the efficacy of ritual as the rituals of, say, Richard II. On the other hand, if we take the plays as dealing consciously with the failure of ritual or as festive subversions of official ceremony, then, one can say, history merely vindicated Shakespeare's insight and imitated his drama.

CHAPTER 3
Mythical Thought and Vision

Myth as 'a story about the gods' may be seen from the point of view of the kind of thinking that goes into its making and the world-view implicit in it. The nature of this mythical thought and vision is the subject of this chapter. As Ernst Cassirer (1874–1945) has written extensively on this subject, it would be appropriate and useful to begin with a brief summary of his views.

According to Cassirer myth is one of the symbolic forms in which we perceive reality, reality being, in his neo-Kantian perspective, a symbolic construct rather than something *given* which we receive passively. Rejecting Freud's psychological reductionism, whereby diverse complex phenomena like myth, magic and art are explained in terms of their origin in a common psychological source, as well as Schelling's attempt to reduce myth to a metaphysical absolute, Cassirer's own phenomenological approach aims at demonstrating the unity of myth not as the unity of its psychological or metaphysical genesis but rather as 'the unity of a specific "structural form" of the spirit'.[1]

The chief characteristic of the mythical form of perception is its concreteness. Cassirer argues that mythical thought is incapable of conceiving abstractions as abstractions. Unlike the scientific mode of thought, which proceeds by synthesis and analysis, myth 'lives entirely by the presence of its object—by the intensity with which it seizes and takes possession of consciousness in a specific moment'. Therefore, myth does not conceal a secret meaning, an 'ideal content'; what we see as 'representation' is a case of 'real identity' for myth. The mythical image does not stand for a 'thing', it is actually identical with it. Mythical thought, as Cassirer puts it, 'lacks the category of the ideal' (p. 38). Any abstraction must therefore be transformed into a material object or being before it can be grasped by the mythical mind.

The difference between the mythical and the scientific mode of thought can be clearly seen in the concept of causality. Whereas scientific causality is concerned with a particular event only as a special instance of a general law, mythical causality is concerned with the 'why' of the particular and the unique in all its particularity and uniqueness. It asks why *this* particular event took place at this particular place and time and 'explains' it with reference to an 'individual act of the will'. Consequently there is nothing accidental to the mythical mind; it 'begins with the intuition of purposive action', all the forces of nature being conceived as expressions of a will. Mere contiguity in space or time is sufficient to link objects or events causally. Thus, whereas scientific thought is concerned with 'change', which it seeks to understand with reference to universal rules, 'mythical thinking knows only a simple metamorphosis' in the Ovidian sense, i.e. change from one individual form to another (pp. 46–7).

Another aspect of the mythical mode of perception is its tendency to hypostatize properties and processes, which are functional or relational concepts, into material objects. Cassirer gives the example of the Hupa Indians, who look upon pain as a substance. Behind the ritual of the scapegoat is a similar belief in the materiality of the evil from which the community is suffering and which, consequently, can be transferred on to the scapegoat. The mythical concept of mana, and its variants like 'manitou', 'wakanda', and 'orenda', are similar hypostatizations of concepts which are relational rather than substantial. Cassirer rightly points out that this tendency persists even in scientific thinking, as in the concept of aether, or of force as a physical substance, or in the various explanations of fire in terms of 'thermal substance' or 'phlogiston' (pp. 55–9, 67). Carl Jung and Gaston Bachelard have also studied the persistence of mythical concepts in science and philosophy, though Jung takes a more positive view of the role of myth in science than either Cassirer or Bachelard. According to him, far from being a hindrance to the development of scientific thought, myth, on the contrary, prepares the ground for scientific discovery. For example, it is the primordial, archetypal idea of a universal magical power which finally leads to the modern concept of energy.[2]

The peculiar immediacy of the mythical perception of the object leads to certain characteristics of mythical thought that Cassirer explains with refence to what he calls 'the law of the concrescence or coincidence of the members of a relation in mythical thinking'. This law can be followed through all the categories of thought. Thus, in the category of quantity, the whole and the part are identified. This identity of the whole and the part is to be distinguished from the idea of harmony, in which the whole is conceived as a unity of diverse elements. In mythical thought the whole *is* the part in the sense that 'it enters into it with its whole mythical-substantial essence, that it is somehow sensuously and materially "in" it'. This principle can be seen at work, according to Cassirer, in totemic organizations, which are based upon a feeling of complete identity with the totem ancestor as well as with all the members of the clan. Cassirer here uses Lévy-Bruhl's idea that the primary characteristic of primitive thought is 'mystic participation', where 'mystic' refers to anything supernatural and 'participation' to the principle by which anything could at the same time be something else.[3] A related explanation of totemism occurs in Jane Harrison's writings. She uses Durkheim's concepts of 'collective representation' and Bergson's idea of 'durée' to explain the nature of totemic society as a stage in epistemology when thinking is as yet 'undifferentiated', so that there is no concept of the distinctively human or individual personality. Magic, according to her, comes at a later stage of totemism when man becomes aware of his personality as distinct from that of the totem. It is only at this stage that the savage realizes that when he dances like an emu he is not actually an emu but only imitating one. Participation therefore comes before imitation, 'methektis' before 'mimesis'.[4] It should be noted that there are two elements in the idea of tribal mystic participation: first, a hypostatization of the whole, the genus or the tribe, and second, the identification of the part, the individual, with this hypostatized whole. As Cassirer remarks, 'the genus, in its relation to the species or individuals it comprises, is not a universal which logically determines the particular but is immediately present, living and acting in this particular'. A similar concrescence can be observed in the categories of quality and similarity. Thus, mythical thought makes no distinction between a thing and its attributes. To the mythical mind a substance does not 'have' different attributes; rather each attribute *is* substance, i.e. 'it can be apprehended only in immediate concretion, in direct hypostatization'. Similarly, similarity is not a mere concept but a physical force, and any perceived similarity becomes an expression of identity of essence (pp. 64–8).

Passing from a consideration of mythical thought to the specifically mythical 'intuition' or 'life-feeling', the 'intuitive unity' that precedes and underlies all forms of mythical thought, Cassirer sees the basic trend of the mythical consciousness as the 'original division of the sacred and profane'. These are not categories for specific classes of objects; any object, even the most commonplace, can acquire the distinctive character of the sacred if it falls under 'the mythical-religious *perspective*', i.e. if it can capture mythical interest or enthusiasm. The sacred is thus a matter of suffusing an object with *value*; without this sense of value, mythical thought could not proceed since it is by introducing differentiation into an 'indifferent reality' that all thought proceeds, and the characteristic mythical differentiation is precisely the one based on a sense of the value of the object that captures the imagination. The primitive concepts of mana and taboo are thus to be understood not in terms of their objects but rather as the *accent* placed on objects which are mythically significant. Mana, according to Cassirer, thus denotes that primordial wonder which is the beginning not only of myth but of religion and science as well (pp. 75–9). Whatever captures the attention of the mythical mind is transformed under the mythical perspective into an object instinct with a mysterious life and power. The universe of the primitive man thus becomes a *living universe*. It has been pointed out earlier that the mythical mind always materializes what is merely ideal; it is now seen that at the same time it also 'spiritualizes' the merely material.

Having described the basic opposition between the sacred and the profane in the mythical mind, Cassirer goes on to discuss how this opposition determines the articulation of space, time and number. Each of these concepts, in keeping with the hypostatizing that is typical of mythical thought, is considered as material rather than merely relational. Hence they are not conceived as continuous, uniform and homogeneous, as in scientific thinking, but as subject to the same qualitative differentiation between the sacred and the profane that marks all the objects of mythical thought. Thus there occurs the idea of a sacred space, which finally evolves into the institution of temples. There is also a sacred time, which is the time of beginnings. The sanctity of a mythical object or being derives from its origin in this absolute mythical past. Mythical time is different from historical time in that whereas in history the past is merely a 'regressum in infinitum', in myth it is absolute:

'The past itself has no "why": it *is* the why of things.' It is in this sense that mythical time may be thought of as 'timeless'. Mythical time is also different from scientific time in that it is qualitative and concrete; temporal as well as spatial intervals and dividing lines are not, for the mythical consciousness, merely conventional distinctions of thought but 'possess an inherent quality and particularity, an essence of their own'. This is most marked in what Cassirer calls the mythical-religious 'sense of phases', by virtue of which any phase of life, human or cosmic, is marked by a character of holiness. The same characteristic mythical differentiation into the sacred and the profane can be observed in the concept of number, as is evident from the widespread belief in the sacredness of certain numbers (pp. 106–9).

In *An Essay on Man* Cassirer writes that 'the real substratum of myth is not a substratum of thought but of feeling' and that the coherence of myth and religion 'depends much more upon the unity of feeling than upon logical rules'. This unity stems from the fact that the mythical view of nature is neither theoretical nor practical but 'sympathetic'; for the primitive man 'the deep conviction of a fundamental and indelible *solidarity of life*' unifies the multiplicity of forms and helps him 'deny and defy the fact of death'. The whole of nature becomes one great society, the *society of life*, in which man shares a place with other creatures as well as with what to us are inanimate objects. The bond between man and nature is thus a bond between, to use Martin Buber's terms, an 'I' and a 'Thou'; myth expresses 'all natural reality in the language of human, social reality and expresses all human, social reality in the language of nature'. David Bidney has criticized Cassirer's identification of the 'feeling of unity' with the 'unity of feeling', and it is true that Cassirer has not given detailed arguments to justify this equation.[5] But poets throughout the centuries have borne witness to the intimate connection between the equilibrium outside and within the mind: if 'the centre cannot hold' within, then 'things fall apart' in the world outside, and vice versa.

In his philosophical orientation Cassirer is a rationalist. For him myth is only one of the ways in which human reality is constructed, and while he does not dismiss it as an illusion his attitude towards it ranges from an appreciation of 'what it can accomplish spiritually' (p. xvii) to an emphasis on its dangers when it intrudes into other realms—such as those of science or politics. Other writers, including literary critics, are less reserved in their enthusiasm for myth, considering it the only mode of apprehending a 'higher' reality. Jung, for example, accepts the common idea (shared, among others, by Freud, Jane Harrison and Cornford) that myths are the 'dream-thinking of a people', but argues that, like some dreams which are pointers to spiritual needs and processes rather than expressions of unconscious sexual urges, they also are a repository of spiritual symbols. Philip Wheelwright defines myth as 'man's primordial way of knowing' and calls for a 'mythico-religious perspective' to replace the predominantly secular attitude that prevails in contemporary society. What is missing from this attitude is 'that haunting awareness of transcendental forces peering through the cracks of the visible universe, that is the very essence of myth'. This transcendental aspect of myth is related by Wheelwright to the fact that it is the product of the communal rather than the individual mind, for the individual mind, he argues, can function only on the horizontal plane of phenomena, whereas the communal mind participates in the mystery that exists on a plane which is, so to speak, vertical to it.[6] It is not clear why only the communal mind can participate in this mystery; it seems to have been invoked in deference to Durkheim's emphasis on the collective aspect of religion as well as to some vaguely defined hippy-like ideal of mystical participation. However, writers generally have both the transcendental and communal aspects of myth in mind when they lament its death or call for its revival.

For Wheelwright myth is almost synonymous with religion, but usage in this area is rather uncertain. Cassirer and the theologian Paul Tillich, for example, both agree that belief in the literal truth of its images is what distinguishes myth from religion. In religion, in Cassirer's view, there is a striving towards a 'progressively purer spiritualization', though there is never a complete emancipation from the world of images (pp. 260–1). Tillich, on the other hand, distinguishes between two senses of the term 'mythical'. According to one, it refers only to the 'unbroken mythical mentality', which makes no distinction between myth, religion and science and is therefore tied to the literal truth of its images. 'Myth' in this sense may be said to be transcended by religion, in which truth is held to transcend all its images. On the other hand the term can refer to every 'intuition of transcendence'. In this sense 'there is no such thing as an unmythical attitude and the myth is shown to be essential'. Thus there is no conflict between myth and religion but only one between one myth and another.

There is greater confusion in the use of the term in literary criticism. According to Cassirer, it is only in art that the tension between image and meaning is 'appeased, if not negated', because in art there is recognition of the image purely as such (p. 261). A similar idea seems to underlie Frank Kermode's distinction between 'myth' and 'fiction', the former demanding literal belief whereas the latter is conceived as a 'model' only which has to be abandoned as soon as it has served its purpose. Literature, according to Kermode, is concerned with such fictions rather than with myth. A precisely opposite definition of myth is given by D. G. James, who makes a distinction between 'myth' and 'dogma' as follows: 'Mythology is the use of symbols which are not bound up with belief in its symbols; but dogma is bound to the denial that it is using mere symbols and to the assertion of the historical truth of its "symbols".'[7] It seems that what is 'myth' to Cassirer, Tillich and Kermode is 'dogma' to James, and what is 'religion' to them is to him 'myth'. The contradiction can be resolved, if at all, if we assume that Tillich and Cassirer are not using the term 'religion' in the sense of a narrowly dogmatic system of beliefs but in the more general sense of any intuition of transcendence. Cassirer's view that myth is marked by belief in its images does seem to be closer to the real nature of myths, but when poets and critics speak of myth (especially when they speak of the need for a mythology) they usually use the term as D. G. James has defined it. There is, however, a curious wavering, of which Yeats's attitude towards his own mythological system is, I think, an example. Tillich's idea of the inner dialectic in the very concept of myth seems to be the best explanation of this wavering as regards the question of belief. But transcendence, which he considers to be characteristic of the mythical attitude, is precisely what distinguishes the idea of the symbol as opposed to allegory or sign-language. Myth and symbol are indeed closely related concepts as the following section attempts to show.

II

There are three ways in which the idea of myth as a mode of thought is applicable to literature and critical theory. First, the term 'mythical' can be applied to the literary work itself, as a whole, or to parts or aspects of it. Mythical literature then would be the kind of literature that shows the characteristic aspects of mythical thought. Not all literature, of course, is mythical in this view, but all myth may be considered to be literature. 'Mythical' can be used either in a positive or in a pejorative sense, depending upon the attitude towards the mythical mode of thought. Usually, however, it is the positive sense that critics have in mind. If a work is described as a myth, then one can expect that the critic has in mind at least some of the characteristics of the mythical mode of thought that we have been describing. Second, a myth or a mythology, considered as the expression of a mythical mode of thought or vision, can be taken as giving a mythical dimension to a work or a body of works as its subject-matter or background. Third, certain critical concepts and procedures themselves could be taken as instances of the mythical mode of thought. In actual usage, of course, such clear-cut distinctions are seldom in evidence.

The early age of man, according to Vico, was one in which 'poetic wisdom' determined all aspects of life, including mythology and religion. What Cassirer describes as 'mythical thought' is termed 'poetic logic' by Vico, and much of his *New Science* (1725) is concerned with tracing the working of this logic. In fact Vichian poetics has been described as basically a theory of myth in which poetry is seen as essentially a myth-making activity. A similar identification of myth and poetry can be found in Herder and other German Romantics, though the identification is seldom total. Also to the point is Shelley's belief that in primitive society all men were poets. In recent times Richard Chase has most consistently maintained that all myth is poetry and that, far from myth being the basis of poetry, it is poetry which is the basis of myths.[8] It is not, however, only in these explicit identifications of myth with poetry that the relevance of the mythical or primitive mode of thought to poetic theory is to be found. In fact an entire tradition of *poetic* theory seems to be behind the theory of myth. This becomes clear when one realizes that each of the characteristics of mythical thought as described by Cassirer and others has also been seen as a characteristic of poetry.

Like mythical thought, poetic thought has also been described as concrete and sensuous. It was Vico who first suggested that primitive language was pre-figurative since figures of speech imply the conceiving of abstractions, of which the primitive mind was incapable. Primitive language is thus pre-metaphoric.[9] The Romantic symbol is also conceived as transcending metaphor or simile by identifying the image and the idea, the general and the particular. The symbolic image, we can say, adapting Cassirer's description of the mythical image quoted earlier, does not stand for the 'thing' or 'idea', it is actually identical with it. In fact, it becomes difficult to determine whether the Romantic concept of myth has been conditioned by its concept of the symbol, or whether its concept of the symbol has been conditioned by its concept of myth. One might add that a similar question arises whether Cassirer's account of the mythical or primitive mind has been, at least partly, determined by the Romantic concept of the symbol. Poetry and myth are not identified by all Romantics, of course. The difference between the two can be described as the difference between the unity which is something *given* prior to the differentiation between the 'idea' and the 'image' and the unity that is *achieved* in spite of the differentiation. The Romantic symbol is a product of the imagination's effort to *recreate* the primordial unity of myth. The dialectic runs from 'undifferentiated' unity through differentiation to what may be called the 'synthetic' unity of the symbol.

In *Language and Myth* Cassirer describes a similar process in the development of language. Myth is the matrix from which language, religion, art, science and history emerge as autonomous symbolic forms in a gradual process of differentiation. In the beginning the signifying function of words is not distinct from their magical function. The distinction between the 'word' and its 'meaning' is not yet apparent. Language attains its autonomy only when this distinction is grasped. Art, however, is always striving to regain this primitive, magical value of words and to synthesize the word and its meaning. The symbol also shows the concrescence of relations that, according to Cassirer, characterizes mythical thought. The most common concrescence is of the whole and the part and of things which are similar. These two categories are neatly combined in the concept of the microcosm. The microcosm is not thought of merely as a part of the macrocosm, but neither is it supposed to be merely analogous to it; it is both, and also something more. The Romantic symbol is conceived as precisely such a microcosm, whether it be in the form of an image within a poem or a poem in its totality. Thus, when

Blake writes about seeing 'Heaven in a Wild Flower', the flower is not merely a metaphor for heaven; rather, heaven itself is thought of as permeating the flower as it permeates everything else.

The wild flower as microcosm also illustrates the similarity between the Romantic symbol and the primitive intuition of the sacred and the profane. I wrote earlier of the transcendental impulse of myth and symbol. The mythical vision has this transcendental dimension because in it everything is marked with the character of the sacred or the holy and so becomes more than a mere 'thing'. The Romantic symbol is similarly transcendental because it too is instinct with the feeling of something larger than itself. The symbolic poet blessing all that he looks upon is like the primitive 'spiritualizing' every object with the accent of the sacred. Thus, to the poetic imagination the whole universe is a universe of living beings rather than dead objects. Richard Chase, in fact, has characterized myth as 'magic literature', that is, 'literature which achieves the wonderful, uncanny, or brilliant reality of the mythical vision of things'. It is precisely this sense of the wonderful that the Romantics were trying to capture, the wonderful ranging from 'the charm of novelty' in everyday things to the sense of the uncanny and the preternatural as in Wordsworth's 'Resolution and Independence', which Chase mentions as an example of a truly mythical poem. Any work, then, which invests things with a preternatural force, with mana, is mythical. The mythical nature of a work does not depend on the use of a mythological story, but rather on this mode of sacralizing vision. Kafka would be considered more truly mythical in this view than, say, Anouilh or Sartre, who have both used stories from Greek mythology in their plays. Kathleen Raine maintains that metaphor, symbol, personification and, 'at the apex, myth', are in an ascending scale of 'increasingly animistic assumptions about the world'. In the mythical view 'the world is, in its whole and in its parts, living and conscious'. Carl Jung has also emphasized the accent of the preternatural, of what, following Rudolf Otto, he terms the 'numinous', that marks the truly archetypal image in dreams, literature or myth.[10] Mythical literature, in this view, is literature that has the numinosity of the true myth.

The feeling of solidarity with the community and with nature that Cassirer thought to be the most important aspect of the mythical attitude is present in Romantic thought, if not as a fact, then at least as an ideal. Once again it is Wordsworth who has most often expressed this feeling of unity as well as the longing for it. The Immortality Ode very nicely illustrates Cassirer's idea that it is the sense of the indestructible unity of life that enables the primitive to negate the fact of death. The 'Recollections of Early Childhood' give 'Intimations of Immortality' precisely because early childhood is an age of complete harmony with nature as well as the age in which everything is apparelled in a numinous, 'celestial light'. The child, in keeping with the principle of the parallel between ontogeny and phylogeny (another example of the mythical concrescence of similars?), represents the primitive vision of an undivided and living universe, hence the Romantic cult of the primitive and of the child.

The theory of literature as the product of a mythical mode of thought has often been criticized for its primitivism. But to view literature as mythical need not necessarily involve this. To the Romantics the primitive and the child were more in the nature of metaphors for a spontaneous, undivided mode of thought than persons to be emulated. Mythical thought tends to explain a logical problem in terms of temporal origins, a characteristic that Kenneth Burke has termed the 'temporizing of essence'.[11] The idea of a past age of undivided, spontaneous sensibility, of undifferentiated unity, may well be seen as an instance of this temporizing of essence, of projecting what is thought to be logically or epistemologically prior as the temporally prior. In this sense it does not matter if the actual primitive consciousness is shown to be different from the pre-logical, 'mystical' consciousness that Cassirer, Lévy-Bruhl, and others have described. The pre-logical may not be temporally prior to the age of logic, but it *is* 'prior' in terms of the value attached to it by the poets. This non-temporal priority is projected as temporal priority in keeping with the mythical mode of thought. One could therefore say that the Romantic cult of the primitive and the child is itself mythical. The primitive and the child *are* myths; the important thing is to try to understand the problems that these myths are trying to solve. Frank Kermode has often, and I believe quite rightly, criticized the primitivism that is involved in the mythical approach to art.[12] But at the same time it should be borne in mind that the primitivism of the Romantics is often an aspect of their poetic theory rather than their poetic theory a consequence of their primitivism. It is true that poetry is considered to be 'primitive', but that is so only because the primitive mind is thought to be 'poetic'.

The concept of mythical thought can also throw light on the formal and stylistic aspects of a work. The most thoroughgoing attempt to trace similarities between literature and primitive language and thought is Wayne Shumaker's *Literature and the Irrational* (1960), which argues that the basic common point is that both are primarily irrational and affective rather than rational and cognitive. One of the examples he gives is the parallel between the absorption of the reader or spectator while experiencing a work of art and the primitive man's habit of intense absorption in anything that catches his attention. Shumaker also relates certain stylistic features to primitive linguistic habits. Both primitive and literary language, for example, are seen as 'concrete' and 'tending to register percepts in *Gestalten*'; also common to both is the irrational conjunction between elements on the basis of mere contiguity, an instance being the frequent occurrence of parataxis. The principle of *pars pro toto* is similarly common to primitive thought and literature, where it is seen in the figure of synecdoche. Primitive animism is also present in poetic language in the form of personifications, the pathetic fallacy, and dead metaphors revived. Shumaker also traces the origins of the major literary forms to primitive rituals and ways of thought. In another book he applies some of these ideas to *Paradise Lost* to show how that poem may be called a myth, but he offers no detailed comments on Shakespeare.[13] Another application of the concept of mythical thought is found in Genesius Jones's study of T. S. Eliot's poetry, where it is argued that Eliot employs the mythical principle of concrescence as a structural device. This is particularly true of *The Waste Land* where, Jones argues, it is not the use of specific mythical parallels to contemporary life that unifies the poem, but rather the merging together of different elements and categories, so that characters melt into each other in a constant mythical metamorphosis and each part becomes a concrescence of the whole.[14] In this way a work can be organized mythically rather than logically or in narrative sequence. Shakespeare's sub-plots could also be seen in this light as 'mythically' or 'magically' related to the main plot.

Myth or mythology as the product of the mythical mode of thought may be considerd as being external to the work of art and providing it with subject-matter or background. Such a myth need not be a story; it can be a system of beliefs or a particular belief, but it must be something that is communally shared and has the characteristics of the mythical mode of thought described above. Philip Wheelwright (1960) distinguishes three attitudes to a given mythology. When it is literally believed in, or at least taken seriously, as in the case of Aeschylus or Dante, the poet's task is the elaboration of some specific myth or myths taken from it. Shakespeare and Virgil illustrate, according to him, the second attitude, a more sceptical one but not entirely positivist. Such writers make thematic use of myths. In the modern age, however, myths are used merely as antiquarian curiosities since the scientific-secular attitude has destroyed any kind of belief in myth. In place of myth, which is the product of the truly communal mind and has a transcendental dimension, the modern age, Wheelwright argues, only has ideology, which is the product of a mob mentality (p. 12).

Finally, some critical procedures and concepts themselves may reflect the mythical mode of thought. For example, the Romantic cult of the primitive and the child and the concept of an age of undivided, spontaneous unity of life and thought, words and meanings, images and ideas, man and nature, the individual and society, seem to be the result, as suggested earlier, of the mythical projection of logical problems into a temporal dimension. Myth criticism may be 'mythical' in another way. It has often been criticized for 'mistaking analogies for identities'.[15] But taking analogies for identities is precisely the characteristic of mythical thought as described by Cassirer. Behind the mode of typological exegesis examined in Chapter 1 is a similar mythical impulsion. A remark made by the Indologist Hermann Oldenburg about the representations of gods in the Vedic religion provides an apt conclusion to this section:

They fear one another, penetrate one another, interweave and pair with one another.... One passes into the other, becomes the other, is a form of the other, *is* the other.... It would seem that once two representations find themselves in a certain proximity, it is impossible to keep them apart.[16]

Once, we might say, the mythological critic finds two literary representations in a certain proximity (usually because of analogy or similarity), he finds it impossible to keep them apart.

III

Cassirer, as we have seen, includes a wide variety of cultural phenomena, such as primitive myths and rituals, totemism, magic, alchemy and astrology, under the category of mythical thought. Several aspects of Shakespeare's works can be seen as instances of mythical thought as thus defined, even when the term myth is nowhere mentioned in discussions of them. An example is the 'Elizabethan World Picture' that Tillyard has seen as the background to the plays. Particularly interesting in this connection is that element in this picture that he describes as 'the corresponding planes'. These planes, according to him, were conceived as 'arranged one below another in order of dignity but connected by an immense net of correspondences'. As examples of such correspondence, Tillyard mentions the one between the microcosm and the macrocosm and also that between the macrocosm and the commonwealth that underlies the famous 'degree' speech in *Troilus and Cressida* (I. iii. 75–137).[17] The causal linking there of the violation of degree in different spheres is an obvious example of 'magical' causation, i.e. the transformation of mere correspondences into causal links. The operation of what Cassirer calls 'the law of concrescence or coincidence of the members of a relation in mythical thinking' can be readily observed in this and in other similar passages. It may not be an exaggeration to say that Shakespeare's universe (much more emphatically than that of any other dramatist of the period) is a magical universe where every significant act is seen as magically affecting the whole structure. Further, while the use of similes and metaphors derived from nature to describe human feelings or affairs is to be found in the poetry of every period, in Shakespeare such comparisons seem to be more than mere comparisons, evoking as they do the primitive sense of identity between man and nature.

An interesting application of the concept of magical causality can be seen in some studies of the Shakespearean sub-plot. It was William Empson who first suggested that the double plot convention depends for its effect on certain magical ideas, a point later taken up by Angus Fletcher and Richard Levin. Empson develops his idea in the course of a discussion of the double plot in Elizabethan drama, more specifically of the double plot in *Troilus and Cressida*. He writes:

The two parts make a mutual comparison that illuminates both parties ('love and war are alike') and their large-scale indefinite juxtaposition seems to encourage primitive ways of thought ('Cressida will bring Troy bad luck because she is bad'). This power of suggestion is the strength of the double plot; once you take the two parts to correspond, any character may take on *mana* because he seems to cause what he corresponds to or be Logos of what he symbolizes.

Richard Levin carries forward this suggestion in his analysis of the function of the multiple plot in Renaissance drama. He points out that in this play the love and war themes are causally related since the sexual motivation lies behind most of the fighting. Thus, for example, even Achilles's savage assault on Hector is in part related to his love for Patroclus. There is, however, according to Levin, a different kind of causation also at work in the relation of the two plots. This, he suggests, is a magical causation as distinguished from the literal kind of causation just mentioned. As a result of this magical causation, not only is war seen as the result of love, but the outcome of the war plot is felt to be dependent on the outcome of the love plot. This is precisely the opposite of the surface plot, in which the lovers are separated by the exigencies of war. According to the causal law of magic, that is, the law of *post hoc, ergo propter hoc*, one tends to feel, not merely that Troy is defeated because Cressida is bad, as Empson argues, but also that

Troy's original military advantage was related to Paris's amatory triumph over Menelaus, who as a scorned cuckold brings bad luck to the Greek side, so that with Troilus's defeat this advantage is lost. The Trojan 'love' hero has been cuckolded by a Greek in one arena, and the magical consequence is that the Trojan 'war' hero is killed by a Greek in the other arena, and that Troy will succumb to the invaders.[18]

Levin also discusses (pp. 141–4) the magical function of the clown subplot in *Henry IV*. This magical function is described in general terms as the providing of vicarious pleasure to the reader or spectator through the clown's indulgence in infantile or primitive desires. The clown also acts as a 'lightning rod' to disarm parodic impulses against the heroic protagonist. His mockery, like ritual cursings or the rituals of rebellion observed in some primitive societies, provides a safe outlet for impulses hostile to order in the community. The festive nature of the clown subplots (Falstaff being considered a clown) is, in fact, implicit in their very nature, as Levin rightly points out, since their 'alternating episodes were shown to offer a kind of emotional vacation from the more serious business of the main action'. Shakespeare, moreover, according to Levin (following C. L. Barber), deliberately emphasizes the saturnalian role of Falstaff, and the latter's 'magical function of providing a licensed release for the drives and fantasies of childhood' applies not only to the audience but also to Prince Hal.

The sense of the magical relatedness of things is especially marked in Shakespeare's presentation of kingship. Generally speaking, his kings are charged with mana, the mystique of what Wilson Knight terms 'royalism', and the well-being of the community is magically linked to their own well-being. That is why regicide (and its familial counterpart in crimes against fathers or brothers) is always, in Shakespeare, more than the violation of legal or ethical codes merely. One of the reasons for dissatisfaction with Bradleyan character analysis may be precisely this sense of the magical and cosmic implications of 'unnatural' crimes that merely psychological studies of character tend to ignore. In *Macbeth*, for example, as M. M. Badawi has pointed out, the murder of Duncan arouses 'not just the usual horror at the breaking of the second commandment, but the more mysterious and terrifying horror at the violation of a primitive taboo'. J. I. M. Stewart also comments on the primitivism of the play, comparing Macbeth's crime to the cannibalistic eating of flesh. 'Nor,' he writes, 'is the parallel so outlandish as it may appear. For it is veritably the crime and not the crown that compels Macbeth, as it is the virtue that lies in the terrible and forbidden, and not the flavour of the human flesh, that compels the savage.'[19]

Belief in word-magic is another primitive feature in *Macbeth*. This is reflected, according to Badawi, in a peculiar stylistic feature of the play, namely the use of euphemisms and indirections to refer to the murder of Duncan (such as the use of pronouns or of more general nouns like 'deed'). This reluctance to name a terrible thing reveals what Otto Jespersen has termed an 'ingrained fear of the right word, a belief, that is, in the more or less supernatural power immanent in the word itself'. It is this power in words that witchcraft seeks to exploit. Language in this play has a mysterious role; one feels that the atmosphere of darkness is a result of the prayers (i.e. words) of Macbeth and Lady Macbeth. The words in this play, as Badawi puts it, 'seem to acquire an independent existence and reality that terrify the characters; they haunt them and keep on reverberating and echoing in their mind' (pp. 42–3).

Yet another primitive feature in the play is pointed out by D. F. Rauber, who comments on the importance of 'threeness' in the play, showing, for example, how the structure of the play seems to be divisible into three parts, in whatever manner we choose to describe this structure. Thus, the play could be seen as depicting the three-part action of Macbeth's rise, kingship and fall, or the progress from Duncan's benign rule, through Macbeth's tyranny, to the restoration of peace. The play could also be divided into three realms of metaphorical space: heaven (symbolized by the pious Edward), hell (the witches) and, between them, earth (Scotland bleeding under the tyrant's rule). In terms of the relation between characters also the three-part structure can be discerned. Thus, in the first part of the play, Macbeth and Lady Macbeth, young and 'strong in their fertile youth, kill the old king-father in classic mythic fashion'; the second part of the play corresponds to the middle age of the protagonists, and Macbeth here kills the middle-aged Banquo; in the third part the old and sterile Macbeth kills the young Lady Macduff and her son and attempts to kill the young and vigorous Macduff. Interestingly enough, at first there is an attempt to kill one person and that succeeds; in the second stage there is an attempt to kill two (Banquo and Fleance) but only one is killed; in the third stage the attempt is to kill three (Macduff and his family) but only two are killed. Thus Rauber goes on, in an interesting and amusing manner, to trace other triadic patterns in the play. These patterns, he suggests, are linked to the 'extensive use of the traditional incantatory and mystical power of this potent number', and indeed in the play the number also appears in its incantatory function in the speeches of the witches, who are, of course, three in number. As another confirmation of his analysis, Rauber points to the otherwise arbitrary introduction of the third murderer.

This kind of reading inevitably leads to numerological analysis. Indeed there is a numerological exegesis of *Venus and Adonis*, but such studies are (mercifully perhaps) not very common. I imagine they do point to a belief in Shakespeare's time in the magical value of numbers. In *Macbeth* certainly the number three appears in a magical context in the witches' speeches, and the fact that threeness seems to extend even to the structure of the play may well indicate a residual belief in the magical efficacy of numbers.

Finally, on this subject of the magical value of words and numbers in Shakespeare, it may be said that a well-known feature of Shakespeare's style, his often tedious play upon words, is also connected with it, though only remotely, since primarily it has the quality of *play* rather than ritual incantation. The delight in words is a marked feature of children's behaviour; they seem to play with them as with toys. Play, of course, is not ritual, but 'the omnipotence of thought' operates in both, and in any case both verbal play and ritual incantation assume the thinginess, as it were, of words. The parallel between the two seems to be closer when we consider that the characteristic form of play on words in Shakespeare's drama is the wit-combat, a combat, that is, in which words take the place of swords and lances or of the counters in a game of chess. Compare, for example, the play on the word 'hit' during the wit-combat in *Love's Labour's Lost* (IV. i. 100) with the use of the same word during the duel in *Hamlet* ('A hit, a very palpable hit', v. ii. 273). Even if one were to deny the ritual function of such use of words, it would, I think, be readily granted that this play upon words is an instance of a primitive (and infantile) habit of thought, in which words acquire a sort of material status. But the puns and verbal jugglery in the plays do seem to link up, in obscure ways, with such things as riddles, catechisms, poetic contests, incantations and the ritual exorcism of evil through cursing, the common element being the belief in the material reality of words. This, therefore, considering the fact that not the least important aspect of Shakespeare's greatness is his verbal felicity, ought to be considered one of the most important aspects of his primitive or mythical habit of thought.

Robert Heilman provides a good example of the use of the term myth in the honorific sense distinguished earlier. Referring to a symposium on 'Myth in the Later Plays of Shakespeare', he writes that it represents an effort to modify the spirit of enlightenment that has led to an 'over-extension of the mythoclastic habit of mind'. The difference between Cassirer's phenomenological approach and the more 'ontological' approach of Heilman is clearly brought out by the next sentence. Cassirer, he writes, 'describes myth as pre-logical; we are now coming to know that it is also post-logical or, better perhaps, co-logical'.[20] Heilman seems to imply that there is a reality that can be grasped only through myth and that it is of a higher kind than the reality that science seeks to master. Consequently, the mythical mode of thought is given a higher status than the scientific (the term 'cological' seems to be merely a rhetorical concession).

Heilman goes on to discuss the mythical aspect of Shakespeare's plays in terms of his definition of myth. He suggests that Shakespeare's later plays are mythic in two senses: they draw upon 'vital myths' and are themselves 'mythic'. This is brought out clearly if one asks the questions: 'What myths were available to Shakespeare, and what is the Shakespeare myth?' Heilman's purpose in this essay is to answer these two qustions. The myths available to Shakespeare, according to him, were the myth of Christianity, the myth of 'love and justice' (the phrase is William Troy's) and the 'myth of love and the myth of divine and earthly governance' (Philip Wheelwright's phrase). Shakespeare's plays are themselves mythic according to the Longinian test of appeal to prosperity and, more importantly, by virtue of the *kind* of appeal to posterity, namely 'the ability to create in posterity a sense of being made to see into the universal. We do not confront Shakespeare with logical dispute: we explicate him.' The plays are also mythic because in them there is a 'residuum of mystery'. Heilman goes on to argue that *Lear, Othello, Hamlet* and *Macbeth* all show Shakespeare's concern with 'myth in crisis'. In fact *Lear*, according to Heilman, is a 'myth about myth' (pp. 36–41, 45). I do not find this use of the term myth very enlightening because many other terms would have done as well. Maybe *Lear* is about myth in crisis, but myth here means no more than traditional beliefs—and not merely traditional beliefs but beliefs which Heilman clearly finds very attractive. He is, in other words, more concerned with the 'ideology' implicit in the myths than in the myths themselves. Besides, if one describes a play as depicting 'myth in crisis', it becomes confusing to describe the same play as also mythic.

Shakespeare's plays are described as mythic not merely because they imply a belief in transcendental reality, but also because they employ non-naturalistic devices to hint at this reality. Thus Maynard Mack suggests that *Lear* is mythic because 'it abandons verisimilitude to find out truth', 'building a deeply metaphysical metaphor, or myth, about the human condition'.[21] The model for this use of the term 'myth' is the Platonic myth rather than the myths of primitive societies. Just as Plato abandons logical discourse in his attempt to describe transcendental reality, so also, it is thought, Shakespeare has recourse to myth to express his intuitions of such a reality. This is the argument put forward by G. Wilson Knight, especially in connection with the 'miraculous' scenes in the romances, and by Richmond Hathorn in his discussion of *Hamlet* and *Lear*. A large number of other studies of the plays mentioned in Chapter 1 would also fall under this category. Although there is an insistence in such studies that the plays express truths symbolically rather than allegorically, in actual practice they turn into a kind of allegorical exegesis since they focus on the *content* of the mythical consciousness (the transcendental truths, the myths of love and divine governance, immortality, and so on) rather than on its formal properties. Exegesis of the mythical work thus inevitably becomes an allegorizing of it, as I tried to show in Chapter 1.

The similarity between the allegorical and symbolic theories of myth and literature should not, however, be exaggerated, for there is a significant difference between the two. The allegorical critic looks upon his role as that of a hierophant or a 'reader of riddles'. If the meaning is hidden, it is solely because it is too sacred for exposure to the common mass of humanity, but the critic has no doubt about his grasp of it or about his ability to lead the right kind of reader to a vision of it. He is like a priest guarding the sanctum sanctorum and allowing entry only to a chosen few. The symbolist critic, on the other hand, casts himself in a humbler role, placing himself at the same level of ignorance and uncertainty as his readers. He is far less certain of his ability to grasp the meaning of the work and feels more like an intruder in the temple than its priest, desecrating rather than revealing. The difference between the two approaches to myth and literature emerges very clearly if we compare the conception of the critic's role as defined by Wigston, Colin Still and several other critics mentioned in Chapter 1 with the following statement by D. G. James about the role of myth in the last plays of Shakespeare—a statement which admirably sums up the dilemma of the symbolist critic:

> The purpose of myth is the showing forth of that which cannot be set out by the representation of a merely human situation; its function is the conveyance, to whatever degree possible, of the divine as well as the human. Yet it is the case that to try to extract its significances, and to

convey them in the prose of statement, is at once a desecration of the work of art, and, in any case, an impossibility; for the justification of the work of art is that it is only thus that an adequate conveyance of the writer's mind can be made.

Nevertheless, we are under compulsion to attempt judgment on the adequacy of myth to its purpose and significance; and if it be said that to do so is to carry out desecration and to attempt the impossible, the only reply must be that we cannot help ourselves. The critic can no more avoid trying to explicate and draw out the significances of Shakespeare's last plays than the theologian can help seeking to draw a philosophical theology out of the structure of Christian dogma.[22]

CHAPTER 4

The Structural Approach to Myth

Somewhere around 1910, according to Virginia Woolf, human character changed.[1] In the realm of aesthetic theory, one could say, Wilhelm Worringer's *Abstraction and Empathy*, first published in 1908, and running into three editions (in German) in two years, is an important manifestation of this change. Worringer attempts a psychological study of style in art, arguing that there are two basic styles, the naturalistic and the abstract, reflecting, respectively, two basic attitudes to the external world: 'a happy pantheistic relationship of confidence between man and the phenomena of the external world', and 'a great inner unrest... a spiritual dread of space'.[2] Characteristic of the abstract style, according to Worringer, are the geometrical forms, deliberately remote from all suggestions of organic life, that we find in Egyptian, Byzantine and Oriental art. Generally speaking, the abstract style is the more primitive, but this does not mean that it is lacking in technical sophistication. Worringer's sympathies are undoubtedly with abstract art as he feels that such art reflects a humbler and spiritually more refined attitude to the world. In England, Worringer's ideas were popularized by T. E. Hulme, whose *Speculations* was published posthumously in 1924. Usually when there is a call for the reappraisal of a particular kind of art of the past, the call is accompanied by—more often than not motivated by—the emergence of a similar kind of art in the present. Worringer and Hulme's reappraisal of abstract art was also accompanied by the emergence of the abstract style in painting and sculpture, an emergence prophesied by Hulme, though perhaps only after the event.

A parallel swing away from naturalism can be observed in literature around this time. The two aspects of naturalism in drama and the novel are, one might say, realistic characterization and a 'realistic' narrative in which events occur in a temporal sequence according to the laws of causality. Both are dispensed with in the novels of James Joyce, Virginia Woolf and D. H. Lawrence. 'Character' is dissolved into a field of psychic forces, of memory and desire, and 'plot' is dislodged by submerged structures of imagery and myth.

Writing about Joyce's *Ulysses* in 1923, T. S. Eliot suggested that it was possible, after its example, to use the mythical method rather than the narrative one to give order and coherence to the immense panorama of futility that is modern life.[3] Eliot was thus the first to formulate the structural possibilities of myth. No doubt he had also his own method in *The Waste Land* in mind. By juxtaposing the First World War with the Punic War in the first section of the poem, for example, he sought to comprehend the contemporary phenomenon. Eliot's use of myth was thus a method by which a contemporary experience could be understood by being placed in the total context of tradition, tradition being, essentially, the history of the particular culture considered synchronically rather than diachronically. The use of myth could also remove the necessity of logical and narrative progression since while reading such a work one does not ask about a part of it: 'Does this necessarily follow that?', but rather: 'Does this correspond with that?' And it could be argued that the perceiving of such imaginative correspondences gives greater aesthetic pleasure than the mere following of a logical or causal progression. It is doubtful, however, whether Eliot and Joyce were really the first writers to realize and use the possibilities of the mythical method. Even poems like Dryden's *Absalom and Achitophel* and Pope's *The Rape of the Lock* use myths, Biblical in one case and Classical in the other, in order to comment upon contemporary experience by placing it in the larger context of the literary and cultural tradition.

The practice of using myth as a structural principle in a work of art is thus older than Eliot made it out to be. In fact even Shakespeare has been seen as using myths in order to give structural and thematic unity to his plays. What is more common and new in contemporary thinking on the subject is the use of myths by *critics* to give shape and coherence to their perception of the work of art, even when there is no evidence of conscious use of myths by the artist. This procedure has been justified by some by arguing for the common origin of works of literature in myths and rituals, and by others by postulating a 'collective unconscious' or a universal human mind. A third group of critics tends to dismiss this question of origins as irrelevant to poetics and dwells, instead, upon the *logical* relationship between myths and literature. In thus adopting a synchronic model of literary tradition the critics of this third group are in harmony with a major trend in several intellectual disciplines, especially anthropology and linguistics.

Foremost among the critics of the third group mentioned above is Northrop Frye, who has become associated in common parlance with the 'myth and ritual' approach and with 'archetypal' critics like Maud Bodkin. Frye himself has, however, pointed out that this indicates a total failure to understand his theories. As he puts it, he resembles Bodkin about as closely as he resembles the late Sarah Bernhardt.[4] Nevertheless, it is easy to see how this association could have occurred. In his fondness for schemas of archetypal images, Frye resembles some of the critics discussed in Chapter 1, especially Colin Still. For example, in an essay entitled 'New Directions from Old', Frye builds up a 'cosmology' of which the basic organizational principles are the changes of the seasons and the dialectic between higher and lower forms of consciousness:

> The basis for organizing the imagery of the physical world has been the natural cycle. The sequence of seasons, times of day, periods of life and death, have helped to provide for literature the combination of movement and order, of change and regularity, that is needed in all the arts. Hence the importance, in poetic symbolism, of the mythical figure known as the dying god, whether Adonis or Proserpine or their innumerable allotropic forms, who represents the cycle of nature.

The physical world, however, is not merely a cyclical world but also a 'middle earth' between a higher and a lower world (an idea very similar to Colin Still's idea of 'planes of consciousness' with their corresponding 'mythical realms'). There are, according to Frye, two points of particular significance in poetic symbolism: one, the point where the upper and the middle world meet, usually conceived as the top of a mountain, and two, the point where this world meets the lower world, usually symbolized by a labyrinthine cave. Behind this foreground of images is 'the background of roughly four levels of existence' which Frye, borrowing a term from Theodor H. Gaster, calls 'topocosm'. These four levels are:

1. The presence of God—grace and providence—the starry heaven;
2. 'Human' nature—symbolized by the garden of Eden;

3. The physical nature—fallen, but morally neutral;
4. Sin, death, and corruption.[5]

These four levels of existence could be subsumed under the more inclusive categories of the world of innocence and the world of experience, and Frye's major critical objective seems to be to place all works of literature within this broad framework.

Passages such as the one above show the influence on Frye's thought of the kind of allegorical and typological exegesis of scriptural material discussed earlier, but the differences between the two are equally significant. Frye is fully conscious of the relation of his tabulations and schemas to such 'myth criticism'. Commenting on his table of apocalyptic imagery in *Anatomy of Criticism* he writes: 'Allegorical alchemy, Rosicrucianism, Cabbalism, Freemasonry, and the Tarot pack are all typological constructs based on paradigms similar to those given here. For the literary critics they are simply reference tables: the atmosphere of oracular harrumph about them, which recurs in some forms of archetypal criticism, is not much to the point.' The 'oracular harrumph' can take several forms. It can, for example, be heard in gestures of reverence towards a hidden universal significance, or in statements about the primordial origins of the narrative and imagistic paradigms, either in the remote past, or in the depths of the individual unconscious, or, deeper still, in the collective unconscious. Frye wants to emancipate his use of the concepts of myth and archetype from all these approaches which, in his terms, would be described as either historical or allegorical. His approach to the concepts claims, in contrast, to be purely literary. Another instance which brings this out is the following comment on 'solar mythology': 'When archetypal criticism revived in the nineteenth century with a vogue for sun myths, an attempt was made to ridicule it by proving with equal plausibility that Napoleon was a sun myth. The ridicule is effective only against the historical distortion of the method. Archetypally, we turn Napoleon into a sun myth whenever we speak of the rise of his career, the zenith of his fame, or the eclipse of his fortunes.'[6]

Frye is thus different from the earlier myth and ritual critics in using the concepts of myth and archetype in a non-allegorical, non-psychological and non-historical sense. He points out in the *Anatomy* that 'one element in our cultural tradition which is usually regarded as fantastic nonsense is the allegorical interpretations of myths'. What the allegorists failed to realize was that myth, being a 'centripetal structure of meaning', can be made to mean an indefinite number of things. In literary criticism, therefore, Frye suggests, myth is best taken not in the sense of a story with a profound moral but as *mythos*, 'a structural organizing principle of literary form'. Similarly, archetype is defined not as an image rising from the collective unconscious but as a symbol, usually an image, 'which recurs often enough in literature to be recognized as an element of one's literary experience as a whole'. Myth, as it is an imitation of recurrent and generic action or ritual, is also defined as 'archetypal narrative'. Myth and archetype are thus, in Frye's terminology, the narrative and significant aspects of the same thing. The major part of the *Anatomy* is concerned with 'archetypal' rather than allegorical criticism, i.e. with the attempt to see literature as a 'total form' rather than as an aggregate of individual works.[7] Frye's kind of 'myth criticism' is directed towards this total form of the verbal universe, and in this respect it seems to be very different from the allegorical-cum-typological criticism examined in Chapter 1.

When, according to Frye, we stand back from particular works in an attempt to see literature as a whole, we perceive that 'all themes and characters and stories that we encounter in literature belong to one big interlocking family'. Frye is not, however, prepared to derive from this any theory of the *origin* of the various forms: he is interested in tracing connections between the members of the family only 'logically, not chronologically'. When we see literature as such a family of works, we can discern in it a single mythical story, 'which may not have existed as a whole story anywhere, but which we can reconstruct from the myths and legends we have'. This story has as its basis the cyclic order of nature and the tension between 'repugnance and desire', between 'identity with, or separation from nature', and may be described as 'the story of the loss and regaining of identity'. It is, according to Frye, the 'framework of all literature'. Inside it 'comes the story of the hero with a thousand faces, as one critic calls him, whose adventures, death, disappearance and marriage or resurrection are the focal points of what later become romance and tragedy and satire and comedy in fiction, and the emotional moods that take their place in such forms as the lyric, which normally does not tell a story'.[8]

This 'ur-myth' in its totality determines the structure of literature as a whole, and the phases of this ur-myth become the structural principles of individual works and classes of works. Frye's description of the process by which myths and rituals enter literature as its structural principle owes a great deal to Jane Harrison's account of the emergence of Greek drama from the rituals of Dionysus. Primitive ritual, he argues, is a recurrent act 'expressive of a dialectic of desire and repugnance: desire for fertility or victory, repugnance to drought or to enemies'. There are thus rituals of integration and rituals of expulsion. These ritual acts are accompanied by a story or myth which 'establishes an inter-related significance among them'.

Literature, in the form of drama, appears when the myth encloses and contains the ritual. This changes the agents of the ritual into the actors of the myth. The myth sets up a powerful pull away from magic: the ritual acts are now performed for the sake of representing the myth rather than primarily for affecting the order of nature. In other words, drama is born in the renunciation of magic, and in *The Tempest* and elsewhere it remembers its inheritance.

The shapes of the myths, when they enter literature, become 'the conventions that establish the general framework of narrative'. Myth, in other words, becomes a structural principle in literature. This is an idea often reiterated by Frye. He argues that myths and folk tales (and in this context the difference between them is not important) are 'pure verbal design'.[9] This is so because they are as near as possible to the structure of human desires; they have not been 'displaced' by the demands of plausibility and morality.[10] But behind even the most realistic works one can discern the basic dialectic of human desire, and archetypal criticism is the process of uncovering this dialectic.

Since conventions are descended from myths, and since, as Frye argues, in myth there is 'identity of personal character and natural object', it follows that the importance of the conventions is that they help to recapture 'the pure and primitive identity of myth'. And as the desire for such identity or unity is deeply rooted in mankind, it also follows that the most popular literature will be that which is most conventional, since it is through the conventions that the primitive identity of myth can be recaptured. Frye thus proposes the equation of the terms, *popular*, *conventional*, and *primitive*. The *popular*, according to him, is 'the continuing primitive, the creative design that makes its impact independently of special education'. The *primitive* is 'not the old fashioned, but the archaic, the region of origins and beginnings'. Shakespeare's art, especially in the comedies and the romances, is popular and primitive in this sense. There are deliberately archaic elements in all his plays, and the effect of this archaizing tendency is 'to establish contact with a universal and world-wide dramatic tradition'.[11]

Frye, it is clear, is interested in myths and conventions only because through them he can have a vision of this world-wide dramatic tradition. But Frye never explains why, if the popular and the conventional are synonymous, some conventional art, in his sense of the word, is far from popular in any acceptable sense of that term. Folk tales, he has argued, are conventional; the more conventional an art-form becomes, the closer it approaches the pure, undisplaced structure of myth; indeed, according to Frye, it becomes pure structure itself. And as communication may be thought to take place through structure rather than surface content, it is easy to see why folk tales, which are almost pure structure, should be popular. But Frye also mentions 'the use of myth and metaphor in contemporary literature', and the analogous tendency in the visual arts to emphasize 'abstract design', as instances of the trend towards pure structure, i.e. one may infer, towards a conventional art.[12] But the fact is that such poetry, fiction and painting have been elite rather than popular forms. Frye's intention, I presume, is to try to make them popular by pointing out their similarity with primitive and hence popular art, but the problem remains that here are instances of conventional and primitive art which are not popular. One can get around the problem by suggesting that the popular is different from the merely fashionable, and this is a distinction which Frye, in fact, is constantly making. His distinction between stereotypes and archetypes is an analogous one. But the psychological and social reasons for the continuing popularity of certain conventional forms of fiction or other forms of art are never argued in detail.

Moreover, although Frye proposes to use myths and conventions as purely structural principles, his analysis of individual works is never really structural. Conventions seem to function in his criticism, as in the criticism of E. E. Stoll, as premature absolutes.[13] They are related to his desire to 'identify' or 'recognize' works of art rather than to evaluate them or to analyse their 'meaning'.[14] But recognition can only be the beginning of structural analysis, not the end. Thus, a number of statements in Frye's criticism referring to the importance of structure seem to be contrary to his actual practice, which is usually to demonstrate that a thing is as it is because it is meant to be that way. For example, he makes the statement that one needs a character like Blifil in *Tom Jones* 'for structural reasons, not merely to symbolize the author's disapproval of hypocrisy'.[15] This could lead to a proper structural analysis if Frye were to tease out the logical implications of the situation presented in the novel and deduce the characters of Blifil and others from this basic situation (a kind of analysis in which Kenneth Burke excels).[16] But instead of elaborating upon such statements in the manner of Burke, Frye usually falls back upon his theory of genres and conventions, these being related to myth through a pseudo-historical regression and to the universal human mind through an extremely generalized psychology of the dialectic of repugnance and desire.

Frye, in fact, is not really interested in the structure of the individual work. His emphasis on myths as structural elements in literature is related to his desire to see literature as a totality, and it is in terms of his interest in the total form of literature that he is able to distinguish his archetypal approach from the allegorical. As he writes in the *Anatomy*, 'translating imagery into examples and precepts [which is allegorical commentary] is a quite distinct process from following images into other poems' (p. 103). Frye's motto would thus seem to be: 'Don't allegorize—only connect.' The ultimate end of this connecting is the realization that

literature as a whole is not an aggregate of exhibits with red and blue ribbons attached to them, like a cat-show, but the range of articulate human imagination as it extends from the height of imaginative heaven to the depth of imaginative hell. Literature is a human apocalypse, man's revelation to man, and criticism is not a body of adjudications, but the awareness of that revelation, the last judgment of mankind.[17]

Visionary experience, we are told, comes from the outside or from above and totally engulfs the consciousness of the subject. It is doubtful if Frye's vision of the human apocalypse is of this order of experience. If the literary order were an objective reality the critic could merely point to it in silence. But of course it is not that. It is, first of all, a verbal construct of Northrop Frye's, which implies that some *interpretation* of it is in-built in its structure, and second, Frye has to explicitly verbalize his sense of the significance of this order. In doing so he cannot avoid allegorization, as I shall try to show presently.

Applauding Frye's liberal intention to 'only connect', we may accept his statement that *Huckleberry Finn* has one of the oldest themes in comedy, 'the freeing of a slave', or that the American Western is a version of the pastoral,[18] resisting the urge to bring up such obvious objections as the point that in view of the presence of slavery as an actual fact of nineteenth-century American society, the connection with classical comedy becomes aesthetically irrelevant even if it were not morally insensitive, or the point that the pastoralization of the West in the Western glosses over the unsavoury realities of the westward extension of the frontier. We resist the urge because Frye has promised us a vision of literature as a whole, and such objections merely lead us away from that goal of literary studies. Similarly, we may agree when Frye says that the 'meaning' of the individual work is not important, it being nothing more than a mere abstraction from our experience of the work. For example, *The Winter's Tale*, according to Frye, is not an allegory. As he puts it: 'In Shakespeare the meaning of the play is the play, there being nothing to be abstracted from the total experience of the play. Progress in grasping the meaning is a progress, not in seeing more in the play, but in seeing more of it.' But 'abstraction' (which is 'meaning') does enter Frye's criticism after all, as Reuben Arthur Brower points out with reference to the passage just quoted. Frye continues from the above passage as follows:

Further progress takes us from the individual plays to the class of things called plays, to the 'meaning' of drama as a whole. That meaning, again, is our total experience of drama. The centre of that experience is the fact that drama is doing, through the identity of myth and metaphor, what its ritual predecessors tried to do by the identity of sympathetic magic: unite the human and the natural worlds.[19]

The cat seems to be out of the bag at last. Frye's use of the term 'meaning' within quotes, and his reference to the 'centre' of the experience of literature as a totality, cannot obscure the fact that he is, in his own terms, allegorizing here. The identity of man and nature in a state of paradisal innocence is, as shown in Chapter 1, a recurrent theme in myth and ritual criticism. Frye describes such criticism as allegorical because it is concerned with the meaning of the individual work. But in spite of all his sophisticated machinery of systems of phases and modes and cycles, he sees in the totality of literature the same kind of thing that these critics saw in the individual works: the seasonal cycle, death and rebirth, the identity of man and nature, the world of innocence and the world of experience. One cannot avoid a sense of anti-climax after this, especially as Frye has brought in the 'oracular harrumph' in his own writing while referring to literature as a totality, the 'human apocalypse'. Lesser minds, as Frederick Crews points out, using the words of Freud about Dostoevsky's piety, have come to the same position with less effort.[20]

II

Although few writers in recent years have written as extensively as Claude Lévi-Strauss on the subject of myth, it may appear awkward to speak of the application of his theory of myth to literature since the structural model that he applies to the study of myths is equally applicable to other forms of cultural expression. What is prior to the study of both myth and literature is, of course, the study of language. Nevertheless, I believe his analysis of myths is of greater value to literary criticism than his analysis of literary works—such as the examination (in collaboration with Roman Jakobson) of Baudelaire's 'Les Chats', a dull technical analysis typical of the linguistic approach—though this view may appear paradoxical in the light of the fact that Lévi-Strauss considers myth and poetry to be polar opposites.

The two most important aspects of Levi-Strauss's approach to myth are his method of analysis and his concept of myth as a logical model designed to overcome a contradiction. His famous analysis of the Oedipus myth (1955) clearly and simply illustrates both these aspects. He begins by dividing the myth (or rather the set of myths concerned with Oedipus and his family) into its constituent units or 'mythemes'. These units are defined as 'bundles of relations'. They are then arranged in four parallel vertical columns as follows:

THE STRUCTURAL APPROACH TO MYTH 159

Column 1	Column 2	Column 3	Column 4
1. Cadmos seeks his sister Europa ravished by Zeus		2. Cadmos kills the Dragon	Labdakos = Lame (?)
	3. The Spartoi kill each other		
	4. Oedipus kills his father Laios		Laios = Left-sided (?)
		5. Oedipus kills the Sphinx	
6. Oedipus marries his mother Jocasta			Oedipus = Swollen-foot(?)
	7. Eteocles kills his brother Polynices		
8. Antigone buries her brother Polynices despite prohibition			

I have added numbers to the units in the table above to indicate the order in which the events occur. In the fourth column; however, the units are not events but a common feature associated with Oedipus's family. Having arranged the units of the myth in the above manner, Lévi-Strauss writes: 'Were we to *tell* the myth, we would disregard the columns and read the rows from left to right and from top to bottom. But if we want to *understand* the myth, then we will have to disregard one half of the diachronic dimension (top to bottom) and read from left to right, column after column, each one being considered as a unit.'[21]

Lévi-Strauss then proceeds to 'decode' the meaning of the myths in the following manner. The first column, he points out, contains relationships in which blood-relations are overemphasized, i.e. shown as more intimate than they should be. The common feature of the second column is the reverse of the first column. All the events here recorded represent the undervaluing of blood-relations. Taken by itself, the interpretation of Antigone's burial of her brother as over-valuing of blood relations may seem forced, but taken in the context of the fact that the brother of Antigone has been killed by his own brothers, it seems quite obviously a contrast to it. The third column refers to monsters being slain. As these monsters are conceived as autochthonous beings, the common feature of this column may be interpreted as 'denial of the autochthonous origin of man'. The fourth column contains references to difficulties in walking straight or keeping upright, and the import of this common feature is the 'persistence of the autochthonous origin of man'. It is thus seen that column two and column four are the reverse of columns one and three respectively. The *difference* between the first two columns is of the same kind as the *difference* between the other two. As Lévi-Strauss puts it, 'the overrating of blood relations is to the underrating of blood relations as the attempt to escape autochthony is to the impossibility of succeeding in it'. Now, the contradiction that the myth is trying to resolve is between the religious theory of the Greeks, according to which man was autochthonous, and the observed fact of nature that men are born of two parents. The myth's way of 'solving' this problem is to relate it to another and derivative problem which is equally insoluble, namely 'born from different or born from the same'. By thus relating one insoluble problem to another analogous and insoluble one the initial problem is 'solved'. 'Although experience contradicts theory, social life validates cosmology by its similarity of structure. Hence cosmology is true' (pp. 215–16).

This very sophisticated method of solving a problem by obfuscating it does not, however, operate at the conscious level. Hence the process of decoding the 'message' of the myth through structural analysis may be described as a process of revealing the 'deep structure' of the myth. In some respects this method of depth analysis is similar to the 'spatial' analysis of Shakespeare's plays advocated by G. Wilson Knight, who suggests that we should try to see the plays of Shakespeare as spatial areas of the mind, dwelling upon the 'set of correspondences which relate to each other independently of the time-sequence which is the story'.[22] These sets of 'correspondences' are analogous, I suggest, to Lévi-Strauss's 'mythemes' or units of 'bundles of relations', and Knight's disregarding of the temporal sequence is parallel to Lévi-Strauss's synchronic analysis. The 'mythemes' could also be described as 'image clusters' or 'recurrent motifs', which are familiar terms in studies of Shakespeare's imagery. Thus, lameness is a recurrent motif in the myth; other critics have noted the recurrence of the motif connected with sight in the version of the myth presented in Sophocles's play. All such studies of recurrent motifs, images and sets of correspondences are examples of the kind of synchronic analysis that Lévi-Strauss is advocating. His contribution to literary studies would thus seem to be the introduction of greater rigour in such analysis rather than a radically new procedure.

In his essay on the Oedipus myth Lévi-Strauss describes the structure of myth as a 'slated' structure which comes to the surface through a process of repetition. These slates are not, of course, entirely identical. Theoretically, an infinite number of slates can be generated, each one slightly different from the others; 'thus myth grows spiral-wise until the intellectual impulse which has produced it is exhausted' (p. 229; it should be borne in mind that 'myth' here means all the variants of the myth rather than a single embodiment of it). This concept of the slated structure of myth also has its parallel in critical theory, especially with regard to the plays of Shakespeare. The idea of the repetition of motifs with a slight difference each time is familiar in what is known as the 'imagery' approach. In fact the musical metaphor of the leitmotif is applied to the structural function of imagery by a number of writers.[23] A similar concept of structure appears in Francis Fergusson's idea of the 'analogical'-structure of the plays of Shakespeare. He shows in his essay on *Hamlet* in *The Idea of a Theater* that most of the events in the play could be interpreted as variations on the theme of finding the hidden imposthume in the kingdom of Denmark. These variations or analogies on the same theme are parallel to the repetition of a theme through the variants of a myth.

Levi-Strauss is, as I have pointed out, usually concerned with a set of myths each of which is a variant of the others. He suggests that this is necessary because a myth lacks the several 'levels' of variables which are to be found in a poem or play: semantic, phonetic, prosodic, etc. And since structural analysis can only proceed where there is a system of variables, one has to find these variables not within the particular embodiment of the myth, but in the multiplicity of versions of the same myth.[24] A work of art, on the other hand, is, in a loose sense, analogous to a *set* of myths and therefore can be analysed in isolation, as Lévi-Strauss demonstrates in the case of Baudelaire's 'Les Chats'. It should also be possible to apply this method of analysis to a number of plays as though they were variants of the same myth. This would be especially appropriate where certain themes and episodes recur in a writer's works, as they do in Shakespeare's. The purpose of such analysis would be to discover the fundamental 'contradictions' that the 'myth' of Shakespeare is trying to reconcile. It should also be possible to choose other 'sets' for analytical attention, depending on the kind of variables we are interested in. A 'set' could, for example, comprise works dealing with similar themes by different authors at one period of time, or different versions of a story over a length of time, considered synchronically rather than diachronically (i.e. in terms of influence), or a group of cultural objects in different media. However, there is very little in the way of such applications of Lévi-Strauss's ideas in the field of Shakespeare criticism. It is, nevertheless, interesting to note the parallels between some of these ideas and ideas already familiar in literary theory and practice.

Kenneth Burke's writings, in particular, contain many anticipations of Lévi-Strauss's ideas. For example, Burke draws attention to the similarity between the structure of music and myths and folk tales, a similarity which Lévi-Strauss brings out in far greater detail and with far greater ingenuity.[25] There is even greater similarity between the two with respect to their broader purpose. Both Burke and Lévi-Strauss are concerned with their respective fields of cultural study as aspects of symbol systems in general. Burke also supplies an interesting variation on the idea of myth as an attempt to overcome a contradiction. He suggests (as pointed out in Chapter 3) that a characteristic of the mythical mode of thought is 'the temporizing of essence', i.e. the projecting of a logical relationship as a temporal, causal one. By thus temporally projecting a logical problem (Lévi-Strauss's 'contradiction') one manages to 'transcend' it. As Burke puts it, '"transcendence" is the solving of the logical problem by stretching it out into a narrative arpeggio, whereby a conflicting element can be introduced as a "passing note", hence not felt as a "discord"'.[26] This can usefully supplement Lévi-Strauss's account of the way myths transcend logical or social contradictions, especially as Lévi-Strauss does not really take the temporality of the mythical structure into account. Moreover, the idea fits in with familiar literary and psychological notions about the way in which literary or artistic form gives one a sense of control over recalcitrant or disturbing emotions.

III

As suggested earlier, the use of what Eliot calls the 'mythical method' does not begin with Joyce's *Ulysses*, though in earlier writers, including Shakespeare, it is used in addition to the narrative method rather than as an alternative to it. Several examples of the kind of criticism which implies or assumes that Shakespeare consciously uses myths to unify his plays have already been given in Chapter 1—for example, Harold Fisch on *Antony and Cleopatra* and Richard Knowles on *As You Like It*. Even Wigston implies that Shakespeare (or rather Bacon) was aware of the true meaning of the Persephone and other myths and used these in a more significant manner than as mere local allusions. Some Christian critics also assume that Shakespeare makes conscious use of Biblical parallels. However, all these critics emphasize the thematic rather than the structural function of the mythical analogues, though it is not always easy to distinguish one from the other.

A particularly clear illustration of Shakespeare's use of myth as structural principle rather than thematic base can be seen in William Godshalk's article on *The Two Gentlemen of Verona*, where it is argued that the play has a 'masterful structure' created through a strategic distribution of allusions to classical myths. Godshalk points out allusions to the myths of Phaethon, Orpheus, Theseus and Ariadne, and Hero and Leander, all of which hint at a tragic outcome for the action in the play 'as the characters become partially or wholly identified with figures in the myths'. In this subtle way, according to Godshalk, 'Shakespeare builds up an almost subliminal sense of crisis, suspense and tension', this 'tragic innuendo' being 'the chief function of the structure of mythological allusion'.

Northrop Frye's Shakespearean criticism consists of three books, one on the comedies and romances, one on the tragedies and one on the problem plays. In addition, he has written numerous articles and brief discussions, including the brilliant essay 'The Argument of Comedy'. Frye has called himself an 'Odyssey' rather than an 'Iliad' critic, i.e. he is more interested in comedy and romance than in tragedy and irony.[27] Therefore it is not surprising that his most substantial contribution to Shakespeare criticism should be *A Natural Perspective*, his book on the comedies and the romances. The other two books, *Fools of Time* and *The Myth of Deliverance*, are also full of brilliant insights, but it seems to me that in them Frye's penchant for schematizing in triadic divisions all but overwhelms the ostensible subject matter.

Frye observes in *A Natural Perspective* that in the comedies and romances Shakespeare 'does not ask his audience to accept an illusion: he asks them to listen to the story'. The ability to listen to a story without asking too many questions is associated by Frye with a primitive response, though as a matter of fact such an uncritical response would be hard to find among actually primitive peoples. Shakespeare, according to Frye, manages to get this response from his audience because he avoids local or specialized details and works towards uncovering 'a primeval dramatic structure that practically anything in the shape of a human audience can respond to'.[28] This involves a deliberate revival of the archaic and the obsolete, and a considerable part of the book is devoted to illustrating such elements in the comedies and the romances. These archaic elements include motifs from folk tales, myths and folk rituals. In addition to his remarks on *A Comedy of Errors, Much Ado, All's Well*, and *The Merry Wives* already cited in Chapters 1 and 2, there are other examples of significance. In *Measure for Measure*, according to Frye, Isabella's chastity is a magical force, and the real problem of the play is not ethical but practical, namely how this magical force 'is going to rescue both the violated Julietta and the jilted Mariana as a result of being exposed to the solicitations of Angelo'. About *Cymbeline* Frye writes that it is not,

to put it mildly, a historical play: it is pure folk tale, featuring a cruel stepmother and her loutish son, a calumniated maiden, lost princes brought up in a cave by a foster father, a ring of recognition that works in reverse, villains displaying false trophies of adultery and faithful servants displaying equally false trophies of murder, along with a great firework display of dreams, prophecies, signs, portents, and wonders.[29]

Frye has similarly brought out the popular, folk-tale or mythical features in the other comedies and romances, but one cannot always agree with his view of the significance of these elements. *Measure for Measure*, for example, certainly has many folk-tale and mythical elements, but this is hardly sufficient ground for dismissing all discussions of the play as a problem comedy.

Frye's argument that Shakespeare's art, particularly in the comedies and the romances, is 'popular', 'conventional' and 'primitive' is, however, a valuable one insofar as it helps to correct the distortions of both naturalistic and formalist approaches. But in this respect his criticism represents a synthesis of earlier findings rather than a fresh departure, for, as shown in Chapter 1, source studies in the nineteenth century had already demonstrated the relationship of almost all the plays to myths or folk tales. Besides, several critics, including William Archer, Israel Gollancz, Freud and J. I. M. Stewart, argued that Shakespeare managed, even while using literary sources, to get to the bedrock of myth underlying those sources. In his emphasis on the conventional elements in Shakespeare, as mentioned earlier, Frye rather strikingly resembles E. E. Stoll. Shakespeare's deliberate use of conventional devices in the last plays was also shown by S. L. Bethell in his book on *The Winter's Tale* (1947), while his earlier book, *Shakespeare and the Popular Dramatic Tradition* (1944) was a more general study along similar lines. G. Wilson Knight's emphasis on the 'miraculous' elements in the plays, especially the romances, also anticipates Frye's shift from the naturalistic to the mythical. In his specific comments on *The Winter's Tale* and *The Tempest* too Frye owes a good deal to Wilson Knight and Colin Still.[30]

Frye has been justly admired for his brilliant local insights, most of which have to do with establishing unexpected connections between the plays and more primitive forms such as myths and folk tales. As these insights are usually built upon the foundation of earlier source studies, to praise him for the insights while dismissing his system, as Frank Kermode, Reuben Arthur Brower and some others have done, is to give him little credit.[31] As it turns out, the two comments that Brower selects for praise in his review of *A Natural Perspective*, namely a comparison of some episodes in *The Tempest* with the ordeals of Aeneas and the description of the structure of *A Comedy of Errors* as a metamorphosis structure, are not really original. Both Wigston and Colin Still refer to the

Aeneid in connection with *The Tempest*, and the metamorphosis structure of *A Comedy of Errors* is related to the theme of loss and recovery or of separation and reconciliation that earlier critics have seen in the play. As far as analysis of individual plays is concerned, Frye's criticism, in fact, breaks little new ground; his contribution mainly lies in the way he places these plays within larger generic structures, and those structures in turn within the still larger structure of the totality of literature.

Frye's description of the structure of Shakespearean comedy derives from the writings of the 'Cambridge' anthropologists and from van Gennep's description of passage rites, and it is similar in many respects to C. L. Barber's paradigm of festive comedy. Frye sees comedy in terms of a composite ritual which has three important phases: a period of preparation, a period of licence and confusion, and a period of festivity proper—the revel or *komos*. Corresponding to these three phases are the three stages of Shakespearean comedy: in the initial stage society is shown under the oppressive dominance of anti-comic persons or principles; this is followed by a temporary loss of identity suffered by the central characters, often symbolized by disguise; finally, there is rediscovery of identity, individual, erotic and social, usually symbolized by marriage. Frye sees the structure of Shakespearean tragedy as the reverse of the structure of comedy; instead of the drive towards identity there is a loss of identity, individual, erotic or social, and there are three main types of tragic structure corresponding to the three kinds of identity. The tragedy of order, which may also be described as 'the tragedy of the killing of the father', depicts the loss of social identity (e.g. *Julius Caesar, Macbeth* and *Hamlet*); the tragedy of passion or 'the tragedy of the sacrifice of the son' depicts the loss of dual or erotic identity (e.g. *Romeo and Juliet, Antony and Cleopatra, Troilus and Cressida* and *Coriolanus*); finally, 'the tragedy of the isolation of the spirit' presents the loss of individual identity (e.g. *Lear, Othello, Timon*). Frye goes on to state that there are two ruling conceptions in tragedy, the order of nature and the wheel of fortune. 'The order of nature provides the *data* of the human situation, the condition man accepts by getting born. The wheel of fortune supplies the *facta*, what he contributes by his own energy and will.' The former conception provides the ironic vision and the latter the heroic.[32] This in turn fits in very neatly into Frye's schema (presented in the third essay of the

Anatomy) of the four *mythoi* of spring, summer, autumn and winter, each of which is a polar opposite of another and moves in phases in a semi-circle between the other pair of polar opposites. Thus tragedy is the opposite of comedy but ranges between romance at one end and irony at the other.

The foregoing discussion shows very clearly Frye's characteristic tendency to lead the reader away from the individual work and into the verbal universe seen as a totality that is schematized in the *Anatomy*. There is no attempt to analyse in detail any single tragedy or comedy in the light of his description of the tragic and comic structures. Instead we are led into higher and higher realms of generality until we come to statements like the following: 'The mythical backbone of all literature is the cycle of nature, which rolls from birth to death and back again to rebirth'; or that Orpheus, the traditional literary symbol of the magical identity of man and nature, 'is the hero of all four romances'.[33] The trouble with the vision of the total verbal universe revealed to us by Frye is that our response to it is quite likely to be less profound than our response to the individual work. Frye's attempt to locate the structural principle of Shakespeare's plays in myth represents a process of *simplification* which is useful in identifying a work at the beginning of structural analysis, but such simplification, if it is not to be a distortion as well, must be supplemented by attention to the minute particulars of the individual work in its formal as well as its mimetic aspect. In other words our sense of the generic and timeless qualities of the work must be modified by an awareness of its historical context and its formal particularity. Like most myth critics, however, Frye emphasizes the general at the expense of the particular. He simplifies the individual work to such an extent that it loses all its complexity; on the other hand the general scheme presented in the *Anatomy* is so complex that only the reader with the mental agility to match Frye's can hold it all together in his mind. Frye's criticism of Shakespeare thus presents a rather remarkable and paradoxical case of oversimplification of the particular combined with over-elaboration of the general.

There have been some interesting applications of Lévi-Strauss's structuralist concepts to the play of Shakespeare, the most notable perhaps being Peter Anderson's study of the 'language of sacrifice' in *Julius Caesar* mentioned in Chapter 2. The idea of myth as a logical model for overcoming contradictions has also been used, though in a modified form, in a study of *King Lear* (see Chapter 2). Surprisingly, there seem to have been few attempts to apply his method of analysing myths, an essay by Jan Kott being the only example that I have come across. Kott attempts to study the different versions of the stories of Hamlet and Orestes so as to get to the basic tragic structure or 'model'. Just as, according to Lévi-Strauss, myth has its own 'unchanging structure' independent of its variable realizations, so also, according to Kott, tragedies can be reduced to a few basic models or unchanging structures. This is the process of structural analysis, which, in contrast to source studies, 'is an attempt to construct the model and define its variable realizations'. After this preliminary reference to Lévi-Strauss and structural analysis, Kott goes on to compare motifs from different versions of the Orestes legend and the story of Hamlet in a manner which does not, except cursorily, resemble Lévi-Strauss's analysis of myths. There are interesting points of comparison between Electra and Hamlet, and Electra and Ophelia, but Kott's model of tragedy seems to owe more to his interest in the question of choice and freedom and in the nature of the absurd than to the ideas of Lévi-Strauss. His conclusion is that 'the dramatic model of Hamlet-Orestes contains all human situations in which choice is enforced by the past, but has to be made on one's own responsibility, and on one's own account'.[34]

CHAPTER 5

Myth, Ritual and Society

The approaches to myth and ritual discussed so far emphasize their collective nature, but in all of them, with the exception of some of the theories discussed in Chapter 2, this collectivity is understood in an entirely non-historical sense. Jung's concept of a collective unconscious, Lévy-Bruhl's of a pre-logical primitive mentality, Cassirer's of a mythical consciousness, and even Lévi-Strauss's idea of a generalized human *esprit* are all non-historical concepts, purporting to explain a diversity of historical phenomena in terms of the working of an autonomous spirit or mind. On the other hand, the psychoanalysts seek to explain myth as but a fantasy shared by a large number of individual subjects. But myth is the expression of neither a transcendental or ahistorical subject, nor an individual subject, but rather of what Lucien Goldmann has termed a 'transindividual subject'. It therefore calls for a socio-historical approach. The advantage of such an approach to cultural creations like myth is obvious (and what is said here and throughout this chapter about myth also applies, more or less, to ritual. First, even the consciousness of the individual, certainly that part of it which is manifested in myth, is determined to a large extent by the social environment; second, although it may be possible to determine the structure of the human mind in the abstract, this structure can hardly be given an autonomous status without unwarranted reification, for it is, to quote Goldmann again, 'not an autonomous and active entity which holds man prisoner, but an *essential characteristic* of the activity of a subject'.[1] The universal mind is never known directly but only as it is mediated through the actions of individual and transindividual subjects. These actions are not, moreover, merely specific embodiments of universal structures, but are rather responses to specific problems in some specific time and place. Lévi-Strauss's interest in myths stems partly from the belief that as they are supposedly the most autonomous of cultural forms, if it could be shown that their autonomy is merely an illusion and that they are determined by fixed structural principles, then *a fortiori* all other cultural forms must be shown to be determined.[2] But the apparent freedom of myths is controlled not only by internal structural principles but also by several external factors, including material conditions of existence and ideological drives. There can therefore be no complete account of myth which disregards these factors.

There are several ways of looking at the role of myth in society, including the psychological, since it is through the individual consciousness that myth can have any social effect. According to Jung, myth is necessary for the health of any society since its function is to compensate for those aspects of experience which are vital for the growth of the personality but which are normally suppressed in modern societies. According to Joseph Campbell, the function of mythology is to alleviate the anxiety of the individual by constituting a 'second womb' for him. Clyde Kluckhohn has similarly argued that the function of myth as well as ritual is 'the gratification (most often in the negative form of anxiety reduction) of a large proportion of the individuals in a society.' By providing socially accepted channels for the expression of anxiety a mythology thus also ensures the solidarity of society. Theodor Reik had earlier discussed the social function of rituals from the viewpoint of psychoanalysis. Rituals, according to his theory, represent the sublimation and displacement of hostile impulses. For example, the function of the pseudo-maternal couvade, in which the husband goes through an act of sharing the labour pains of his wife, is primarily 'to protect the woman against the latent hostility and sexual aggression of the man'. It is easy to extend this to cover the function of myths, since they too are forms of symbolic actions. Another writer makes a correlation between characters in myths and the various identities whose struggle according to him constitutes the personality of the individual. Myth thus functions as a 'shaper of identities'. In society as well as in the life of the individual, the corpus of myths provides 'a set of possible programmatic identities', which the society and the individual imitate.[3] One could perhaps put it more simply by saying that myth provides a society with ideals to which it can aspire, though these ideals themselves are but the externalization of inner impulses. In the absence of adequate myths, individuals are compelled to search for their own inner identities rather than to identify with the ideals of the society.

The idea of myth is indeed closely linked to that of identity, both at the collective and the individual level. Identity is created by unifying experiences with reference to significant events in the past. In a sense, therefore, without myth the life of an individual as well as of a society is chaotic and fragmentary, since it is myth which provides this essential point of reference in the past. It was probably thinking along these lines that led to Schelling's argument, since repeated by numerous writers, that mythology could not have originated from a nation since a nation cannot exist without a mythology. Ernst Cassirer, from whom I have taken the reference to Schelling, writes:

The mythical-religious consciousness does not simply *follow* from the empirical content of the social form but is rather one of the most important *factors* of the feeling of community and social life. Myth itself is one of these spiritual syntheses through which a bond between 'I' and 'thou' is made possible, through which a definite unity and a definite contrast, a relation of kinship and a relation of tension, are created between the individual and the community.[4]

Similar views about the necessity of myth have been expressed by writers as diverse as Nietzsche, Yeats and T. S. Eliot. There are numerous other writers who attempt to relate the fragmentariness of modern life to the loss of the sustaining power of myth. Thus Philip Wheelwright, as pointed out earlier, feels that many of the ills of modern life are due to the loss of the transcendental and unifying function of myth, which has been replaced by the pseudo-collectivity of the mob united only by an ideology.[5] In other words, without myth a society does not possess a sense of identity and hence cannot, strictly speaking, be a society at all.

According to this view, then, it is myth which determines society rather than vice versa. It is a metaphysical theory of society rather than a sociological theory of myth that is being propounded. A people are united, not because of material circumstances but because they believe in a common mythology; it is this common mythology which makes them a coherent society or a nation. Mythology, according to Cassirer, is one of the modes in which the mythical consciousness is expressed. The essence of this consciousness is a feeling of the solidarity of all life in nature and society. It is, in fact, the essence of the religious experience as well. But if this feeling of the unity of all life were really one of the factors of social life, it would be difficult to explain why there are so many different societies and nations and so many mythologies, which are, moreover, usually hostile to each other. It is an empirical fact that mythologies separate as much as they unite nations and societies. The yearning for a lost paradise may be one of the important aspects of myths of all nations, but this can barely obscure their implicit or explicit recognition of the ordinary world of differences and enmities.

The coherence imparted by mythology to a group of people has been seen in two ways: either as the coherence of an 'organic community' or as the coherence of a nation-state. But both are examples of a 'spiritual' rather than a merely material unity. Also, a clear separation between the two is not always possible. Yeats's attempt to create a living myth for the people of Ireland on the basis of Irish folk tales and legends may be seen as an attempt towards the creation of an organic community as well as a unified nation-state. It has a political as well as a spiritual dimension. This is inevitably the case since a view of cultural unity presupposes a certain kind of political and economic structure, and political unity is usually based on, or supported by, appeals to the cultural unity of the people. In T..S. Eliot's announcement that he was a classicist in literature, anglo-catholic in religion, and royalist in politics there was a clear recognition of the interrelatedness of the three spheres, though he would probably have opposed their reduction to any one sphere.[6]

It is true, as we shall see, that mythology functions as a force of unity, but this does not justify the importance given to myth as the cause of unity and as something prior to society rather than as an expression of social needs. Such an overvaluation of mythology is misleading as well as dangerous. The most notorious example of a dangerous myth is, of course, the Nazi myth of the superior race. It was linked to the concept of the nation-state as well as to that of the organic community since it stressed, at least in theory, the 'organic' unity of a race that transcended national boundaries, the word 'organic' in this connection reassuming its original biological sense, so that an organic community became one which was held together by the biological bond of blood. But even in its less extreme forms the theory of the priority of myth over society is generally misleading. Thus myth is often defined as the transcendent perspective on human life. If this means nothing more than that a desire to transcend the barriers imposed on man because of his position in time and place is universal and fundamental, it can be accepted without hesitation. Myth expresses, according to this view, the fundamental and universal desire to transcend human barriers. But, apart from the inevitable barriers of death and diseases, the others have their origin in society, and hence the trancendence expressed in myth is the transcendence of social as much as of natural human limitations. To understand a myth, therefore, it would be necessary to place it in the context of its time and place and the social problems it is trying to resolve through imaginative transcendence. Besides, the shape that this transcendence takes, even when the problems are universal to humanity, is determined by the structure of society and serves a social function. It is when this fact is ignored, and stress is laid simultaneously on the autonomy of myth and on its role as a model for social action or organization, that it becomes a dangerous force. Not all models are designed for the improvement of society as a whole; some may seek, or in any case function, to maintain the status quo by giving priority to spiritual transcendence, while others may merely provide outlets for the anxieties of a group through the mechanism of the scapegoat. The only way to keep the undoubted power of myth in check is to recognize that, like other cultural forms, it too is a product of a particular time and place and has to be seen in this context.

The difference between the sociological and the metaphysical approach to myth is clearly brought out by the following example. We have seen that according to many writers modern society has lost its organic character and become fragmentary and chaotic because it has lost the sustaining power of myth. In other words it is myth which binds people together in an organic community. The idea that myth and an organic community are closely linked is also found among the sociologically oriented writers, but with a reversal of the causal sequence. For example, Christopher Caudwell argues that a living mythology arises from an organic, i.e. an undifferentiated, society. In other words it is an organic community that can create a living mythology rather than vice versa. Caudwell writes: 'The gods live for the primitive in the collective festival and the collective emotion. Because so little division of labour exists, because society is still so undifferentiated, the collective world of emotion in which the gods live penetrates every hour of the individual's life.' He goes on to argue that mythology is the opposite of religion because, unlike the latter, it demands no formal assent. This is so because it so 'interpenetrates the daily life of the primitive' that the question of belief does not arise:

Faith becomes necessary when mythology ossifies into 'true' religion. Faith and dogma are the signs of lack of faith and suspicion of doctrine. They show that mythology has in some way separated itself from society.

How has this come about? Only because society has separated itself from itself; because the matrix of religion has become only a part of society, standing in antagonism to the rest of society. Because of this, religion becomes isolated from the rest of society. 'True' religion marks the emergence of economic classes in society. The end of mythology as a developing thing is the end of undifferentiated tribal life.[7]

The desirability of an undifferentiated or organic life is thus widely shared. But whereas some would seek to bring it about by creating and propagating a unifying myth, others would argue that we must begin by recreating an organic community, since it is the decline of such a community that leads to the death of mythology. A corollary of this view would be that to seek the reinstatement of myth without first trying to change the structure of society would amount to obscurantism or 'mystification'. I believe that this would not be an unfair description of much of the modern interest in myth. Another way of describing the difference between the two approaches to myth is to examine the various senses of the term 'organic' as applied to a community. It will be found the sense varies from 'organic' as distinct from 'mechanical' or 'material' to 'organic' as the opposite of 'differentiated' or 'divided', especially on the basis of class. Among poets and literary critics, the former meaning of 'organic' is by far the more frequent.

So far we have discussed myth considered either as a cause or a product of an organic community. The term is, however, used in a more general sense to refer to the creation of any collectivity, whether 'organic' or not. E. M. W. Tillyard's definition will provide a convenient illustration. By the term myth, he writes:

I refer to the universal instinct of any human group, large or small, to invest, almost always unconsciously, certain stories or events or places or persons, real or fictional, with an uncommon significance; to turn them into instinctive centres of reference; to make among stories A, B, C, D, all roughly having the same theme or moral, *one*, and one only, the type. Made thus typical, the story becomes a communal possession, the agreed and classic embodiment of some way of thinking or feeling.

Thus defined, mythical literature (i.e. literature which draws upon some myth, or which has itself become mythical), since it is tied to the needs and aspirations of particular communities, is the very opposite of literature with a universal appeal.[8] This approach to myth and mythical literature becomes not merely appropriate but necessary when dealing with the myths of modern rather than primitive societies since we can assume, if only because of our inadequate knowledge of primitive societies, that the differences among modern societies are more important than, or at least as important as, the similarities, whereas the similarities among primitive societies are more marked. Even in the case of primitive societies, however, their myths have been studied in their concrete cultural and social context by several anthropologists.

The works of Bronislaw Malinowski provide an early and important example of this approach. His basic idea is that myth is neither symbolic-allegorical, nor explanatory, but, as he puts it, 'a pragmatic charter of primitive faith and moral wisdom'. Its function is to 'strengthen tradition and endow it with a greater value and prestige by tracing it back to a higher, better, more supernatural reality of initial events'. It is a 'constant by-product of living faith, which is in need of miracles; of sociological status, which demands precedent; of moral rule, which requires sanction'. Myth, then, is important not for its truth-value but for its pragmatic value. Further, myth is not, in Malinowski's view, merely the expression of an organic (i.e. 'undifferentiated') community. In fact, according to him, the role of myth is especially important on occasions of social strain, 'such as in matters of great difference in rank and power, matters of precedence and subordination, and unquestionably where profound historical changes have taken place'.[9] Myth, in other words, acts as a cohesive force in society through its unverifiable validation of the existing order of society, by invoking supernatural sanctions for material relations.

The function of myth as described by Malinowski thus relates myth to ideology. If the term ideology is taken in a broad sense, then of course this is a truism. But myth is ideological in a narrower sense as well, expressing the fundamental interests of the ruling classes or groups and working to justify and maintain the status quo or the existing social order. Karl Mannheim uses the term to refer to 'the total structure of the mind' of an epoch or a group, tracing the development of the concept from Kant's philosophy of consciousness, through Hegel and the Historical School, with their belief in the *Volksgeist*, to philosophies of 'the historical-social process', in which the concept of a homogeneous 'folk' is replaced by that of class divisions and hence class consciousness and ideology. As an expression of class consciousness, ideology presents a distortion of reality in the interests of that class or group. Another mode of thinking in which there is a distortion of reality is the 'utopian' mode, and Mannheim draws a sharp distinction between ideology and utopia. Though both attempt to transcend the social reality of the time, in ideology such ideas of transcendence are confined to a world beyond history and society. They therefore do not affect the status quo but actually give support to it. Utopia also reflects class consciousness, but instead of supporting the status quo it works in opposition to it and seeks to disintegrate it. Myths, according to Mannheim, are examples of wishful thinking and as such associated, along with fairy tales, otherworldly promises of religion, humanistic fantasies, and travel romances, with ideology rather than utopia.[10] As an ideological expression myth need not, of course, present class interests in a direct manner; it may not even be conscious of them as the interests of a specific class or group, seeing them only as part of an eternal and immutable 'natural' order, but in doing so it only serves to validate existing customs, institutions and privileges.

In contrast to Mannheim, Georges Sorel uses the term myth to refer to the activating force behind revolutionary movements. Myth, for him, is 'a means of acting on the present'. This view of myth stems from his belief that it presents an image or 'a body of images' capable of evoking sentiments which impel men to social action. But in a study of the relationship between 'myth' and 'ideology' as they are used in contemporary writings, Ben Halpern suggests that the apparently antithetical views of Mannheim and Sorel are so only on the surface and that at a deeper level there is agreement between the two. He defines this agreement thus: 'Myth, as the irrational pole of the origin and function of beliefs, is a zone of contact between irrational drives and rational communication—that is, we may add, it is an area where beliefs arise and social consensus is established; ideology, as the rational pole of the origin (moulding) and function of beliefs, is a zone of rational communication and social competition.'[11]

We can define the relationship between myth and ideology not merely in terms of rationality and irrationality, as Halpern suggests, but also, and more simply, with reference to their modes of expression. Ideology is discursive, whereas myth is imaginative and narrative. Most myths have an ideological function (either conservative or revolutionary, depending upon the definition of the term we choose), but in a sense myth *is* prior to ideology, as Halpern argues, since imagination may be said to be prior to reason, and images and stories make their impact more immediately than ideas. Moreover, it is difficult to refute a story or image. That is why mythology is the very foundation of all religions and dogmas. Conversely, most ideologies have a myth behind them, some temporal structure made up of events that are supposed to have taken place in the past and which directly explain or justify (and sometimes criticize) some aspects of the present. A myth, one can say, is the narrative or imagistic structure of an ideology, the 'mythos' behind the 'logos'. This is the sense in which Ian Watt, for example, has used the term with reference to *Robinson Crusoe*, explaining the book's popularity in terms of the mythical status of the hero: as *Homo economicus* he brings into focus the nascent ideology of economic individualism. Similarly the 'Tudor myth' was ideological insofar as it was designed to validate the Tudor claim to the throne.

This is not, however, the sense in which the term myth is generally used in literary criticism, where it is more common to find myth contrasted rather than compared with ideology. John Holloway has, it is true, used some of the insights of the functionalist approach to myth exemplified by Malinowski and others, but although he relates the function of literature in modern societies to that of myth in primitive cultures, this function is seen in a purely psychological way. Thus the function of literature, according to him, is to give a sense of power rather than knowledge; like myth it is 'fidejussive', not explanatory.[12] But Holloway explains this sense of power purely in universalist psychological terms, ignoring the possibility that it may be related to the historical context of the work as well as of the reader or audience. The psychological approach to the question of the function of myth and of mythical literature is, in fact, limited by its assumption, first, of an ahistorical subject, and second, of an integral society. Even Malinowski, who clearly recognized the ideological role of myth in primitive society, could not proceed from this to an analysis of myth in terms of its function in maintaining the privileges of a class or group, speaking only in holistic terms of social cohesion or equilibrium. In other words he is still limited by the holistic concept of the *Volksgeist*. Only thus could he see it as a positive force in primitive societies, for, once we realize that myth often serves to maintain the status quo (and it is usually a privileged class that seeks to do so), the proper approach to myth would be a neutral rather than a partisan one.

The ideological function of myth does not depend on any inherent quality in it, unless it be its capacity to sustain a wide variety of interpretations, for it is through these that the ideological potential of myth is most often realized. So long as a work has a mythical status, it invites ideological interpretations; conversely, such interpretations sustain, and sometimes even raise, the mythical status of a work. A myth gives imaginative expression to an ideology, but precisely because it is an *imaginative* expression there are bound to be differences over what the ideology is, since trying to discover it involves translating the myth's imaginative terms into discursive ones. The ideology discovered might therefore be as much the ideology of the interpreter as of the mythmaker. One finds an acute awareness of this in some recent criticism, where the ideology of the critic is as much in focus as the ideology of the writer.[13]

The most obvious ideological aspect of myth criticism is its anti-historicism. Myth critics are at pains to emphasize the universality of myth and of mythical literature. Along with this goes the tendency to stress various 'extraneous' aspects of literature—moral, psychological, and religious—without ever mentioning the socio-historical context. Northrop Frye's elaborate scheme in the *Anatomy of Criticism* seems to have been designed to disinfect literature of all taint of historical origin and social concern. Elsewhere he writes that the function of 'generic criticism' is to enable the structural critic (who is said to be concerned with 'such matters as myth and ritual') to get clear of the 'tyranny of historical categories'.[14] One can sympathize with this view insofar as it reflects a desire to escape from dreary historical studies of genres and styles, but the myth critic ignores the historical context of literature altogether, getting away from the tyranny of history only in order to be able to contemplate the world of struggling mortals from the serenity of Olympian heights.

The anti-historicism of the myth critic generally goes with a conservative socio-political outlook. Discussing the social function of the arts, Frye writes that it 'seems to be closely connected with visualizing the goal of work in human life. So in terms of significance, the central myth of art must be the vision of the end of social effort, the innocent world of fulfilled desires, the free human society.'[15] On the face of it this seems to ascribe to art a 'utopian' function in Mannheim's sense of the term, but it does not take into account the possibility that this 'vision' of the ideal life can serve as well to maintain the status quo in this world, leaving the world of fulfilled desires in the lap of the almighty. Whether it is 'ideological' in this sense or truly 'utopian' can be determined only in relation to the historical context of the individual work. A theory which does not recognize this has to be called 'ideological', even if the vision of literature and society presented by it be as attractive and liberal as Frye's.

The point may be clarified by approaching it from a slightly different angle. Frye insists upon the autonomy of art, and his theory is intended to establish criticism as an autonomous discipline. So long as the autonomy is insisted upon for pedagogic and methodological reasons it is quite understandable. But very often behind the cry for autonomy (though perhaps this does not apply to Frye) there is a desire to be left alone, not to be interfered with, to let things remain as they are. Is that why, as Frederick Crews suggests, the whole field of American studies is 'taciturn about such themes as racism, imperialism, and monopoly, but eloquent about myths, motifs, and morals—the Fulbrighter's stock-in-trade'?[16] Once we begin to discuss myth in its subjective aspect, as here or in Chapter 3, there is no option but to apply the same principles to the students of myth as to the creators. If myth implies an ideology, so does myth criticism.

II

Shakespeare, as we have seen, has been seen as a writer who not only draws upon the vital myths of his time but also creates his own myths. His works still have a mythical role in English culture (he is, after all, the first major poet, and the greatest, of English nationalism). Since even in primitive societies myths have an ideological function, it would be surprising if he were mythical solely by virtue of belonging to a supposedly organic community. It should be possible, therefore, to examine the ideological role of Shakespeare's plays-as-myths. As long as Shakespeare's works have a mythical status, ideological interpretations of them will continue to be a possibility. Conversely, ideological interpretations will continue to sustain the mythical status of the works, though in most cases the critic will not be conscious of the ideological content of his interpretation. As a matter of fact, in spite of the great variety of ideological interpretations of Shakespeare, there is very little criticism which makes conscious use of the sociological approach to myth to make the ideology explicit.

E. M. W. Tillyard's discussion of the use of the Tudor myth in the history plays of Shakespeare is one of the very few instances in Shakespeare criticism where the word myth has the sense of a story or a narration of historical events which serves to validate existing customs or institutions. Myth, in other words, becomes a synonym for ideologically distorted history. It might be argued that there is very little history that is not thus 'distorted' and that Tillyard's statement that 'the Elizabethans took history in a much less detached way than we do',[17] is an oversimplification of the difference between Elizabethan and modern historiography. Indeed it is now fairly common to point to the mythical aspects of the writings of historians like Spengler and Toynbee. Besides, to use the term myth for such ideologically distorted history is to obscure the distinction between two different concepts of time. It will be remembered that Cassirer made a distinction between the mythical and the historical concept of time: mythical time, or rather the time in which the events which the myth narrates are supposed to have taken place, is the time of the absolute past, the time of beginnings, and not the relative past of the historians. Among the aborigines of Australia, for example, it is believed that mythical events occurred in 'dream time'. Nevertheless, while it may be true that 'mythical' history is thus different from myth proper, it is at the same time similar with respect to the *function* that it performs within a particular culture, namely the validation of present institutions and customs with reference to events in the past. At any rate the term myth *is* used in this sense, and indeed for any idea that is considered to be subjectively motivated.

Tillyard suggests that the Tudor myth was actually made up of two interrelated myths. The first, which was derived from the shakiness of Henry VII's title to the English throne, is described as the 'Myth of Pedigree'. According to this myth, Henry was a direct descendant of Cadwallader and also, in a vague way, associated with the second coming of Arthur. The second myth, according to Tillyard, was that 'the Tudors had been divinely appointed to put an end to a long spell of civil war and to lead the country out of an unspeakable tyranny into happiness'. Tillyard argues that Shakespeare thoroughly imbibed the Tudor myth, both from popular sources and from the Chronicles of Hall, and that the first tetralogy of the history plays is founded on it. Aspects of the myth are also to be found in the second tetralogy, though there are other complicating factors in this group. But the first tetralogy can, according to Tillyard, be described as truly mythical in that it takes over and propagates a contemporary myth.[18] One could also introduce the concept of ritual here (although Tillyard does not do so) to bring out Shakespeare's individual contribution to the myth. A myth by itself is only potentially a cohesive and adaptive agent. It is its ritual enactment or recitation (or exegesis) that brings out its full power. Similarly, the historical myth concerning the rights and virtues of the Tudors becomes a truly potent unifying force in Elizabethan England only when enacted on the popular stage. The drama, in other words, performs the same function as ritual does in primitive society. And if we consider, as many scholars are now agreed, that Shakespeare may well have been an innovator in the field of historical plays, we would have to give him credit for bringing a national myth to a focal point in the communal consciousness. His role *vis à vis* the Tudor myth was thus not confined to mere passive acceptance of this myth and its transformation into drama, but was rather the much more active one of giving ritual form to it and thereby bringing out its full integrative power.

Critics are not in complete agreement, however, about Shakespeare's attitude to the Tudor myth. There are some who feel that Shakespeare's attitude is either ironic or ambivalent, especially in *Henry V*. Mention may be made here of two critics who hold views different from Tillyard's on the role of the Tudor myth in the history plays. In an unpublished doctoral dissertation, J. P. Brockbank agrees with the general argument advanced by Tillyard but introduces some qualifications. He argues that while Shakespeare's orthodoxy concerning the Tudor myth cannot be denied it must also be pointd out that 'he tested Hall's myth thoroughly and critically and did not accept it casually and passively'. More recently, Henry Ansgar Kelly has argued that in the histories, chronicles, and memoirs of the fifteenth and sixteenth centuries we can discern not one but three myths about the period of English history from the time of Richard II to that of Henry VII, namely the Yorkist myth, the Lancastrian myth and the Tudor myth proper. After a survey of these myths in a large body of historical works of the period, he discusses Shakespeare's relation to these three myths and comes to the following conclusion:

Shakespeare's great contribution was to unsynthesize the syntheses of his contemporaries and to unmoralize their moralizations. His genius for sounding the realities of human passion and action . . . enabled him to sort out the partisan layers that had been combined in rather ill-digested lumps in Hall and Holinshed and to distribute them to appropriate spokesmen. Thus the sentiments of the Lancastrian myth are spoken by Lancastrians, and opposing views are voiced by anti-Lancastrians and Yorkists. And the Tudor myth finds its fullest statement in the mouth of Henry Tudor. In this way Shakespeare often reproduced by instinct the viewpoints of fifteenth-century documents which for the most part were either completely unavailable to him or present only in their assimilated forms in the large compilations which he drew upon.[19]

In contrast to Tillyard, then, both Brockbank and Kelly suggest that the histories present a balanced critique of contemporary historical myths rather than a mere reflection of them, a view which certainly does greater justice to the complexity of Shakespeare's drama as well as to the complexity and diversity of ideological positions within Elizabethan society. Not 'myth-making', then, but 'critique of myth' would be a fairer description of the history plays, a conclusion in keeping with the analysis of Shakespeare's attitude to ritual and to mythical or magical thought in Chapters 2 and 3. At the same time perhaps it could be said that the plays performed the mythical function of integrating the community by giving powerful expression to the nascent nationalism of the age and its mystique of royalty.

As shown earlier, the idea of myth is often associated with that of the organic community, i.e. a community held together by a common mythology rather than by merely material needs and relations. According to T. S. Eliot the Elizabethan age lacked 'a coherent system of thought' such as Dante could take for granted,[20] and although Eliot stresses the point that this does not mean that Dante is necessarily a greater poet than Shakespeare, it is clear that his preference is for the kind of society in which Dante lived (which is in keeping with the neo-Christian reaction against the Renaissance). We could, I think, following common usage, though perhaps with some distortion of Eliot's views, substitute 'mythology' for 'system of thought', and say that for Eliot Elizabethan society did not form an organic community because it lacked a common mythology. Other writers, however, argue that Elizabethan society did form an organic community and that it was much closer to the Middle Ages than to these sadly secular times, even though it left much to be desired by way of a system of 'orderly and strong and beautiful' thought. They also argue that Shakespeare's greatness is to some extent related to his belonging to such an organic community. I shall mention just one critic to illustrate this view.

Philip Wheelwright, who has already been referred to more than once, laments the loss of the 'mythico-religious consciousness' without which society becomes a mere mob instead of a genuine community. The two aspects of the mythico-religious perspective are a sense of togetherness and a sense of a transcendental mystery. As I have indicated earlier, there is no necessary connection between even a genuine sense of togetherness (as opposed to mere collectivity) and a belief in what Wheelwright calls 'transcendental forces peering through the cracks of the visible universe'. The haunting awareness of these forces can very well go with the most ruthless exploitation and self-seeking; on the other hand, we have present-day examples of societies which do seem to have a genuine sense of togetherness without the transcendental awareness. Besides, when Wheelwright argues (like many others) that myth is essential to the poet because it provides a background of familiar references by which the sensibilities of the poet and his readers are oriented, it is not clear why this background of familiar references must be 'myth' in his sense and not just *any* body of accepted beliefs. Moreover, to consider the loss of a widely shared body of myths as the cause of the writer's alienation is to mistake the symptom for the disease. The loss of a common body of knowledge and beliefs, insofar as it is common, may be a consequence of other and more material factors, such as changes in the economic structure of the society.

I suggested in Chapter 3 that among literary critics myth is more often associated with a belief in transcendental forces than with 'organic' community in a material sense (as in Christopher Caudwell). This is brought out very clearly in Wheelwright's discussion of the myths of Shakespeare. Shakespeare, according to him, is great because even though in his time 'a more sophisticated attitude is beginning to set in', it has not yet made such headway as to 'drain the myths of all vitality'. These myths that Shakespeare could fall back upon, and which give unity to his work are 'the myth of love and the myth of divine and earthly governance'. There is a third 'myth' running through the works of Shakespeare, and that is 'the myth of tragedy itself'. We in the modern age have lost faith in the tragic myth and fallen back on the 'shabbier' myth of comedy. It is not clear what all this has got to do with the ills of contemporary society, but Wheelwright is obviously agitated about them. I would like to end this section with a slightly lengthy quotation from Wheelwright's essay because in its sustained irrelevance to Shakespearean tragedy and comedy and to the problems of modern society, it is, I suggest, symptomatic of a rather drastic form of contemporary mythomania:

We today have lost this sense of cyclical fulness and therewith of transcendental significance in human affairs; accordingly we no longer produce great tragedy because we no longer believe in the tragic myth. In its place we have substituted the shabbier myth of comedy, which Shakespeare utilized for a time and then, when it had lost its power to move him dramatically, unleashed his contempt by expressing it as the title of one of his worst plays, 'All's Well That Ends Well'. This wretched quartertruth is exploited in most of the novels and nearly all of the movies of our day—no longer as healthy comedy merely, but decked out with false sentimentality in the trappings that once belonged to tragedy. Our failure in tragic intuition, our substitution for it of bathos and business practicality in loose-wedded conjunction, is not the least among the disastrous factors of the contemporary world.[21]

So far I was discussing the concept of myth in its social aspect, but the function assigned to myth can also, *mutatis mutandis*, be considered as the function of ritual. One such function assigned to ritual and myth by anthropologists is, to quote the words of Clyde Kluckhohn again, 'the gratification (most often in the negative form of anxiety reduction) of a large proportion of the individuals in a society'. Even the Tudor myth as defined by Tillyard can be seen as a form of anxiety reduction since, as Tillyard points out, it was Henry's sense of the shakiness of his title to the throne that produced the myth. The function of myth as defined by Levi-Strauss, namely the overcoming of contradictions, can also be seen as one form of anxiety reduction, since all contradictions, even those of a logical and speculative nature, create mental tensions. Many of these contradictions, of course, are of a purely social nature. Kenneth Burke has used the concept of the scapegoat to analyse the ways in which a play attempts to resolve tensions which are either peculiar to a particular society or to human society in general. This, as I have suggested, is a more valuable application of the concept of ritual than the mere tracing of primitive ritual patterns in the plays.

Burke's analysis of *Coriolanus* is an example of this sociological extension of the concept of the scapegoat. He argues that since the play is a tragedy it is concerned with 'some notable form of victimage' imitated for 'the purgation, or edification of an audience'. All the elements in the play are to be seen as relating to the fulfilling of the expectations and desires aroused in the audience. These expectations and desires will be shaped by conditions within the play. 'But,' Burke writes, 'the topics exploited for persuasive purposes *within* the play will also have strategic relevance to kinds of "values" and "tensions" that prevail *outside* the play.' Burke goes on to define these tensions as related to the conflicting claims of nation, class, family and the individual, and suggests that although to some extent these conflicts are present in most societies, in Shakespeare's day they were felt more acutely because of such immediate events as the unrest caused by the Enclosure Acts, as well as because of the more gradual but still perceptible change from feudalism to nationalism.[22] Burke's historical analysis is meant to be suggestive rather than thorough, but I believe that he does suggest a valuable way of reconciling the Aristotelian concept of catharsis, the anthropological concept of the scapegoat ritual, and the socio-historical analysis of works of art.

One of the advantages of Burke's use of the scapegoat concept is that analysis based on it can avoid the charge of reductionism that is frequently levelled against myth and ritual critics, and not always without justice. One of the reasons why the latter are reductionist is that they approach myth and ritual in an entirely non-historical manner. The problems that the myths and rituals are concerned with are thus formulated in extremely general terms like death and rebirth, sacrifice for the propitiation of the gods, expulsion of evil, and so on. Burke suggests, on the other hand, that the evil which is sought to be purged through scapegoat rituals is not evil in general, but tensions and problems peculiar to a given society. Thus, where John Holloway has to 'reduce' the diversity of elements in the plays of Shakespeare to a basic pattern which he finds recurring in the major tragedies, namely the pattern of the increasing alienation and the final sacrifice of the tragic hero, Burke is able to relate this pattern of the scapegoat ritual to different tensions within the plays as well as in their society. In an analysis of *Othello*, for example, he argues that Iago, not Othello, is the 'katharma' or 'pharmakos', his function being to purge the tensions inherent in what he describes as 'a tragic trinity of ownership in the profoundest sense of ownership, the property in human affections, as fetishistically localized in the object of possession'. Similarly, he discusses *Julius Caesar* and *Antony and Cleopatra* in terms of tensions exploited by Shakespeare for cathartic effects.[23] Burke conceives the tensions as both socio-political and psychological, and in any case the line between the two cannot be easily drawn. His discussions tend to be suggestive and exploratory rather than well-researched papers. Moreover, his style has become more and more difficult and allusive, too caught up in his own terminological network for any particular article to be easily comprehensible in itself. Nevertheless, I believe that an extension of anthropological and psychological insights to literature in the manner suggested in his writings is the most useful way of looking at the relationship between literature, myth, ritual and society.

Conclusion

It is difficult to offer any simple concluding generalization about the achievements of 'the myth and ritual approach' to Shakespeare in view of the diversity of critical assumptions and strategies included under the term. What follows therefore is largely a recapitulation of the issues raised by the different kinds of criticism along with some tentative suggestions about the possibility of a synthesis.

The most common kind of myth criticism of Shakespeare, as we have seen, is concerned with relating the plays to some specific myths or, more frequently, to a universal paradigm or 'monomyth' which is seen as expressing such 'timeless themes' as death and rebirth, the loss and recovery of paradise, the disruption of an original harmony or unity followed by the achievement of a higher unity, the cycle of the seasons, loss and recovery, and estrangement and reconciliation. Northrop Frye too sees Shakespeare in the light of a monomyth whose theme he defines as the loss and recovery of identity. His main difference from the allegorical critics lies in the fact that he divests myth and ritual of their extra-literary associations, considering them purely as principles of literary structure and using the monomyth without any 'oracular harrumph' as a sort of 'fiction' to organize the whole of literature. But the oracular harrumph is not quite inaudible in his criticism either.

Although such criticism does usually have as its foundation some causal hypothesis about the origin of art in myths and rituals or in the collective unconscious, such hypotheses are generally used, as R. S. Crane has pointed out, as 'validating principles for the method in general rather than as premises to be invoked in support of particular interpretations'.[1] In practice such criticism avoids the question of origins and sources altogether, something which Northrop Frye defends theoretically by arguing for the autonomy of criticism, i.e. for the position that criticism derives its principles from literature, not from other disciplines. But in the absence of any causal hypothesis such criticism becomes, according to Crane, merely analogical and hence ultimately arbitrary, a charge whose justness is well borne out by the criticism surveyed in Chapter 1. Nothing can prevent one from seeing quincunxes everywhere if one is determined to do so, and much of this criticism is of the type practised by Shakespeare's Fluellen in *Henry V*: 'There is a river in Macedon; and there is also moreover a river at Monmouth... and there is salmons in both... for there is a figure in all things' (IV. vii. 24).

The arbitrariness, even wildness, of some of the analogizing does not, however, invalidate the method, as Crane himself admits, for that would be to invalidate all 'interpretation' (as opposed to the kind of structural analysis favoured by Crane), interpretation being, like poetry itself, 'ultimately metaphorical and symbolic'.[2] One cannot think of any 'objective' and 'non-metaphorical' (i.e. Aristotelian) analysis of the structure of a work that makes it reverberate or resonate beyond itself as the best of myth criticism can. The pointing out of the mythical analogy results in 'the dawning of a perspective' in which the reader just cannot ignore the connection between the work and its mythical analogues, though it must be admitted that such cases are rather rare in the myth criticism of Shakespeare. Further, in spite of the fact that the individual analyses of the plays may be weak or far-fetched, the cumulative effect of the criticism surveyed is to place Shakespeare in relation to a wider tradition.

This centrifugal pull outwards from the individual work has, however, to be balanced by a centripetal movement towards its unique particularity. It is not enough to show a connection between Shakespeare's plays and some mythical or archetypal pattern; one must also show how this pattern is used by Shakespeare, for often the plays present ironic rather than straight versions of the myths or play strange variations on them. They are thus not merely mythical but also critiques of myth, a fact which is also reflected in the mixture of realism and fantasy in the content and of naturalism and convention in the dramaturgy. The world-wide dramatic tradition also ought to be defined in more specific terms than moral or psychological universals, which are often defined in such general terms as to be banal. Perhaps what is needed is a shifting of focus from structure back to history once more, for there is much work still to be done on sources, influences and diffusion, particularly in regard to prose tales in Arabic and

Sanskrit. Such research would give a historical underpinning to the comparativist work of the myth critic and place Shakespeare in a more sharply defined tradition than Frye's human apocalypse.

In the case of ritual criticism too there is need to relate the broad ritual patterns to the specificities of Shakespeare's art and culture. The works of C. L. Barber, Marjorie Garber and Edward Berry have already shown how this can be done, and in fact the tradition of criticism coming down from E. K. Chambers and Janet Spens to C. L. Barber and Robert Weimann is one of the strongest traditions of Shakespeare criticism. The work of Mikhail Bakhtin has given a new dimension to ritual criticism by shifting the focus decisively from the broadly conservative figure of the hero as scapegoat to the more subversive figure of Carnival, though one must point out that more empirical studies of popular culture have shown that carnival does not always represent social protest.[3] The question of the social role of Shakespeare's plays as rituals thus remains an open one: one cannot say whether in general the rituals work to ensure readjustment to society or whether they are intended to transform society, for this is a question that will have to be asked in the case of each play, and a lot of work still needs to be done in this direction. One point that has emerged from the ritual criticism of Shakespeare is that it is too simplistic to talk about ritual in the plays without also discussing Shakespare's attitude to ritual. Among the critics who have addressed themselves to this question the consensus seems to be that Shakespeare's plays are better seen as critiques of ritual rather than as themselves ritualistic. We see a similar view emerging with regard to Shakespeare's attitude to myth, whether we take the term in the sense of a story of universal appeal or in the sense of a reflection of a higher reality. In either case we see Shakespeare maintaining a delicate balance between scepticism and faith, between engagement and detachment.

The ideas of Cassirer and Lévi-Strauss have not had the kind of direct impact on the criticism of Shakespeare that the ideas of Frazer and Jung have had, though Cassirer has certainly been very influential at the theoretical level. It is perhaps also the case that this influence is not as visible in specifically mythic criticism of Shakespeare as in other kinds of criticism, for criticism using Lévi-Strauss's method of analysis is not necessarily classifiable as 'myth criticism'. The idea of myth as a logical model designed to overcome a contradiction is, of course, an extremely suggestive one and can be linked to the Marxist analysis of social contradictions as well as to the Freudian analysis of psychological conflicts. The analogy between myth and art here gives us the picture of the artist as a mythmaker trying to resolve contradictions in the manner of myths, with the critic trying to deconstruct the artist's synthesis to reveal these hidden contradictions.

The sociological approach to myth has not found much favour among the critics of Shakespeare. If the approach discussed in Chapter 1 represents one pole of myth criticism, the socio-historical approach represents the other, and the ideal myth criticism would be a synthesis of the two. While the defect of the first approach is excessive generalization, often amounting to vapidity, the wider cross-cultural perspective is also its strength, for one has to see Shakespeare as equally of an age and for all time. Similarly, there has to be a synthesis of the general and the particular at the level of formal criticism, a synthesis, as to speak, of the methods of Northrop Frye and R. S. Crane, so that we can see the work both in relation to other works and in all its unique particularity.

The fact that the socio-historical approach to myth has not been popular among the majority of the myth critics of Shakespeare may be a reflection of the ideological orientation of these critics. An exclusive focus on the transcendent and the universal often goes with a conservative or reactionary ideology. This is probably true of most of the critics discussed in this book, though the statement needs to be modified and complicated a bit. The immediate background for the major tradition of myth criticism of Shakespeare was the growth of Indo-European philology and comparative mythology. In England interest in these areas was generally confined to amateur and eccentric scholars, including retired civil servants, and reflected a paternalistic attitude towards Indian culture and civilization. Nevertheless, the cross-cultural perspective it opened up had a subversive potential, especially where a writer like Shakespeare was concerned, for he had become the central instrument in the policy to civilize the colonies through English, and his Indian connection must have been a source of embarrassment to imperialist attitudes and assumptions. This was probably one of the reasons for the marginalization of such interests and studies.

The final point that I have to make is even more conjectural than the previous one. Broadly speaking, as we have seen, 'myth' in contemporary literary criticism still primarily has the honorific sense of a story which conceals a profound and universal truth. Very often the idea is given greater complexity by insisting that this truth could not be conveyed in any other way, myth being, in this respect, different from allegory. But this does not prevent the critic from allegorizing the myth. In fact the more 'mythical' a work of art in this sense, the more numerous are the possibilities of allegorical interpretaions. Perhaps the converse is even truer, namely the more numerous the possibilities of allegorical interpretation, the higher the mythical status of the work. Clearly Shakespeare is mythical in this sense, having undergone so many transformations during the last four hundred years. It is hardly surprising that even so protean a concept as myth is unable to catch the even more protean, shape-shifting genius of Shakespeare.

Shakespeare may be thought of as mythical in another sense. In the light of our knowledge of the social role of myth and ritual in primitive cultures it is possible to argue that his plays have a mythic role in British society. There is of course the obvious way in which Shakespeare can be seen as a culture-hero. But his plays may be said to be mythical in yet another way. Every community or nation has its body of myths which gives it its sense of identity and purpose. These myths may be in the form of stories about gods or they may appear as just distorted history, but in either case the purpose is the same. It seems that the way the British see themselves, which includes the way they see their past, has been greatly influenced by Shakespeare's version of English history, though very few critics apart from G. Wilson Knight have dwelt on this aspect of Shakespeare. It is perhaps not an exaggeration to say that he is the first poet of English, even British, nationalism. In the battlefield of Agincourt and in the prophetic vision of Cranmer inspired by the infant Elizabeth we see, as it were, the birth of a new nation. The history plays thus express the national identity of the English, their sense of who they are and whence they have come. At the present time, when British society is going through a period of ideological reorientation after the decline of colonialism, it is not surprising that the canonical status of all major writers, including Shakespeare, should be questioned, or rather, more precisely, that the established evaluations of these writers should be questioned. But few will doubt the ability of this supremely protean genius to assume a shape more congenial to the spirit of the times.

Notes

Citations have been given in abbreviated form in the Notes. For details the reader should refer to the relevant section of the Bibliography. The roman numeral within brackets at the end of a note or after a group of references indicates the section of the Bibliography where the relevant entry or entries can be found. Where several items from the same section are cited in a note, this number follows the last such item to be mentioned. Section 3 of the Bibliography lists items under the individual works that they refer to, and the works have been arranged alphabetically. No page reference is given in the Notes in the case of a reference in the text to a brief article, or where the reference is to the whole argument rather than to a specific passage. In such cases the reader should go directly to the relevant section of the Bibliography. In the case of a work cited frequently in the text, page references are given there in parentheses immediately after the passage cited.

INTRODUCTION

1. Herbert Weisinger and Harry Levin have written essays with identical titles: 'Some Meanings of Myth'. Weisinger's essay can be found in *The Agony and the Triumph*, and Levin's in *Refractions* (I). See also the following: Haskell M. Block, 'Cultural Anthropology and Contemporary Literary Criticism', *Journal of Aesthetics and Art Criticism*, 11 (1952), 46–54; reprinted in Vickery (1966), pp. 129–36 (I); Daniel Russell Brown, 'A Look at Archetypal Criticism', *Journal of Aesthetics and Art Criticism*, 28 (1969–70), 465–72; Ruby Cohn, 'Myth about Myths', *Modern Drama*, 12 (1969), 319–23; W. W. Douglas, 'The Meanings of "Myth" in Modern Criticism', *Modern Philology*, 50 (1953), 232–42; reprinted in Vickery, pp. 119–28; O. B. Hardison, Jr, 'Symbol and Myth: More Questions than Answers', *Bucknell Review*, 12 (1964), 17–28; E. W. Herd, 'Myth Criticism: Limitations and Possibilities', *Mosaic*, 2 (1969), 69–77; C. S. Lewis, 'The Anthropological Approach', in *Selected Essays by C. S. Lewis*, edited by Walter Hooper, (London, 1969); Walter J. Ong, 'The Myth of Myth: Dialogue with the Unspoken', in *The Barbarian Within and Other Fugitive Essays* (New York, 1962); Donald A. Stauffer, 'The Modern Myth of the

Modern Myth', in *English Institute Essays, 1947* (New York, 1948), pp. 23–49; and William Troy, 'A Note on Myth' and 'Myth, Method, and the Future', in *Selected Essays*, edited by Stanley Edgar Hyman (New Brunswick, 1967). For useful collections of essays on myth and literature see the entries under the following in Section I of the Bibliography: *Chimera*, Henry A. Murray, Thomas A. Sebeok, and John B. Vickery.
2. Weisinger (1957), p. 142 (II); Wimsatt and Brooks, p. 733; Crane, pp. 109–39, *passim* (I).
3. Weisinger (1964a), pp. 38–9, (1964b); Hapgood, p. 121 (II).
4. The term 'mythicist' is used by John W. Velz, p. 127 (II), and the other term by Lawrence J. Ross in a review of *Approaches to Shakespeare*, edited by Norman Rabkin, in *Shakespeare Quarterly*, 16 (1965), 358.
5. It may be clarified here that the terms 'myth criticism' and 'the myth and ritual approach' have been used throughout this book as convenient shorthands for some such expression as 'criticism that makes use of any of the several theories of myth or ritual'.
6. See Evans, p. 193 (II).
7. For a different classification see Percy Cohen, p. 338 (I).
8. See Chapter 4 for further discussion of this point.

Chapter 1

1. See J. A. Stewart, pp. 223, 235 (I).
2. See the chapters on the 'Physical' and the 'Encyclopedic' traditions in Seznec (I).
3. Seznec, p. 87.
4. See the essay 'The Biblical Origins and Patristic Development of Typology' in Lampe and Woollcombe (I). See also J. A. Stewart, pp. 226–30.
5. Quoted in Lampe and Woollcombe, p. 58.
6. See Smart, pp. 114–15 (I).
7. Cited in Lampe and Woollcombe, p. 36.
8. Ibid., pp. 32–3.
9. Ibid., p. 63.
10. Seznec, pp. 90 ff.
11. Ibid., pp. 98–9, 248, 315; Bush, p. 5 (I).
12. Cited in Hungerford, p. 57 (I).
13. Max Müller, pp. 69–73, 87–91, 110 (I).
14. Jung, V, 97–9, 132–41 (I). The reference to Rufus is in a footnote on p. 99.
15. Jung, XV, 80–1; VIII, 203; Levi-Strauss (1968), p. 65(I); see also his interview with George Steiner in *Encounter*, 26, no. 4 (April 1966), 32–8 (p. 35).

16. Jung, VIII, 213–14.
17. Freud, XIII, 149 (I).
18. Burke (1969), p. 220; Frye *Anatomy*, p. 89. See also Fletcher, p. 14 (I).
19. Still, pp. 4–6 (III). Still's study of *The Tempest* was first published in 1921 as *Shakespeare's Mystery Play*, but all references to Still are to *The Timeless Theme* (1936) which is an expanded version of the earlier study.
20. Ibid., Chapters 2 and 3, esp. pp. 21–3, 33.
21. Ibid., pp. 62 ff., 121, 135.
22. Knight (1933), pp. 70–6 (I); (1929), (II).
23. Frye, *Anatomy*, p. 90; Hathorn, p. 25 (I); James, p. 213 (II).
24. Honig, pp. 22–3 (I).
25. Knight (1936), 1964, p. 157; Frye (1965), p. 147 (II): Weisinger (1953), p. 10 (I). See also Lord Raglan, pp. 178–9 (I).
26. Wigston, pp. 190–2 (II). Unless otherwise stated, subsequent references to Wigston are to this book and are usually incorporated in the text. For Honigmann see under *The Winter's Tale* (III).
27. Paris, pp. 94–7 (II).
28. Knight (1932), 1971, p. 120; Frye (1965), pp. 77–8, 106–7 (II). For a discussion of the wandering in the wilderness as a part of the Eleusinian mysteries, see Colin Still, pp. 97ff.
29. *Shakespeare's Life and Art* (London, 1939), p. 71, cited in Tillyard (1965), pp. 210–11 (II). See also Brunvand (III).
30. Wigston, pp. 296–7, 343. See also Wigston (1888), pp. 130–2 (II). Line references are given throughout to the Tudor edition of Shakespeare, edited by Peter Alexander (1951); London, 1964.
31. Halliwell, *An Introduction to Shakespeare's 'Midsummer Night's Dream'* (London, 1841), p. 23. See also W. J. Thoms, *Three Notelets on Shakespeare* (London, 1859?); W. Bell, *Shakespeare's Puck and His Folklore*, 3 vols (London, 1852–64). Bell relates Puck to the 'universal deity Bog (whence the purely Eastern god Bacchus)', II, 343–4. See also the New Variorum edition of the play (reprinted New York, 1963), p. 307.
32. Nutt, p. 25, front and back inside covers (III).
33. Paris, pp. 106–9 (II).
34. Freud, 'The Theme of the Three Caskets', pp. 291–3, 296, 299 (I). See also Reik (1952) (I); Sinsheimer, Spivakovsky (III).
35. Reik, pp. 88–9, 96 (I); Holland (1964), p. 99 (II).
36. See note 34 above. See also the New Variorum edition of the play (reprinted New York, 1964), pp. 309–10, where passages from *The Wandering Jew* (1881) by M. D. Conway are cited.
37. Reik (1952), pp. 47–8, 55 (I); Sinsheimer, pp. 114–17 (III). See also Ruggles and Lewalski (III).
38. Arnold, esp. pp. 94 ff.; Paris, p. 106 (II).

39. Frye (1965), pp. 63–4 (II).
40. Lake, p. 310 (II).
41. Sennet, pp. 24, 38–40, 56–62, 92–7 (III).
42. Knowles, pp. 2–5, 9–12, 21 (III).
43. Lewalski, esp. pp. 169–70, 176–8 (III).
44. Frye (1965), p. 64; Lake, pp. 314–18; Lawrence, p. 33; Simrock, pp. 96–8 (II).
45. See esp. pp. 275, 279, 287–8 (III).
46. Knight, pp. 150 ff; Pogson, *Three Plays*, the Foreword and pp. 21–3, 38 (II).
47. Sachs, pp. 85–91 (I).
48. Matthews, pp. 14–15; Tillyard (1944), p. 267 (II).
49. p. 66 (I).
50. Goddard, pp. 39–40; Matthews, p. 171; Holland, p. 336 (II); Leech, pp. 90–4 (III).
51. See, for example, Heninger (III).
52. Bryant, pp. 21–5; Wickham, p. 179 (II). For the phrase 'Christian myth criticism' see Hyman, p. 29, under *Othello* (III).
53. Chapter 3, p. 46 (I).
54. Lings, pp. 18; 22 (II).
55. Maitra, pp. 93–103, 127 (II).
56. Knight (1947), 1969, Chapter 6, esp. p. 331 (II); Foakes, p. lxiv; Felperin, pp. 43–6 (III).
57. Wheelwright (1960), pp. 30–1; Frye, *Anatomy*, pp. 211–16 (I); Knight (1936), 1964, p. 157; Battenhouse, p. 91 (II).
58. Matthews, p. 171 (II).
59. Simrock, pp. 8–9 (II).
60. Heline, pp. 35–6 (III).
61. Maitra, p. 46; Pogson, *Three Plays*, p. 1 (II); Levin, p. 8 (III).
62. *The Academy*, 1 June 1871, pp. 277–9.
63. Fiske, pp. 195–6 (I); *Poet-Lore*, 1 (1889), 100–1; MacCurdy (III). See also Gollancz (III); Rank (1932), 1950, pp. 67–9 (I); and Holland (1966), p. 187 (II).
64. Murray, p. 41 (III).
65. See Hathorn, p. 262 (I).
66. Campbell, pp. 7 (footnote), 122–3, 328 (I).
67. Vannovsky, pp. 52, 86 (III).
68. Hathorn, pp. 146–7, 164, 173 (I).
69. Armens, pp. 14, 122, 146–8 (I).
70. Slochower, pp. 15, 155–7, 168–71 (I).
71. Winstanley, '*Othello*', pp. 12, 30–36, 50, 61ff.; see also her '*Macbeth*', pp. 3, 10, *passim* (III).
72. Brown, esp. pp. 149–51 (III); see also Battenhouse, Bryant (II); Heilman, Bethell (III).
73. Bodkin, pp. 217–24, 244–5 (I).

74. *In the East*, pp. 16–22 (II).
75. Matthews, p. 174 (II); Kaula, p. 116 (III).
76. Vol. 11 (1899), 109.
77. Creighton, pp. 7–8 (III).
78. 'The Theme of the Three Caskets', p. 300 (I).
79. Hiebel, p. 35 (II); Bickersteth, pp. 169–70 (III).
80. Stewart, p. 21 (II).
81. Lake, p. 307 (II).
82. Hathorn, pp. 177–93, 268 (I).
83. Matthews, p. 171 (II); Armens, pp. 174, 183 (I); Stevenson, p. 262 (III).
84. Quoted in the New Variorum edition of the play, (reprinted New York, 1963), pp. 398–9.
85. Sachs, *International Journal of Psychoanalysis*, 2 (1921), 98; Jekels, 'The Riddle of Shakespeare's Macbeth' (1917), 'The Psychology of the Festival of Christmas' (1936), in *Selected Papers* (I).
86. Matthews, pp. 165, 170 (II); Walker, pp. 55, 107–8, 195, 221 (III).
87. Goddard, pp. 498, 504, 520 (II); Holland (III); Morris, reported in *The Shakespeare Newsletter* (February, 1962), 3.
88. Frye (1965), p. 62 (II).
89. Warner; Waddington, pp. 210, 222–4; Fisch, pp. 59, 64 (III).
90. David M. Bergeron, 'Alchemy and *Timon of Athens*', *College Language Association Journal* (Morgan State College, Baltimore), 13 (1970), 364–73, reported in *The Shakespeare Newsletter* (February, 1971), 10.
91. Goddard, p. 623; Rank cited in Holland (1966), pp. 161–2 (II).
92. Bush, p. 85, Knight (1947), 1969, p. 30; Tillyard (1938), p. 26; Spens, pp. 101–2; James; Wincor (II).
93. Dowden, pp. 47–8 (II).
94. Weisinger (1957), p. 144; also 'Myth, Method, and Shakespeare', p. 48; Leavis, p. 344; Kermode, p. 256; Kott, p. 266; Edwards, p. 11; Hunter, p. 28 (II).
95. Knight (1967), pp. 306–7; (1947), 1969, pp. 14–17 (II). The copy of 'Marina', along with 'Thaisa' and some other material, has been deposited in the Shakespeare Memorial Library in the Central Reference Library, Birmingham.
96. Quoted by Sachs, p. 80 (I).
97. *In the East*, pp. 48, 53–5 (II).
98. Thorne, p. 146 (III).
99. Pogson, *Three Plays*, pp. 39–51, *passim* (II); Arnold, p. 512 (III).
100. Honigmann, pp. 33–6; Scott, pp. 411, 417 (III).
101. Bryant, pp. 211–14, 219; Hoeniger, pp. 11, 14; Thorne, p. 34 (III).
102. Hugo, quoted in the New Variorum *Tempest* (1892), pp. 357–8; Levey, p. 1 (III).

103. *Notes and Queries*, 3rd series, 6 (10 Septemebr 1864), 202; Grimm, quoted in the New Variorum *Tempest*, pp. 346–8; Newell, esp pp. 245–8; Allen (III).
104. Still, pp. 19ff., 70, 124, 240–1, *passim* (III). See also Wigston (1888), pp. 62–9, 156 (II).
105. Rosenheim, pp. 120–32 (I).
106. Butler and Fowler, p. 125 (III).
107. Wigston, pp. 10, 109–10; Knight (1955), pp. 30ff.; Fiedler, p. 48 (II); Frye (1963), pp. 92, 105 (I).
108. Eliade, pp. ix, 4 (I).
109. See the chapter on 'Myth' in Holland, esp. pp. 246–50 (I). For an explanation of 'resonance' in terms of Jungian theory and the concept of *dhvani* in Indian aesthetics, see Maitra, pp. 27–8 (II).
10. The following titles, for example, are listed under the 'Bacon-Shakespeare Controversy' in the catalogue of the Shakespeare Memorial Library, Birmingham, though not all of them are by Baconians: C. C. Cattell, *Shakespeare: Was he a Myth? Or, What did he Write?* (1880); J. A. Morgan, *The Shakespeare Myth* (1881); Ignatius Donnelly, 'The Shakespeare Myth' (1887); J. Watts de Peyster, *Was the Shakespeare, after all, a myth?* (1888); E. Durning-Lawrence, 'The Shakespeare Myth' (1912); Mary Rose, *Baconian Myths* (1913); Sydenham of Comte and H. C. Batchelor, 'The "Shakespeare" Myth: A Challenge' (1924); H. W. Wack, '"Shakespeare": Man—Mask—Myth?' (1930). While on the subject of bardolatry, mention ought to be made of the books by 'Clelia' (pseudonym of Charles Downing): *The Shakespearean Reconciliation* (1888); *God in Shakespeare* (1889); and *The Messiahship of Shakespeare* (1901). For Clelia, Shakespeare was none other than the Messiah himself.
11. Harbage (1964), (II). For discussion of the mythical or religious role given to Shakespeare see also Heilman; Wasserman; and Harbage (1966): 'The Myth of Perfection' (II).

Chapter 2

1. *The Religion of the Semites*, 1889 (London, 1894), p. 18.
2. For an account of the influence of *The Golden Bough* on modern poetry, see Vickery (1957) (I).
3. Frazer, Chapter 57, pp. 755–6 (I). For a critical account of Frazer as an anthropologist, see Leach (I).
4. *Themis*, pp. 42–5, 328; *Ancient Art and Ritual*, pp. 129, 206, 222 (I).
5. *Prolegomena*, p. 568 (I).
6. *Themis*, pp. 330–4. Some words which appear in Greek in the original passage have been transliterated.
7. Ibid., p. 341.

8. See Marienstras, Chapters 2–4 (II).
9. Hardison (1965), pp. 285–91 (I).
10. Turner, pp. 168–9 (I); Berry, pp. 14–17; Garber, pp. 5–13 (II). The passage from van Gennep is cited by Berry, pp. 14–15.
11. Barber, Chapter 1 (II).
12. Bakhtin, the Introduction, esp. pp. 6–8 (I).
13. Ibid., pp. 18–19, 273–5.
14. Turner, Chapters 3–5, esp. pp. 96, 129, 131–7.
15. Schechner (1966), pp. 26–39; (1970), p. 125 (I).
16. See, for example, Pickard-Cambridge, pp. 126–9 (I). For further arguments against Frazer and the ritual theory of myth see Evans Pritchard; Fontenrose; Kluckhohn; Lévi-Strauss (1963), pp. 232–; Schechner (1966); and the concluding chapter of Kirk (I). It may be mentioned here that of the four members of the so-called 'Cambridge School' (Jane Harrison, Gilbert Murray, A. B. Cook, and F. M. Cornford), Murray was actually an Oxford man.
17. Piaget, pp. 84–5 (I).
18. Piaget himself (ibid., pp. 197–8) draws attention to the similarities between the thought of the child and primitive modes of thought, though he dissociates his theory from any assumption of a 'collective unconscious'.
19. Fergusson, pp. 236–40 (I).
20. Garber, p. 26, *passim* (II).
21. Bakhtin, p. 275 (I); Bristol, Part IV, Chapters 10–12, esp. pp. 172, 18 200, 207–9 (II).
22. Knight (1936), 1964, p. 150 (II); Fergusson, pp. 113–19 (I); Holloway p. 176 (II).
23. Spens, pp. 33–8, 49 (II); Frye (1949), 85ff. (II).
24. Barber, pp. 205, 239, *passim*.
25. pp. 15–17, *passim*.
26. pp. 483–4, 489–90, 495 (III).
27. Cited by Velz, p. 162 (II).
28. Spens, p. 45; Barber, p. 194, note; Chapter 7, esp. pp. 166–8.
29. Tiddy, p. 126 (I); Spens, pp. 45–9; Barber, Chapter 9.
30. Montégut, cited in the New Variorum *Twelfth Night* (reprinted New York, 1964), pp. 382–3; Spens, pp. 41–3; Barber, Chapter 10 (I) Seiden, pp. 113–14 (III).
31. Frye (1949), p. 86; Maitra, p. 129 (II); Bryant, reported in *The Shakespeare Newsletter* (February 1971) p. 6.
32. See esp. pp. 245–6 (III).
33. La Guardia, pp. 70–1; Kernan, p. 3; Bevington, pp. 147–8, 172 (II).
34. Brockbank, p. 39; Burckhardt, pp. 157–8 (III). Perhaps it ought to be mentioned that in spite of the later date of this publication, it was Burckhardt who influenced La Guardia.

35. Rossiter, pp. 73–4 (III); see also Leech, p. 286 (I).
36. Walter Pater, *Appreciations*, pocket ed. (London, 1924), pp. 205–6; Tillyard (1944), p. 251; McCollom, pp. 447–8; Bryant, pp. 21–5 (II); Wilson (III).
37. Raglan, pp. 215–22 (I); Barber, Chapter 8, pp. 220–1; Bristol, pp. 204–7 (II); Wilson, p. 128 (III). Although Bristol does not explicitly say that the expulsion of Falstaff is aesthetically unsatisfactory, he does say that it leaves a piece of 'unfinished cultural and political business' at the end of the play (p. 207). For a general discussion of the ritual origins of the Fool, see, besides Raglan, Enid Welsford, Chapters 3–4 (I).
38. Stewart, p. 139 (II); Williams, esp. p. 363 (III).
39. Hapgood (1962), p. 120; Holloway, pp. 98, 120, 135 (II).
40. Hapgood (1965), pp. 494–6 (II).
41. Hapgood, ibid.; Desmonde (III).
42. Marienstras, Chapter 3 (II); Anderson, pp. 3–8, 11–12, 25; Stirling (III). For Lévi-Strauss on sacrifice see *The Savage Mind*, pp. 223–8 (I).
43. Fergusson, pp. 109–14 (I).
44. Ibid., pp. 117–19.
45. Montgomerie, pp. 220, 226; Morley, pp. 9–10, 18–22 (III).
46. Eckert, pp. 324–8, 336 (III).
47. Davidson, 118–22 (III).
48. Ibid., pp. 122–5, 129–32.
49. Hewitt, pp. 10–11, 15, 22 (II).
50. Empson, p. 157 (III).
51. Frost, pp. 577–80, 584; Mack, pp. 107–8; Stampfer, p. 10 (III); Bristol, pp. 209–13 (II).
52. Riley, pp. iii–v (III).
53. Ibid., pp. 188, 233.
54. Elliott, pp. 165–6 (I).
55. Burke (1966), p. 94 (I).
56. See esp., pp. 346–7, 358, 364 (III). Tinkler's 'savage humour' invites comparison as well as contrast with the carnival humour of Bakhtin.
57. Kermode (1967), p. 39 (I).
58. Heilman in Robertson, p. 45 (II); Wheelwright (1960), p. 12 (I).
59. Yeats, p. 241 (I).
60. Schechner (1970), p. 125 (I). Consider also Yeats's remark, made in 1899, that the theatre began in ritual and must return to it in order to be great again (Yeats, p. 170).

Chapter 3

1. *Symbolic Forms*, II, 17 (I). Unless otherwise stated, further references to Cassirer are to this work and are given after quotations in the text.

2. Bachelard, *The Psychoanalysis of Fire*, translated by Alan C. N. Ross (London, 1964); Jung, VII, 66–7 (I).
3. Lévy-Bruhl, pp. 7, 55, *passim* (I). It ought to be mentioned that Lévy-Bruhl's idea of 'mystic participation' is now generally discredited. Lévi-Strauss, for example, sees the supposed totemic 'identification' of the individual with the genus or species in terms of the logic of 'universalization and particularization'. See *The Savage Mind*, Chapter 6; p. 268 (I).
4. *Themis*, pp. xiii, 120–7 (I).
5. Cassirer, *Essay on Man*, pp. 81–2; *Symbolic Forms*, p. 192; Bidney, in Sebeok, pp. 13–14 (I).
6. See G. S. Kirk, p. 273; Wheelwright (1960), pp. 10–13 (I).
7. Kermode (1967), p. 39 (I); James, p. 245 (II).
8. See Caponigri, pp. 167–8; Chase (1948), p. 10; (1949), p. 78, *passim* (I).
9. Vico, para 409, p. 90 (I).
10. Chase (1948), p. 10; Raine, p. 109; Jung, the introductory essay in *Man and his Symbols* (I).
11. Burke (1966), p. 381 (I).
12. Kermode (1963), especially 'The Myth Kitty' and 'Northrop Frye' (I); see also Wallace W. Douglas, cited in note 1 to the Introduction.
13. See the chapter '*Paradise Lost* as Myth' in *Unpremeditated Verse: Feeling and Perception in 'Paradise Lost*' (Princeton, 1967).
14. Jones, pp. 59–60 (I).
15. Hapgood (1962), p. 123 (II).
16. Quoted by Cassirer in *Symbolic Forms*, p. 45.
17. Tillyard (1943), p. 77 (I).
18. Empson, p. 34; Fletcher, Chapter 4: 'Allegorical Causation: Magic and Ritual Forms'; Richard Levin, pp. 160–8, esp. p. 167 (I).
19. Stewart, pp. 93–4 (II); Badawi, pp. 43–5 (III).
20. Heilman, 'The Lear World', pp. 43–5 (III).
21. Mack, pp. 97, 115 (III).
22. James, pp. 213–14 (II).

Chapter 4

1. 'Mr Bennet and Mrs Brown', in *Collected Essays*, 4 vols (London, 1968), I, 320.
2. *Abstraction and Empathy*, translated by Michael Bullock (London, 1953), p. 15.
3. Eliot (1923), p. 483 (I).
4. (1969), p. 6 (I).
5. (1963), pp. 58–9, 63 (I).
6. *Anatomy*, pp. 359–60, 110 (I).

7. Ibid. pp. 341–2, 365–7.
8. (1964), pp. 28, 48, 51–5; *Anatomy*, p. 109 (I).
9. *Anatomy*, p. 106 (I); (1965), pp. 59, 61 (II); (1970), p. 63 (I).
10. For a definition of 'displacement' see *Anatomy*, p. 365.
11. (1965), pp. 53–4, 58–61 (II).
12. (1970), p. 63 (I).
13. Frye has been described as 'an anthropologically sophisticated E. E. Stoll' by Eastman, p. 381 (II).
14. Krieger, p. 29 (I).
15. (1965), p. 40 (II).
16. See for example the essay 'Myth, Poetry, and Philosophy' in Burke (1966) (I).
17. (1964), p. 105 (I).
18. *Anatomy*, pp. 43, 180.
19. (1965), pp. 116–17 (II). For Brower's comment see his review of this book in *Partisan Review*, 33 (1966), 132–6.
20. Crews (1970 b), p. 5 (I).
21. 'The Structural Study of Myth', in Lévi-Strauss (1963), pp. 211–14, 229 (I). The essay was first published in 1955 in Sebeok (I).
22. *The Wheel of Fire*, p. 3 (II).
23. Consider, for example, the use of the musical term in Caroline Spurgeon's *Leading Motives in the Imagery of Shakespeare's Tragedies* (London, 1930). It is significant that Lévi-Strauss greatly admires Wagner; see *The Raw and the Cooked*, p. 15 (I).
24. 'Les Chats', pp. 202–3 (I).
25. Compare Burke (1931), 1968, p. 36, and Lévi-Strauss (1970), the 'Overture' (I).
26. Burke (1941), 1957, p. 84 (I).
27. (1965), pp. 1–2 (II).
28. Ibid., pp. 12–13, 53, 58. For an amusing and instructive account of a far from uncritical response to the story of *Hamlet* by a tribal group in West Africa, see Laura Bohannan, 'Miching Mallecho, That Means Witchcraft', *London Magazine*, 1, no. 5 (June. 1954), 51–60.
29. (1965), pp. 64, 67 (II).
30. Compare for example, Frye's essay on *The Winter's Tale* in *Fables of Identity* with Knight's essay on the play in *The Crown of Life*.
31. Kermode (1963), 'Northrop Frye'; for Brower, see note 19 above.
32. (1965), pp. 73–8; (1967), pp. 5–6, 13–16, 35, 48–9 (II).
33. (1965), pp. 119, 147 (II).
34. Kott, pp. 304, 309–10, 313 (III).

Chapter 5

1. Goldmann, p. 903 (I).

2. *The Raw and the Cooked*, p. 10 (I).
3. Jung, the introductory essay in *Man and His Symbols*; Campbell, in Vickery (1966), p. 21; Kluckhohn, p. 57; Reik, *Ritual*, p. 56; Jerome S. Bruner, 'Myth and Identity', in Henry A. Murray, p. 281 (I).
4. *Symbolic Forms*, II, 177 (I).
5. See note 6 to Chapter 3.
6. *For Lancelot Andrewes: Essays on Style and Order* (London, 1938), p. ix.
7. Caudwell, pp. 35–7 (I).
8. Tillyard (1961), pp. 10, 13–15 (I).
9. Malinowski (1926), pp. 23, 79, 125 (I).
10. Mannheim, pp. 49–50, 57–60, 173, 184 (I).
11. Sorel, pp. 125-7; Halpern, p. 143 (I).
12. Holloway, p. 170 (II).
13. See, for example, Chris Baldick *The Social Mission of English Criticism* (Oxford University Press, 1983); *Political Shakespeare: New Essays in Cultural Materialism*, edited by Jonathan Dollimore and Alan Sinfield (Manchester, 1985); and Terence Hawkes, *That Shakespeherian Rag: Essays on a Critical Process* (London, 1986). The description of the relationship between myth and its ideological interpretation, it may be noted, restates Edwin Honig's description of the relationship between text and allegory cited in Chapter 1.
14. Frye (1951), p. 544 (I).
15. (1963), p. 18 (I).
16. Crews (1970a), p. 424 (I).
17. Tillyard (1961), p. 45 (I).
18. Ibid., pp. 48–9, 53, 61–3.
19. Kelly, pp. 304–5 (II); Brockbank (under *Henry VI*), p. 46 (III).
20. *Selected Essays*, p. 136 (I).
21. Wheelwright (1960), pp. 27–31 (I).
22. Burke (1966), pp. 81, 88–92 (I).
23. Burke (1964), pp. 153–4; (1966), pp. 102–5 (I).

Conclusion

1. Crane, p. 137 (I).
2. Ibid., p. 138.
3. See Peter Burke, pp. 199–204 (I).

Bibliography

Original dates of publication or composition, where these are different from those of the editions or reprints used, have been given in parentheses immediately after the titles of the works. Every work cited in abbreviated form in the Notes is cited in full here, but some books and articles cited in full in the Notes have not been included in the Bibliography, and some items listed here have not been cited in the Notes. The following abbreviations have been used:

SQ	Shakespeare Quarterly
ShS	Shakespeare Survey
ShakS	Shakespeare Studies

I. Myth, Ritual, Drama and Literature: Theoretical and Historical Works

Armens, Sven Magnus, *Archetypes of the Family in Literature*, Seattle, 1966

Bakhtin, Mikhail, *Rabelais and His World*, translated by Helene Iswolsky, Cambridge, Mass., and London, 1968

Baskervill, Charles Read, 'Dramatic Aspects of Medieval Folk Festivals in England', *Studies in Philology*, 17 (1920), 19–87

Bidney, David E., 'Myth, Symbolism, and Truth', in Sebeok, pp. 3–24; reprinted in Vickery (1966), pp. 3–13

———, 'The Philosophical Anthropology of Ernst Cassirer', in Schilpp, pp. 465–545, esp. Sections 8–17

Bodkin, Maud, *Archetypal Patterns in Poetry: Psychological Studies of Imagination* (1934), London, 1984

Brody, Alan, *The English Mummers and Their Plays: Traces of Ancient Mystery*, London, 1971

Burke, Kenneth, *Counter-Statement* (1931), Berkeley, 1968

———, *Philosophy of Literary Form: Studies in Symbolic Action* (1941), revised and abridged edition, New York, 1957.

———, *A Rhetoric of Motives* (1950), Berkeley, 1969

———, *Perspectives by Incongruity* and *Terms for Order*, edited by Stanley Edgar Hyman, Bloomington, 1964

———, *Language as Symbolic Action: Essays on Life, Literature, and Method*, Berkeley, 1966

Burke, Peter, *Popular Culture in Early Modern Europe* (1978), Aldershot, 1988, Chapter 7: 'The World of Carnival'

Bush, Douglas, *Pagan Myth and Christian Tradition in English Poetry*, Philadelphia, 1968

Campbell, Joseph, *The Hero with a Thousand Faces* (1949), New York, 1961

Caponigri, A. Robert, *Time and Idea: The Theory of History in Giambattista Vico*, Notre Dame, 1968: Chapter 9, 'Poetry, Myth and Language'

Cassirer, Ernst, *The Philosophy of Symbolic Forms*, 3 vols., translated by Ralph Manheim, New Haven, 1965: vol. II, *Mythical Thought*

———, *Language and Myth*, translated by Susanne K. Langer, New York, 1946

———, *An Essay on Man: An Introduction to a Philosophy of Human Culture*, New Haven, 1947

———, *The Myth of the State*, New Haven, 1946

Caudwell, Christopher, *Illusion and Reality: A Study of the Sources of Poetry*, London, 1946

Chambers, E. K., *The English Folk-Play*, London, 1933

Chase, Richard, 'Myth as Literature', in *English Institute Essays* (1947), New York, 1948, pp. 3–22

———, *Quest for Myth*, Baton Rouge, 1949

Chimera, 4, No. 3 (Spring 1946)

Cohen, Percy S., 'Theories of Myth', *Man*, 4 (1969), 337–53

Cornford, Francis Macdonald, *The Origin of Attic Comedy* (1914), edited by Theodor H. Gaster, Gloucester, Mass., 1968

Crane, R. S., *The Languages of Criticism and the Structure of Poetry* (1953), Toronto and Buffalo, 1970

Crews, Frederick, 'Do Literary Studies Have an Ideology', *PMLA*, 85 (1970a), 423–8

———, ed., *Psychoanalysis and Literary Process*, Cambridge, Mass., 1970b

Eliade, Mircea, *The Myth of the Eternal Return*, translated by Willard R. Trask, New York, 1965

Eliot, T. S, '*Ulysses*, Order and Myth', *The Dial*, 75 (1923), 480–3
——, *Selected Essays*, London, 1932
Elliott, Robert C., *The Power of Satire: Magic, Ritual, Art* (1960), Princeton, 1970
Empson, William, *Some Versions of Pastoral: A Study of the Pastoral Form in Literature* (1935), Harmondsworth, 1965
Evans-Pritchard, E. E., *Social Anthropology and Other Essays* (1951), New York, 1962: 'The Divine Kingship of the Shilluk of Nilotic Sudan', pp. 192–212
Fergusson, Francis, *The Idea of a Theater* (1949), Princeton, 1968
Fischer, Ernst, *The Necessity of Art: A Marxist Approach* (1959), translated by Anna Bostock, Harmondsworth, 1970
Fiske, John, *Myths and Myth-Makers: Old Tales and Superstitions Interpreted by Comparative Mythology*, London and Boston, 1873
Fletcher, Angus, *Allegory: The Theory of a Symbolic Mode*, Ithaca, 1964
Fontenrose, Joseph, *The Ritual Theory of Myth*, Berkeley and London, 1966
Frazer, James George, *The Golden Bough: A Study of Magic and Religion*, abridged edition (1922), St Martin's Library edition, London, 1963
Freud, Sigmund, *The Standard Edition of the Complete Psychological Works of Sigmund Freud*, edited by James Strachey and others, 24 vols, London, 1953–74
——, 'The Theme of the Three Caskets' (1913), XII, 289–302
——, *Totem and Taboo* (1913), XIII, 1–162
——, 'The "Uncanny"' (1919), XVII, 217–52
Frye, Northrop, 'A Conspectus of Dramatic Genres', *Kenyon Review*, 13 (1951), 543–62
——, *Anatomy of Criticism* (1957), Princeton, 1971
——, *Fables of Identity: Studies in Poetic Mythology*, New York, 1963
——, *The Educated Imagination*, Bloomington, 1964
——, 'Mythos and Logos', *Yearbook of Comparative and General Literature*, 18 (1969), 5–18
——, *The Stubborn Structure: Essays on Criticism and Society*, London, 1970
Gaster, Theodor H., *Thespis: Ritual, Myth and Drama in the Ancient Near East*, New York, 1950
Gennep, Arnold van, *The Rites of Passage* (1908), translated by

Monika B. Vizedom and Gabrielle L. Caffee, Chicago, 1960
Goldmann, Lucien, 'Ideology and Writing', *TLS*, 28 September 1967, pp. 903–5
Guépin, J.-P., *The Tragic Paradox: Myth and Ritual in Greek Tragedy*, Amsterdam, 1968
Halpern, Ben, '"Myth" and "Ideology" in Modern Usage', *History and Theory*, 1 (1960–1), 129–49
Hardison, O. B., Jr, *Christian Rite and Christian Drama in the Middle Ages*, Baltimore, 1965, esp. the Epilogue: 'A Note on the Continuity of Ritual Form in European Drama'
Harrison, Jane Ellen, *Prolegomena to the Study of Greek Religion*, (1903), Cambridge, 1922
———, *Themis: A Study of the Social Origins of Greek Religion* (1912), London, 1963
———, *Ancient Art and Ritual*, London, 1913
Hathorn, Richmond Y., *Tragedy, Myth, and Mystery*, Bloomington, 1963
Holland, Norman N., *The Dynamics of Literary Response*, New York, 1968
Honig, Edwin, *Dark Conceit: The Making of Allegory* (1959), New York, 1966
Hungerford, Edward B., *Shores of Darkness*, New York, 1963
Hyman, Stanley Edgar, 'Myth, Ritual, and Nonsense', *Kenyon Review*, 11 (1949), 455–75
Jekels, Ludwig, *Selected Papers*, London, 1952
Jones, Genesius, *Approach to the Purpose: A Study of the Poetry of T. S. Eliot*, London, 1964
Jung, C. G., *The Collected Works*, edited by Herbert Read, Michael Fordham and Gerhard Adler, 20 vols, London, 1953–79:
———, V: *Symbols of Transformations*, bound in two parts (1956)
———, VII: *Two Essays on Analytical Psychology* (1953)
———, VIII: *The Structure and Dynamics of the Psyche* (1960)
———, XI: *Psychology and Religion* (1958)
———, XV: *The Spirit in Man, Art and Literature* (1966)
———, 'Approaching the Unconscious', in *Man and His Symbols*, edited by C. G. Jung and M.-L. von Franz, London, 1964
Kermode, Frank, *Puzzles and Epiphanies*, London, 1963
———, *The Sense of an Ending: Studies in the Theory of Fiction*, New York, 1967
Kirk, G. S. *Myth: Its Meaning and Functions in Ancient and Other Cultures*, Cambridge, 1970

Kluckhohn, Clyde, 'Myths and Rituals: A General Theory', *Harvard Theological Review*, 35 (1942), 45–79; reprinted in abridged form in Vickery (1966), pp. 33–44

Knight, G. Wilson, *The Christian Renaissance*, Toronto, 1933

Krieger, Murray, ed., *Northrop Frye in Modern Criticism: Selected Papers from the English Institute*, New York, 1966

Lampe, G. W. H. and K. J. Woollcombe, *Essays on Typology* (Studies in Biblical Theology, 22), London, 1957

Langer, Susanne K., 'On Cassirer's Theory of Language and Myth', in Schilpp, pp. 379–400

Leach, Edmund, 'Frazer and Malinowski', *Encounter*, 25, no. 5 (November 1965), 24–36

Leech, Clifford, 'Document and Ritual', *Durham University Journal*, 30 (1937), 283–300

Levin, Harry, *Refractions: Essays on Comparative Literature*, New York, 1966

Levin, Richard, *The Multiple Plot in English Renaissance Drama*, Chicago and London, 1979

Lévi-Strauss, Claude, *Structural Anthropology*, translated by Claire Jacobson and Brooke Grundfest Schoepf, New York, 1963

———, *The Savage Mind*, London, 1968

———, *The Raw and the Cooked*, translated by John and Doreen Weightman, London, 1970

———, 'Charles Baudelaire's "Les Chats"', in *Structuralism: A Reader*, edited by Michael Lane, London, 1970, pp. 202–21

Lévy-Bruhl, Lucien, *Primitive Mentality*, translated by Lilian A. Clare, Boston, 1966

Malinowski, Bronislaw, *Myth in Primitive Psychology*, London, 1926

Mannheim, Karl, *Ideology and Utopia: An Introduction to the Sociology of Knowledge*, London, 1936

Max Müller, F., *Chips from a German Workshop*, vol. II, London, 1880

Murray, Gilbert, 'Excursus on the Ritual Forms Preserved in Greek Tragedy', in *Themis* by Jane Harrison, pp. 341–63

Murray, Henry A., ed., *Myth and Mythmaking*, New York, 1960

Nietzsche, Friedrich, *The Birth of Tragedy* and *The Genealogy of Morals*, translated by Francis Golffing, New York, 1956

Piaget, Jean, *Play, Dreams and Imitation in Childhood*, translated by C. Gattegno and F. M. Hodgson, London, 1951

Pickard-Cambridge, A. W., *Dithyramb Tragedy and Comedy*, 2nd ed., revised by T. B. L. Webster (1966), London, 1970

Raglan, Lord, *The Hero: A Study in Tradition, Myth, and Drama* (1936), London, 1949

Raine, Kathleen, *Defending Ancient Springs*, London, 1967

Rank, Otto, *The Myth of the Birth of the Hero* (1909), edited by Philip Freund, New York, 1959

———, *Psychology and the Soul* (1932), translated by William D. Turner, Philadelphia, 1950

Reik, Theodor, *Ritual: Psycho-Analytic Studies*, London, 1931

———, *The Secret Self: Psychoanalytic Experiences in Life and Literature*, New York, 1952

Rosenheim, Richard, *The Eternal Drama: A Comprehensive Treatise on the Syngenetic History of Humanity, Dramatics, and Theater*, New York, 1952

Rougemont, Denis de, *The Myths of Love*, translated by Richard Howard, London, 1964

Sachs, Hanns, *The Creative Unconscious*, Cambridge, Mass., 1951

Schechner, Richard, 'Approaches to Theory/Criticism', *Tulane Drama Review*, 10, no. 4 (Summer 1966), 20–53

———, 'Actuals: A Look into Performance Theory', in *The Rarer Action: Essays in Honour of Francis Fergusson*, edited by Alan Cheuse and Richard Koffler, New Brunswick, 1970, pp. 97–135

Schilpp, Paul Arthur, ed., *The Philosophy of Ernst Cassirer*, New York, 1958

Sebeok, Thomas A., ed., *Myth: A Symposium*, Bloomington, 1965 (first published in the Bibliographical and Special Series of the American Folklore Society, vol. 5, 1955)

Seznec, Jean, *The Survival of the Pagan Gods: The Mythological Tradition and its Place in Renaissance Humanism and Art*, translated by Barbara F. Sessions, New York, 1961

Shumaker, Wayne, *Literature and the Irrational: A Study in Anthropological Backgrounds*, Englewood Cliffs, 1960

Slochower, Harry, *Mythopoesis: Mythic Patterns in Literary Classics*, Detroit, 1970

Slote, Bernice, ed., *Myth and Symbol*, Lincoln, Nebraska, 1963

Smart. J. D. *The Interpretation of Scripture*, London, 1961

Sorel, Georges, *Reflections on Violence* (1908), translated by T. E. Hulme and J. Roth, New York, 1970

Stewart, J. A., *The Myths of Plato*, edited by G. R. Levy, London, 1960
Strelka, Joseph, ed., *Perspectives in Literary Symbolism* (*Yearbook of Comparative Criticism*, 1), University Park and London, 1968
Tiddy, R. J. E., *The Mummers' Play*, London, 1923
Tillich, Paul, 'The Religious Symbol', in *Myth and Symbol*, edited by F. W. Dillistone, London, 1966
Tillyard, E. M. W., *The Elizabethan World Picture*, London, 1943
———, *Some Mythical Elements in English Literature*, London, 1961
Tindall, William York, *The Literary Symbol* (1955), Bloomington, 1967
Turner, Victor, *The Ritual Process: Structure and Anti-Structure*, London, 1969
Vickery, John B., '*The Golden Bough* and Modern Poetry', *Journal of Aesthetics and Art Criticism*, 15 (1957), 271–88
———, ed., *Myth and Literature: Contemporary Theory and Practice*, Lincoln, 1966
Vico, Giambattista, *New Science*, translated by Thomas Goddard Bergin and Max Harold Fisch, abridged edition, New York, 1961
Watt, Ian, '*Robinson Crusoe* as a Myth', *Essays in Criticism*, 1 (1951), 95–119
Weisinger, Herbert, *Tragedy and the Paradox of the Fortunate Fall*, London, 1953
———, *The Agony and the Triumph: Papers on the Use and Abuse of Myth*, East Lansing, 1964
———, 'The Proper Study of Myth', *Centennial Review*, 12 (1968), 237–67
Welsford, Enid, *The Fool: His Social and Literary History*, London, 1935
Weston, Jessie L., *From Ritual to Romance*, London, 1920
Wheelwright, Philip, 'Notes on Mythopoeia', in Vickery (1966), pp. 59–66; originally published in *Sewanee Review*, 59 (1951), 574–91
———, 'Poetry, Myth, and Reality', in *The Language of Poetry*, edited by Allen Tate, New York, 1960
Wimsatt, William K., Jr and Cleanth Brooks, *Literary Criticism: A Short History* (1957), Calcutta, Bombay, New Delhi, 1964

Yeats, William Butler, *Essays and Introductions*, London, 1961

II. MYTH AND RITUAL IN SHAKESPEARE: GENERAL STUDIES

Arnold, Paul, 'Occultisme Elisabethain', *Cahiers du Sud*, 308, (1951), 88–101

Barber, Cesar L., *Shakespeare's Festive Comedy: A Study of Dramatic Form and its Relation to Social Custom* (1959), Princeton, 1972

Battenhouse, Roy W., *Shakespearean Tragedy: Its Art and its Christian Premises*, Bloomington and London, 1969

Berry, Edward, *Shakespeare's Comic Rites*, Cambridge, 1984

Bevington, David, *Action Is Eloquence: Shakespeare's Language of Gesture*, Cambridge, Mass., and London, 1984, Chapter 5: 'The Language of Ceremony', and Chapter 6: ' "Maimed Rites": Violated Ceremony in *Hamlet*'

Briggs, Katharine M., 'The Folds of Folklore', *ShS*, 17 (1964), 167–79

Bristol, Michael D., *Carnival and Theatre: Plebeian Culture and the Structure of Authority in Renaissance England*, New York and London, 1985

Bryant, J. A., *Hippolyta's View: Some Christian Aspects of Shakespeare's Plays*, Lexington, 1961

Bush, Douglas, 'Classical Myth in Shakespeare's Plays', in *Elizabethan and Jacobean Essays: Presented to Frank Percy Wilson in Honour of his Seventieth Birthday*, edited by Herbert Davis and Helen Gardner, Oxford, 1959, pp. 65–85

Dowden, Edward, *Shakespeare*, Literature Primer Series, London, 1895

Eastman, Arthur M., *A Short History of Shakespearean Criticism*, New York, 1968

Edwards, Philip, 'Shakespeare's Romances: 1900–1957', *ShS*, 11 (1958), 1–18

Evans, G. B. ed., *Shakespeare: Aspects of Influence* (Harvard English Studies 7), Cambridge, Mass., and London, 1976

Fiedler, Leslie A., 'Shakespeare and the Paradox of Illusion', in *No! in Thunder: Essays on Myth and Literature*, London, 1963, pp. 45–60; originally published as 'The Defense of Illusion and the Creation of Myth', in Robertson (II)

Frye, Northrop, 'The Argument of Comedy' (1949), in *Shakespeare: Modern Essays in Criticism*, edited by Leonard F. Dean,

New York, 1968, pp. 79–89; first published in Robertson (II)
———, *A Natural Perspective: The Development of Shakespearean Comedy and Romance*, New York, 1965
———, *Fools of Time: Studies in Shakespearean Tragedy*, London, 1967
———, *The Myth of Deliverance: Reflections on Shakespeare's Problem Comedies*, Brighton, 1983
Garber, Marjorie, *Coming of Age in Shakespeare*, London, 1981
Goddard, Harold C., *The Meaning of Shakespeare*, Chicago, 1951
Hapgood, Robert D., 'Shakespeare and the Ritualists', *ShS*, 15 (1962), 111–24
———, 'Shakespeare's Maimed Rites: The Early Tragedies', *Centennial Review*, 9 (1965), 494–508
Harbage, Alfred, 'Shakespeare as Culture Hero', *Huntington Library Quarterly*, 27 (1964), 211–27
———, *Conceptions of Shakespeare*, Cambridge, Mass., 1966
Heilman, Robert B., 'The Role We Give Shakespeare', in *Essays on Shakespeare*, edited by Gerald W. Chapman, Princeton, 1965, pp. 3–34
Hewitt, Douglas, 'The Very Pompes of the Divell—Popular and Folk Elements in Elizabethan and Jacobean Drama', *Review of English Studies*, 25 (1949), 10–23
Hiebel, F., *Shakespeare and the Awakening of Modern Consciousness*, translated by Barbara Betteridge, New York, 1940
Holland, Norman N., *The Shakespearean Imagination*, New York, 1964
———, *Psychoanalysis and Shakespeare*, New York, 1966
Holloway, John, *The Story of the Night: Studies in Shakespeare's Major Tragedies* (1961), London, 1965
Hunter, G. K., 'The Last Tragic Heroes', in *Later Shakespeare*, Stratford-upon-Avon Studies, 8, London, 1966, pp. 11–28
James, D. G., 'The Failure of the Ballad Makers', in *Scepticism and Poetry* (1937), London, 1960
Kelly, Henry Ansgar, *Divine Providence in the England of Shakespeare's Histories*, Cambridge, Mass., 1970
Kermode, Frank, *Shakespeare, Spenser, Donne: Renaissance Essays*, London, 1971
Kernan, Alvin, 'The Henriad: Shakespeare's Major History Plays', *Yale Review*, 59 (1969), 3–32
Knight, G. Wilson, 'Thaisa: An Essay on Myth and Allegory in Shakespeare's Final Plays' (*c.* 1928), unpublished; typescript

in the Shakespeare Memorial Library in the Central Reference Library, Birmingham

———, *Myth and Miracle: An Essay on the Mystic Symbolism of Shakespeare*, London, 1929; reprinted in *The Crown of Life*

———, *The Wheel of Fire: Essays in Interpretation of Shakespeare's Sombre Tragedies* (1930), London, 1970

———, *The Shakespearian Tempest* (1932), London, 1971

———, *Shakespearian Production*, London, 1964; incorporating the essays originally published as *Principles of Shakespearian Production* (1936)

———, *The Olive and the Sword: A Study of England's Shakespeare*, London, 1944

———, *The Crown of Life: Essays in Interpretation of Shakespeare's Final Plays* (1947), London, 1969

———, *The Mutual Flame: On Shakespeare's Sonnets and The Phoenix and the Turtle*, London, 1955

———, *The Sovereign Flower*, London, 1958

———, *Shakespeare and Religion*, London, 1967

Kott, Jan, *Shakespeare Our Contemporary* (1961), translated by Boleslaw Taborski (1964), London, 1970

La Guardia, Eric, 'Ceremony and History: The Problem of Symbol from *Richard II* to *Henry V*', in *Pacific Coast Studies in Shakespeare*, edited by Waldo F. McNeir and Thelma N. Greenfield, Eugene, Oregon, 1966, pp. 68–88

Lake, H. Coote, 'Some Folklore Incidents in Shakespeare', *Folk-Lore*, 39 (1928), 307–28

Lawrence, W. W., *Shakespeare's Problem Comedies*, New York, 1931

Leavis, F. R., 'The Criticism of Shakespeare's Last Plays: A Caveat', *Scrutiny*, 10 (1942), 339–45

Lings, Martin, *Shakespeare in the Light of Sacred Art*, London, 1966

McCollom, William G., 'Formalism and Illusion in Shakespearian Drama: 1595–1598', *Quarterly Journal of Speech*, 31 (1945), 446–53

Maitra, Sitansu, *Psychological Realism and Archetypes: The Trickster in Shakespeare*, Calcutta, 1967

Marienstras, Richard, *New Perspectives on the Shakespearean World*, translated by Janet Lloyd, Cambridge, 1985

Matthews, Honor, *Character and Symbol in Shakespeare's Plays*, London, 1962

Paris, Jean, *William Shakespeare*, translated by Richard Seaver, New York, 1960

Pogson, Beryl, *In the East My Pleasure Lies: An Esoteric Interpretation of Some Plays of Shakespeare*, London, 1963

———, *Three Plays by Shakespeare: An Esoteric Interpretation of 'Romeo and Juliet', 'All's Well' and 'The Winter's Tale'*, , London, 1963 (These two works are published in one volume but with separate pagination.)

Ribner, Irving, 'Shakespeare and Legendary History: *Lear* and *Cymbeline*', *SQ*, 7 (1956), 47–52

Robertson, D. A., ed., *Myth in the Later Plays of Shakespeare: English Institute Essays, 1948*, New York, 1949

Schueller, Herbert M., ed., *The Persistence of Shakespeare Idolatry: Essays in Honour of Robert W. Babcock*, Detroit, 1964

Simrock, M. Karl, *The Remarks of M. Karl Simrock on the Plots of Shakespeare's Plays*, with notes and additions by J. O Halliwell, London, 1850

Spens, Janet, *An Essay on Shakespeare's Relation to Tradition*, Oxford, 1916

Stewart, J. I. M., *Character and Motive in Shakespeare: Some Recent Appraisals Examined*, London, 1949

Tillyard, E. M. W., *Shakespeare's Last Plays* (1938), London, 1951

———, *Shakespeare's History Plays* (1944), London, 1969

———, *Shakespeare's Early Comedies*, London, 1965, esp. pp. 25–31, and the Appendix: 'The Fairytale Element in *The Taming of the Shrew*', pp. 209–16

Velz, John W.., *Shakespeare and the Classical Tradition: A Critical Guide to Commentary*, Minneapolis, 1968

Wasserman, Earl W., 'Shakespeare and the English Romantic Movement', in Schueller, pp. 77–104 (II)

Weimann, Robert, *Shakespeare and the Popular Tradition in the Theatre: Studies in the Social Dimension of Dramatic Form and Function* (German edition, 1967), edited by Robert Schwartz, Baltimore and London, 1978, esp. Chapters 1 and 2

Weisinger, Herbert, 'The Myth and Ritual Approach to Shakespearean Tragedy', *Centennial Review*, 1 (1957), 142–66; reprinted in *The Agony and the Triumph* (I)

———, 'An Examination of the Myth and Ritual Approach to Shakespeare', in Murray, Henry A. (I)

———, 'Myth, Method, and Shakespeare', *Journal of General*

Education, 16 (1964a), 29–49; reprinted in *The Agony and the Triumph* (I)

———, 'Myth and Ritual Approaches', *Shakespeare Newsletter* (April-May 1964b), 28–9

Wickham, Glynne, *Shakespeare's Dramatic Heritage: Collected Studies in Medieval, Tudor and Shakespearean Drama*, London, 1969

Wigston, W. F. C., *A New Study of Shakespeare: An inquiry into the connection of the plays and poems, with the origins of the classical drama, and with the Platonic philosophy, through the mysteries*, London, 1884

———, *Bacon, Shakespeare, and the Rosicrucians*, London, 1888

Wincor, Richard, 'Shakespeare's Festival Plays', *SQ*, 1 (1950), 219–40

III. Myth and Ritual in Shakespeare: Individual Works

All's Well That Ends Well

Calderwood, James L., 'Styles of Knowing in *All's Well*', *Modern Language Quarterly*, 25 (1964), 272–94

La Guardia, Eric, 'Chastity, Regeneration, and World Order in *All's Well That Ends Well*', in Slote (I), pp. 119–52

Antony and Cleopatra

Fisch, Harold, '*Antony and Cleopatra*: The Limits of Mythology', *ShS*, 23 (1970), 59–67

Waddington, Raymond B., '*Antony and Cleopatra*: "What Venus did with Mars"', *ShakS*, (1966), 210–27

Warner, Alan, 'A Note on *Antony and Cleopatra*', *English*, 11 (1957), 139–44

As You Like It

Knowles, Richard, 'Myth and Type in *As You Like It*', *ELH*, 33 (1966), 1–21

Sennet, M., *His Erring Pilgrimage: A New Interpretation of 'As You Like It'*, London, 1949

Coriolanus

Burke, Kenneth, 'Coriolanus—and the Delights of Faction', in *Language as Symbolic Action* (I); orig. printed in *Arts in Society*, 2, no. 3 (1963); reprinted in *Hudson Review*, 19 (1966), 185–202

Cymbeline

Thorne, Willam Barry, '*Cymbeline*: "Lopp'd Branches" and the Concept of Regeneration', *SQ*, 20 (1969), 143–59

Hamlet

Crane, William Ward, 'The Allegory in *Hamlet*', *Poet Lore*, 3 (1891), 565–9

Eckert, Charles W., 'The Festival Structure of the Orestes-Hamlet Tradition', *Comparative Literature*, 15 (1963), 321–37

Gollancz, Sir Israel, *The Sources of Hamlet: With an Essay on the Legend*, London, 1926

Korner, Sinclair, '*Hamlet* as Solar Myth', *Poet Lore*, 3 (1891), 214–16

Kott, Jan, 'Hamlet and Orestes', translated by Boleslaw Taborski, *PMLA*, 82 (1967), 303–13

MacCurdy, John T., 'Concerning Hamlet and Orestes', *Journal of Abnormal Psychology*, 13 (1918), 250–60

Montgomerie, William, 'Folk Play and Ritual in *Hamlet*', *Folk-Lore*, 67 (1956), 214–23

Morley, F. V., 'The Impersonal Hamlet', *University of Arizona Bulletin*, 30, no. 5 (July 1959)

Murray, Gilbert, 'Hamlet and Orestes', in *The Critical Performance*, edited by Stanley Edgar Hyman, New York, 1956; orig. published as the Annual Shakespeare Lecture of the British Academy, London, 1914

Paris, Jean, 'The Three Sons in *Hamlet*', *Atlantic Monthly*, 203 (June 1959), 68–76

Savage, Derek Stanley, 'Alchemy in Shakespeare's *Hamlet*: An Essay in Creative Interpretation', *The Aryan Path*, 33 (1952), 366–9

Taupin, René, 'The Myth of Hamlet in France in Mallarme's Generation', *Modern Language Quarterly*, 14 (1953), 432–57

Vannovsky, Alexander A., *The Path of Jesus from Judaism to Chris-*

tianity, as Conceived by Shakespeare: Disclosure of a Hidden Jewish Plot in Shakespeare's Tragedy 'Hamlet', Tokyo, 1962

Henry IV and Henry V

Auden, W. H , 'The Fallen City: Some Reflections on Shakespeare's *Henry IV*', *Encounter*, 13, no. 5 (November 1959), 21–31

Heath-Stubbs, John, 'The Mythology of Falstaff', *Occult Observer*, 1 (1949), 21–30

Williams, Philip, 'The Birth and Death of Falstaff Reconsidered', *SQ*, 8 (1957), 359–65

Wilson, J. Dover, *The Fortunes of Falstaff* (1943), London, 1944

Henry VI

Brockbank, J. P., 'Shakespeare's Historical Myth: A Study of Shakespeare's Adaptation of His Sources in Making the Plays of *Henry VI* and *Richard III*', unpublished Ph.D. dissertation, University of Cambridge, 1953

Burckhardt, Sigurd, '"I am but shadow of myself": Ceremony and Design in *1 Henry VI*', *Modern Language Quarterly*, 28 (1967), 139–58

Pratt, Samuel, 'Shakespeare and Humphrey Duke of Gloucester: A Study in Myth', *SQ*, 16 (1965), 201–16

Henry VIII

Felperin, Howard, 'Shakespeare's *Henry VIII*: History as Myth', *Studies in English Literature 1500–1900*, 6 (1966), 225–46

Foakes, R. A., Introduction to the Arden Edition, London, 1957, xv–lxvii

Julius Caesar

Anderson, Peter S., 'Shakespeare's *Caesar*: The Language of Sacrifice', *Comparative Drama*, 3 (1969), 3–26

Herbert, Edward T., 'Myth and Archetype in *Julius Caesar*', *Psychoanalytic Review*, 57 (1970), 303–8

Stirling, Brents, '"Or else this were a savage spectacle"', *PMLA*, 66 (1951), 765–74

King Lear

Bickersteth, Geoffrey L., 'The Golden World of *King Lear*', *Proceedings of the British Academy*, 32 (1946), 147–71
Creighton, Charles, *An Allegory of King Lear*, London, 1913
Davidson, Sarah Anne, 'King Lear, Scapegoat', *Vassar Journal of Undergraduate Studies*, 5 (1931), 117–36
Empson, William, 'Fool in *Lear*', in *The Structure of Complex Words*, London, 1951; orig. published in *Sewanee Review*, 57 (1949), 177–81
Frost, William, 'Shakespeare's Rituals and the Opening of *King Lear*', *Hudson Review*, 10 (1957–8), 577–85
Gollancz, Israel, Introduction to the Temple edition of *King Lear* (1895), London, 1898
Heilman, Robert, B., 'The Lear World' in Robertson, pp. 29–57 (II)
Mack, Maynard, *'King Lear' in Our Time*, London, 1966
Pauncz, Arpad, 'The Lear Complex in World Literature', *American Imago*, 11 (1954), 51–83
Ribner, Irving, see under *Cymbeline*
Riley, Michael Howard, 'Ritual and Hero in English Renaissance Tragedy', unpublished Ph.D. dissertation, Boston University, 1970
Stampfer, Judah, 'The Catharsis in *King Lear*', *ShS* 13 (1960), 1–10
Stevenson, Warren, 'Albany as Archetype in *King Lear*', *Modern Language Quarterly* 26 (1965), 257–64
Winstanley, Lilian, *'Macbeth', 'King Lear' and Contemporary History*, London, 1922

Macbeth

Badawi, M. M. 'Euphemism and Circumlocution in *Macbeth*', *Cairo Studies in English* (1960), 25–46
Holland, Norman, 'Macbeth as Hibernal Giant', *Literature and Psychology*, 10 (1960), 37–8
Rauber, D. F., 'Macbeth, Macbeth, Macbeth', *Criticism*, 11 (1969), 59–67
Walker, Roy, *The Time Is Free: A Study of Macbeth*, London, 1949
Winstanley, Lilian, See under *King Lear*

Measure for Measure

Nuttall, A. D., '*Measure for Measure*: Quid Pro Quo?', *ShakS*, 4 (1968), 231–51

The Merchant of Venice

Brody, Paula, 'Shylock's Omophagia: A Ritual Approach to *The Merchant of Venice*', *Literature and Psychology*, 17 (1967), 229–34

Heline, Theodore, *The Occult in Shakespeare: The Merchant of Venice*, New York. 1936

Lewalski, Barbara K., 'Biblical Allusion and Allegory in *The Merchant of Venice*', *SQ*, 13 (1962), 327–43

Midgley, Graham, '*The Merchant of Venice*: A Reconsideration', *Essays in Criticism*, 10 (1960), 117–33

Ruggles, Julia, *The Metaphysical Shakespeare: The Merchant of Venice*, Pasadena, Calif., 1908

Sinsheimer, Hermann, *Shylock: The History of a Character or the Myth of the Jew*, London, 1947

Spivakovsky, Erica, 'The Shylock Myth', *Chicago Jewish Forum*, 18 (1960), 131–4

The Merry Wives of Windsor

Steadman, John M., 'Falstaff as Actaeon: A Dramatic Emblem', *SQ*, 14 (1963), 231–44

A Midsummer-Night's Dream

Cambillard, C., 'Le Songe D'Une Nuit D'Été: Theme Astrologique', *Études Anglaises*, 3 (1939), 118–26

Fisher, Peter F., 'The Argument of *A Midsummer Night's Dream*', *SQ*, 8 (1957), 307–10

Korner, Sinclair, 'Solar Myth in *A Midsummer Night's Dream*', *Poet Lore*, 3 (1891), 17–20

Nutt, Alfred, *The Fairy Mythology of Shakespeare*, London, 1900

Robinson, James E., 'The Ritual and Rhetoric of *A Midsummer Night's Dream*', *PMLA*, 83 (1968), 380–91

Way, Arthur S., 'Relics of Ancient Aryan Folk-Lore in Shakespeare', *London Quarterly Review*, 105 (1906), 258–75

Othello

Bethell, S. L., 'Shakespeare's Imagery: The Diabolic Images in *Othello*', *ShS*, (1952), 62–80

Brown, Hugh, 'The Divine Drama', *Hibbert Journal*, 29 (1930–1), 134–51

Heilman, Robert B., *Magic in the Web: Action and Language in 'Othello'*, Lexington, 1956

Hyman, Stanley Edgar, *Iago: Some Approaches to the Illusion of His Motivation*, London, 1971

Kaula, David, 'Othello Possessed: Notes on Shakespeare's Use of Magic and Witchcraft', *ShakS*, 2 (1966), 112–32

Winstanley, Lilian, *'Othello' as the Tragedy of Italy*, London, 1924

Richard II

Heninger, S. K., 'The Sun-King Analogy in *Richard II*', *SQ*, 11 (1960), 319–27

Wilson, J. Dover, Introduction to *King Richard II*, Cambridge, 1939, pp. xiii-xvi

Richard III

Brockband, see under *Henry VI*

Leech, Clifford, 'Shakespeare, Cibber, and the Tudor Myth', in *Shakespearean Essays*, edited by Alvin Thaler and Norman Sanders, Knoxville, 1964, pp. 79–95

Rossiter, A. P., 'The Structure of *Richard the Third*', *Durham University Journal*, 31 (1938), 44–75

Romeo and Juliet

Archer, William, 'The Myth of Romeo and Juliet', *The National Review*, 4 (1884), 441–50

Heline, Theodore, *The Occult in Shakespeare: Romeo and Juliet*, New York, 1936

Levin, Harry, 'Form and Formality in *Romeo and Juliet*', *SQ*, 11 (1960), 3–11

The Taming of the Shrew

Brunvand, J. H., 'The Folktale Origin of *The Taming of the Shrew*', *SQ*, 17 (1966) 345–59

Thorne, William Barry, 'Folk Elements in *The Taming of the Shrew*', *Queen's Quarterly*, 75 (1968), 482–96

The Tempest

Allen, Don Cameron, *Image and Meaning: Metaphoric Traditions in Renaissance Poetry*, Baltimore, 1964, Chapter 3: 'William Shakespeare: *The Tempest*'

Baum, Bernard, '*Tempest* and *Hairy Ape*: The Literary Incarnation of Mythos', *Modern Language Quarterly*, 14 (1953), 258–73

Levey, Sivori, *The New Study of Shakespeare, No. 1: The Source of 'The Tempest': A Suggestion*, London [1921]

Newell, W. W., 'Sources of Shakespeare's *The Tempest*', *Journal of American Folklore*, 16 (1903), 234–57

Still, Colin, *The Timeless Theme: A Critical Theory Formulated and Applied*, London, 1936

Titus Andronicus

Desmonde, William H., 'The Ritual Origin of Shakespeare's *Titus Andronicus*', *The International Journal of Psychoanalysis*, 36, part 1 (1955), 61–5

Troilus and Cressida

Foakes, R. A., '*Troilus and Cressida* Reconsidered', *University of Toronto Quarterly*, 32 (1963), 142–54

Twelfth Night

Lewalski, Barbara K., 'Thematic Patterns in *Twelfth Night*', *ShakS*, 1 (1965) 168–81

Seiden, Melvin, 'Malvolio Reconsidered' *University of Texas City Review*, 28 (1961), 105–14

The Two Gentlemen of Verona

Godshalk, William Leigh, 'The Structural Unity of *Two Gentlemen of Verona*', *Studies in Philology*, 66 (1969), 166–81

Scott, William O., 'Proteus in Spenser and Shakespeare: The Lover's Identity', *ShakS*, 1 (1965), 283–93

Venus and Adonis

Butler, Christopher and Alastair Fowler, 'Time Beguiling Sport: Number Symbolism in Shakespeare's *Venus and Adonis*', in *Shakespeare: 1564–1964*, edited by Edward A. Bloom, Providence, Rhode Island, 1964, pp. 124–33

The Winter's Tale

Arnold, Paul, 'Ésotérisme du *Conte D'Hiver*', *Mercure de France*, 318 (1953) 494–512

Bryant, J. A., 'Shakespeare's Allegory: *The Winter's Tale*', *Sewanee Review*, 63 (1955), 202–22

Hoeniger, F. David, 'The Meaning of *The Winter's Tale*', *University of Toronto Quarterly*, 20 (1950), 11–26

Honigmann, E. A. J., 'Secondary Sources of *The Winter's Tale*', *Philological Quarterly*, 34 (1955), 27–38

Scott, William O., 'Seasons and Flowers in *The Winter's Tale*', *SQ*, 14 (1963), 411–17

Thorne, William Barry, '"Things Newborn": A Study of the Rebirth Motif in *The Winter's Tale*', *The Humanities Association of Canada Bulletin*, 19 (1968), 34–43

Tinkler, F. C., '*The Winter's Tale*', *Scrutiny*, 5 (1937), 344–64

Index

References to specific themes or characters from myth, religion, legend, folk tale and fairy tale, as well as to some characters from fiction, are listed under 'folk tales' or in the appropriate group under 'myths'.

Aeschylus 42, 140
Alexander, Peter 25
Allen, Don Cameron 34, 69
Ancient Mariner, The Rime of the 29
Anderson, Peter S. 106–7, 167
Anouilh, Jean 137
Archer, William 44, 165
archetype 6, 10–12, 51, 57, 60, 72, 151–6
Aristophanes 91
Aristotle 43, 78, 125, 185, 188
Armens, Sven 51, 57
Arnold, Paul 22, 31, 67
Artaud, Antonin 125
Aryan folklore and mythology 19, 24, 25, 27, 44, 66; *see also* Sanskrit, mythology
Auden, W. H. 41

Bachelard, Gaston 129
Bacon, Francis 54, 61, 66–7, 163
'Baconian' theory 74–5, 197
Badawi, M. M. 143–4
Bakhtin, Mikhail 2, 81–3, 88–9, 119, 189
Baldick, Chris 202
Barber, Cesar L. viii, 2, 81–3, 87, 90–8, 102–3, 123–4, 143, 166, 189,
Battenhouse, Roy 43, 99
Bell, W. 194
Bergson, Henri 14, 130
Berry, Edward 91–2, 189
Bethell, S. L. 165

Bevington, David 100
Bickersteth, Geoffrey L. 55
Bidney, David 132
Blake, William 9, 137
Block, Haskell M. 192
Boccaccio 7, 82
Bodkin, Maud 53, 60, 74, 151
Bohannan, Laura 201
Bradley, A. C. viii, 21, 59
Bristol, Michael D. 88–9, 102–3, 116
Brockbank, J. P. 100–1, 182
Brody, Paula 31, 95
Brooks, Cleanth 1
Brower, Reuben Arthur 157, 165
Brown, Daniel Russell 192
Brown, Hugh 52–3
Bryant, J. A. 40, 68, 98, 101–2
Buber, Martin 83, 132
Bullough, Edward 77
Burckhardt, Sigurd 100, 198
Burke, Kenneth 12, 16, 118, 123, 124, 125, 126, 138, 156, 162, 185–6
Burke, Peter 202
Bush, Douglas 5, 8, 34, 62
Butler, Christopher 70

Cabbalism 22, 67, 152
Calderwood, James L. 36–7
Cambillard, C. 27–8
Campbell, Joseph 35, 49, 170
Carnival and Lent 2, 80–3, 88–9, 95, 97, 98, 102–3, 121, 189
Cassirer, Ernst 4, 125, 128–38, 140,

INDEX

141, 145, 169, 171, 180, 189
Caudwell, Christopher 173, 184
Chambers, E. K. 76, 189
Chase, Richard 135, 137
Cocchiara, G. 56
Cohen, Percy 193
Cohn, Ruby 192
Cornford, F. M. 21, 76, 78, 102, 133, 198
couvade 170
Cox, George 19, 25, 66
Crane, R. S. 1, 187–8, 190
Crane, William Ward 49
Creighton, Charles 54
Crews, Frederick 158, 179

Dante 33, 140, 183
Davidson, Sarah Anne 112–13
Demeter (Ceres) 19–20, 66–67, 69, 105
Desmonde, W. H. 105–6
Diana 24, 33, 45, 64–5, 70
Digges, Leonard 67
Dionysus (Bacchus) 26, 27, 45, 60, 65, 78, 102, 105, 113, 154, 194
Dollimore, Jonathan 202
Douglas, W. W. 192
Dowden, Edward 62
Dryden, John 150
Dunne, W. J. 73
Durkheim, E. 84, 130, 133
'dying god' 27, 45, 76, 79, 81, 84, 86; see also scapegoat, sacrifice

Eckert, Charles 109–11
Edwards, Philip 63–4
Eleusinian mysteries see under mysteries
Eliot, George 8
Eliot, T. S. 5, 64, 76, 163, 171–2, 183; *The Waste Land* 36, 139, 150
'Elizabethan World Picture' 114, 141
Elliott, Robert C. 117–18
Empson, William 114, 141
Eniautos-daimon 10, 78, 85

esotericism 19–20, 22–3, 28, 41, 45, 53, 66, 67, 75
Euhemerism 8, 52, 54
Evans-Pritchard, E. E. 198

Felperin, Howard 42
Fergusson, Francis 86, 89, 104, 107–8, 124, 126, 161
festivals, festive rites 4, 28, 56, 79–84, 87–9, 93, 97, 98, 102, 109, 110, 113, 119; see also Carnival, folk drama, May Day, misrule, mummers' play, saturnalia
Fiedler, Leslie 71
Fisch, Harold 60–1, 163
Fisher, Peter, F. 94
Fiske, John 47
Fletcher, Angus 141, 194
Foakes, R. A. 42, 52
folk drama, folk play 76, 79, 86–7, 90, 93, 96, 113, 119; see also festivals, mummers' play
folklore 25, 27–8, 41, 54
folk tales 23, 26, 28, 29–30, 33, 36, 44, 46, 55, 65, 66, 69, 154–5, 164–5
Fontenrose, Joseph 198
Fowler, Alastair 70.
Frazer, James G. 2, 4, 10, 18, 36, 71, 76–7, 80, 86, 93, 97, 101, 112, 120–1, 189
Freemasons 31, 41, 152
Freud, Sigmund 4, 10, 12–13, 28, 30, 46, 55, 57, 72, 73, 74, 128, 133, 158, 165, 190
Frost, William 114–15
Frye Northrop viii, 4–5, 12, 14, 15–16, 17, 21, 23, 32, 35, 36, 43, 59, 71, 72, 90, 98, 151–9, 163–7, 178–9, 187, 189–90

Garber, Marjorie 87–8, 189
Gaster, Theodor H. 151
Gennep, Arnold van 4, 79–81, 83, 87, 91, 166
Gluckman, Max 116

INDEX

Gnostics 7, 19, 64
Goddard, H. C. 39–40, 59, 62
Godshalk, William 163
Gollancz, Israel 54, 55, 165
Goldmann, Lucien 169
Granville-Barker, H. 107
Gregory of Nyssa 7
Grimm, Hermann 69

Halliwell, James O. 25
Halpern, Ben 176–7
Hapgood, Robert 2–3, 104, 106, 109, 120, 14
Harbage, Alfred 75, 197
Hardison, O. B. 79, 192
Harrison, Jane Ellen 10, 76–8, 85, 112, 125, 130, 133, 155, 198
Hathorn, Richmond Y. 15, 50, 56, 147
Hawkes, Terence 202
Heath-Stubbs, John 41
Heilman, Robert 124, 145–6
Heline, Theodore 45
Herbert, Edward T. 46
Herd, E. W. 192
Herder, J. G. 135
Hermeticism 19, 64
Hewitt, Douglas 113–14, 126
Hiebel, F. 55
Hoeniger, F. David 68
Holland, Norman 30, 40, 73, 101
Holloway, John 89, 104, 114, 117–18, 121, 124–6, 177, 185
Homer 6, 26, 78
Honig, Edwin 16–17, 202
Honigmann, E. A. J. 19, 67–8
Hugo, Victor 68
Hulme, T. E. 149
Hungerford, E. B. 8–9
Hunter, G. K. 64

ideology 170–1, 175–9
initiation 15, 18, 31, 56, 65, 66, 67, 70, 80, 87, 105, 109, 112; *see also* mysteries, rites

James, D. G. 15, 62–3, 134, 147–8
Jekels, Ludwig 57
Jespersen, Otto 143
Jones, Genesius 139
Jonson, Ben 91, 125
Joyce, James, *Ulysses* 150, 163
Jung, Carl G. 10–12, 129, 133, 169–70, 189, 198

Kafka, Franz 137
Kaula, David 54
Kelly, Henry Ansgar 182
Kermode, Frank 63, 122, 134, 138, 165
Kernan, Alvin 100
Kluckhohn, Clyde 170, 185, 198
Knight, G. Wilson viii, 2, 15, 17, 19, 21, 23, 37, 42, 62–3, 64–5, 68, 71, 89, 99, 103, 127, 143, 147, 160, 165, 191
Knowles, Richard 34, 61, 163
Korner, Sinclair 26, 48–9
Kott, Jan 63, 168
Krieger, Murray 3

La Guardia, Eric 38, 100, 198
Lake, H. Coote 32, 36, 39
Lawrence, D. H. 76, 150
Lawrence, W. W. 36
Leavis, F. R. 63, 127
Leech, Clifford 40, 101
Levey, Sivori 68
Levin, Harry 46
Levin, Richard 141–3
Lévi-Strauss, Claude 4–5, 11, 107, 116–17, 158–63, 167–70, 185, 189–90, 198, 200, 201
Lévy-Bruhl, Lucien 130 138, 169
Lewalski, Barbara 35
Lewis, C. S. 192
Liebrecht, Felix 47
Lings, Martin 41

McCollom, William G. 101
MacCurdy, John T. 47

INDEX

Mack, Maynard 114–15, 126, 146
Maitra, Sitansu 41, 98, 197
Malinowski, B. 5, 125, 175–8
mana 16–17, 72, 108, 129, 131, 137, 142, 143
Mannheim, Karl 176–7, 179
Marienstras, Richard 106, 198
Matthews, Honor 38, 40, 43–4, 53–4, 56–7, 58
Max Müller, F. 6, 9–10
May Day, May festival, May games 57, 90, 92, 93–4, 113, 117; *see also* festivals, folk drama, mummers' play
Midgley, Graham 31
misrule, Lord of Misrule 80, 81, 89, 92, 97, 116–17
Mithraism 66
Montegut, E. 97
Montgomerie, William 109
Morley, F. V. 109
Morris, Harry 59
mummers' play 66, 79, 92, 96; *see also* folk drama
Murray, Gilbert 48, 76, 86, 107, 112–13, 120, 198
mysteries 14 15, 19, 23, 24, 25, 26, 31, 33, 53, 55, 66, 67, 69, 70, 86, 105, 194; *see also* initiation, Orphism
myth *and* dogma 133–4; *see also* ideology, symbol
mythography: ancient 6; medieval 7; Renaissance 7–8, 24, 34, 36, 60–1, 68–9, 70
mythology, comparative 4, 8–9, 19, 66, 190; *see also* Aryan folklore, solar myth
myths: Biblical 7–8, 15, 17, 18, 22, 30, 34 5, 38, 40–1, 43, 45, 49, 50, 53, 55, 57, 58, 59, 60, 68, 70, 79, 99; British, Celtic, Irish 26, 28, 41, 44, 54, 66, 113, 181, 194; Classical (*see also under* Demeter, Diana, Dionysus, Oedipus, Orestes, Persephone) 7, 8, 9, 10, 17, 19–20, 22, 23–4, 26, 27, 28, 29, 30, 32, 33, 34, 36, 41, 42, 44, 45, 46, 47–8, 49, 51, 54, 55, 56–7, 60, 64, 65, 66–7, 69, 70, 71, 78, 89, 102, 105, 106, 107–8, 109–11, 112, 142, 154, 158, 159, 161, 163, 167–8, 194; Germanic, North European 10, 26, 30, 41, 44, 46–7, 57, 59, 117; Indian 8–9, 25, 26, 42, 49, 51, 65, 69, 70, 102; miscellaneous 28, 30, 32, 51, 60, 66, 67, 70

Nashe, Thomas 27
Nazi 122, 172
Newell, W. S. 69
Nietzsche, F. 171
Nutt, Alfred 26–7
Nuttall, A. D. 99

Oedipus 30, 49, 54, 89, 105, 107–8, 158, 159, 161
Oldenburg, Hermann 140
omophagia 95
Ong, Walter J. 192
Orestes 32, 49, 109–11, 168
Origen 6, 15
Orphism 28, 45
Otto, Rudolf 137
Ovid 105, 129

Paris, Jean 22, 27–8, 31, 49–50
Pauncz, Arpad 55–6
Persephone (Proserpine) 20, 33, 45, 64–9, 105–6, 163
Philo 6, 7, 11
Piaget, Jean 85, 198
Pickard-Cambridge, A. W. 198
Plato 1, 6, 8, 19, 26, 111, 146
Plautus 23, 30
Plumptre, James 52
Pogson, Beryl 37, 45, 53, 65, 67
Pope, Alexander 150
Pratt, Samuel 39

Raglan, Lord 35, 102
Raine, Kathleen 137
Rank, Otto 39, 62
Rauber, D. F. 144
Regifugium 109–10
Reik, Theodor 39, 105, 170
Riley, M. H. 116–17
rites: Christian rites 43, 79, 97, 101–2, 115; rites of passage 4, 79, 80, 83; 84, 87, 91, 92; rites of puberty 105; rites of purgation 109–12; *see also* initiation, mysteries, rituals
ritual *and* play 84–5; *and* imitation 85–6, 131
rituals, *see under* couvade, 'dying god', festivals, initiation, omophagia, Regifugium, rites, sacrifice, scapegoat, sphagia, thusia
Robinson, James E. 94
Romanticism 135–8
Root, Robert Kilburn 5
Rosenheim, Richard 70
Ross, Lawrence J. 193
Rosicrucianism 19–20, 22, 41, 64, 67, 152
Rossiter, A. P. 101
Rufus, Mutianus 8, 10

Sachs, Hanns 38, 58
sacrifice 79, 84, 100–1, 103–4, 106–7, 117–18; *see also* 'dying god', scapegoat
Śakuntala 32, 36
Sandys, George 70
Sanskrit 4, 8, 25, 69, 188–9
Sartre, Jean-Paul 137
saturnalia 80–1, 91, 92, 94
Savage, D. S. 49
scapegoat 43, 76, 79, 84, 86, 94–9, 102–6, 112, 114–24, 129, 184; *see also* 'dying god', sacrifice
Schechner, Richard 84, 125
Schelling, F. W. 128, 171
Scott, William O. 23–4

Seiden, Melvin 97
Sennet, M. 33–4
Seznec, Jean 7–8
Shakespeare, William: the comedies 21–3, 90–2, 166–7; the history plays 38–9, 99–100, 180–3, 191; the romances 62–4, 118–19; the tragedies 43, 79 103–4, 166–7; *All's Well That Ends Well* 36–8, 98–9, 164, 184; *Antony and Cleopatra* 60–1, 117, 163, 166, 186; *As You Like It* 22, 32–5, 91, 96–7, 163; *The Comedy of Errors* 22–3, 35, 92, 164, 165, 166; *Coriolanus* 62, 118, 121, 166, 185; *Cymbeline* 22, 65–6, 119, 164; *Hamlet* 31, 32, 38, 46–51, 52, 53, 56, 63, 88, 104, 107–12, 117, 124, 126, 145, 146, 147, 161, 166, 168; *Henry IV* 39, 41–2, 88, 91, 102–3, 121, 123, 142–3; *Henry V* 41–2, 102–3, 188; *Henry VI* 38–9, 100–1; *Henry VIII* 42–3, 103, 191; *King John* 40, 101; *Julius Caesar* 46, 104, 106–7, 166, 167–8, 186; *King Lear* 44, 52, 53, 54–7, 63, 68, 112–17, 126, 146, 147, 166, 168; *Love's Labour's Lost* 24–5, 91, 93, 94, 145; *Macbeth* 32, 40, 42, 44, 52, 57–60, 63, 72, 88, 117, 121, 123, 143–4, 146, 166; *Measure for Measure* 38, 99, 121, 164, 165; *The Merchant of Venice* 28–32, 91, 94–6, 121, 123; *The Merry Wives of Windsor* 36, 98, 164; *A Midsummer-Night's Dream* 22, 25–8, 48, 88, 91, 93–4, 194; *Much Ado About Nothing* 32, 96, 164; *Othello* 52–4, 63, 109, 112, 121, 123, 146, 166, 186; *Pericles* 22, 23, 45, 64–5; *Richard II* 40–1, 101–2, 104, 127; *Richard III* 39–40, 101, 104; *Romeo and Juliet* 37, 44–6, 104, 106, 121, 166; *Sonnets* 70–1; *The Taming of the Shrew* 23, 92–3; *The Tempest* 13,

INDEX

19–20, 22, 50, 63, 67, 68–70, 83, 102, 154, 165–6; *Timon of Athens* 61, 117–18, 166; *Titus Andronicus* 43–4, 104, 105–6, 121; *Troilus and Cressida* 52, 112, 141–2, 166; *Twelfth Night* 33, 35–6, 91, 95, 97–8, 121; *The Two Gentlemen of Verona* 22, 23–4, 90, 93, 163; *Venus and Adonis* 12, 37, 70, 144–5; *The Winter's Tale* 19–20, 32, 33, 37, 63, 65, 66–8, 69, 119, 157, 165
shaman 116–17
Shelley, P.B. 135
Shumaker, Wayne 139
Simrock, Karl 36, 44, 46–7, 48–9, 57–8, 59
Sinsheimer, Hermann 30
Slochower, Harry 51
Smith, W. Robertson 76
solar myth 9–10, 18, 26, 40, 47, 48, 54, 70, 152
Sophocles 42
Sorel, Georges 126, 176,
Spens, Janet 62, 90, 96, 112, 117, 119–20, 189
sphagia 110
Spurgeon, Caroline 46, 201
Stauffer, Donald A. 192–3
Steadman, John M. 36
Stevenson, Warren 56
Stewart, J. I. M. 21, 55, 103, 121, 143, 165
Still, Colin 13–15, 48, 69–70, 147, 151, 165
Stirling, Brents 106
Stoll, E. E. 155, 165, 201
symbol, symbolism 15–16, 135–7, 145–8
syncretism 17, 21, 43, 45, 61

Terence 32
Thoms, W. J. 25
Thorne, William Barry 68, 92, 118
thusia 110
Tiddy, R. J. E. 76, 96

Tillich, Paul 133–4
Tillyard, E. M. W. 38, 100–1, 114, 141, 174, 180–2, 185
Tinkler F. C. 119
Troy, William 146, 193
Tudor Myth 40, 127, 177, 180, 181–2, 185
Turner, Victor 82
typology 6–8, 17, 35, 41, 152

Underhill, Evelyn 34

Vannovsky, Alexander A. 50
Vedic deities 140
Vegetation Spirit, *see* Eniautosdaimon
Velz, John W. 193
Vico, Giambattista 135
Virgil 26, 140; *Aeneid* 69
Vyvyan, John 35

Waddington, Raymond 60
Walker, Roy 58
Walpole, Horace 52
Warner, Alan 60
Watt, Ian 177
Way, Arthur S. 25
Weisinger, Herbert 1–2, 18, 21
Weimann, Robert 189
Weston, Jessie 76
Wheelwright, Philip 43, 124, 133, 140, 146, 171, 183–4
Wickham, Glynne 41
Wigston, W.F.C. 19–20, 22, 24, 25–6, 33, 35, 44–5, 61, 62–3, 64–5, 66–7, 69, 70–1, 75, 106, 147, 163, 165–6
Williams, Philip 103
Wilson, John Dover 101–2
Wilson, Monica 116
Wimsatt, William K. 1
Wincor, Richard 62
Winstanley, Lilian 52, 54
Woolf, Virginia 149, 150
Wordsworth, William 137–8
Worringer, Wilhelm 149

Yeats, W. B. 76, 125, 171–2, 199